The Early Republic and the Sea

The Early Republic and the Sea:

Essays on the Naval and Maritime History of the Early United States

Edited by **William S. Dudley**
and **Michael J. Crawford**

Brassey's, Inc.

WASHINGTON, D.C.

Library of Congress Cataloging-in-Publication Data

The early republic and the sea : essays on the naval and maritime history of the early United States / edited by William S. Dudley and Michael J. Crawford.— 1st ed.
    p.   cm.
Includes bibliographical references and index.
ISBN 1-57488-371-2 — ISBN 1-57488-372-0
    1. United States—History, Naval—18th century. 2. United States—History, Naval—19th century. 3. Navigation—United States—History—18th century. 4. Navigation—United States—History—19th century. 5. United States. Navy—History—18th century. 6. United States. Navy—History—19th century. I. Dudley, William S. II. Crawford, Michael J.

E182.E2 2001
359'.00973—dc21

2001025607

Hardcover ISBN 1-57488-371-2   (alk. paper)
Paperback ISBN 1-57488-372-0   (alk. paper)

Some of the essays have been previously published in the *American Neptune:* in Volume 57, Number 4 (Fall 1997), the four essays on James Fenimore Cooper's writings, by Hugh Egan (pp. 343–50), Robert Madison (pp. 323–34), Wayne Franklin (pp. 351–57), and Thomas Philbrick (pp. 315–21); and in Volume 57, Number 3 (Summer 1997) Mary A. Y. Gallagher's "Charting a Course for the China Trade: The Late Eighteenth-Century American Model," in an earlier version. These essays, originally edited by the *American Neptune's* editor-in-chief, Barry Gough, are printed here with the permission of the *American Neptune,* Peabody Essex Museum, East India Square, Salem, MA 01970-3783, which holds the copyright.

Printed in the United States of America on acid-free paper that meets the American National Standards Institute Z39-48 Standard.

Brassey's, Inc.
22841 Quicksilver Drive
Dulles, Virginia 20166

Design by Pen & Palette Unlimited

First Edition

10 9 8 7 6 5 4 3 2 1

Contents

Illustrations

Introduction

The early naval and maritime history of the United States is embraced by the years 1781 and 1860. Most of the essays in this volume focus on the early years, an era characterized by the shift from British colonial status to that of American independence, from a mercantile economy to an entrepreneurial economy, from dependence on Great Britain for military and naval protection to the need for self-defense at home and abroad. No longer would the heavy hand of British control be present to thwart the will of local government and to suppress freedom of expression and freedom of trade. Moreover, within the decade following the Peace of Paris in 1783, the great powers of Europe were engaged in the wars of the French Revolution, a long drawn out conflict that did not end until 1815.

Consequently, during the late 1780s the United States entered a period of dynamic growth of international trade during which the nation chose the role of a neutral party among the hostile European states. This role was not without risk or harm, as both Britain and France tried to limit U.S. trade to themselves and deny it to their enemy. American merchant ships were at risk in trading with European nations and their Caribbean colonies, and in the Mediterranean as well, with no naval protection available for escorting merchantmen in the dangerous waters off the Barbary Coast. But even though the United States was without a navy for about fifteen years, many former Continental Navy and privateer officers served in the growing merchant marine on voyages to the Far East.

With the implementation of the U.S. Constitution in 1789, internal U.S. trade barriers were eliminated and uniform customs regulations were established. Congress enacted various forms of protective legislation to stimulate domestic shipbuilding and the use of American shipping firms, instead of foreign. By 1795, 92 percent of all U.S. imports and 85 percent of all exports traveled in American flag vessels.

American exports and imports quintupled from 1790 to 1800 from a base of about $20 million in each case to more than $100 million in product valuation. The population of New York City, a major trade center, grew rapidly during this period, more than doubling between 1790 and 1805. American merchant activity spread to the Indian Ocean via the French island of Mauritius, to China via the Pacific Northwest to exchange furs for trade goods, and via Hawaii to pick up sandalwood and put in at Sumatra for pepper, and to the Arabian coast for coffee. American merchants' attempts to trade with Mediterranean states met resistance and frustration at the hands of the "Barbary Pirates." The states of Algiers, Tripoli, Morocco, and Tunis sent out swift-sailing feluccas with armed crews to capture any undefended ships they could. The British Royal Navy had formerly protected American merchantmen, but after 1783 the Royal Navy naturally withdrew its protection. In effect, these Barbary vessels were state warships sent out to capture ships, cargoes, and crews that could be held for ransom. The pitiful accounts penned by sailors captured, imprisoned, or enslaved reached the United States, and before long there was an outcry that the government do something about the situation. The U.S. government found that its options were limited: it could pay tribute and ransom its citizens, or it could build a navy to protect its rights. At first, the government agreed to provide tribute, an armed ship of war, and other items. In the meantime, however, Congress in 1794 authorized the expenditure of funds on the construction of several frigates, three of which, *Constellation, United States*, and *Constitution*, were ready to sail by 1798. Three more frigates followed, *Congress, Chesapeake*, and *President*, with the last not being completed until 1801.

By a great coincidence, the first three ships of the reborn United States Navy were nearly ready for duty in the Mediterranean when hostilities broke out between the United States and the French Republic. That nation was undergoing rapid societal and political changes under the duress of war and revolution, and by 1795 the governing Directory was angered that the United States had not provided the aid the French expected under the Treaty of Alliance of 1778. After failed negotiations with the United States, the Directory ordered French Navy ships and licensed privateers to attack U.S. ships trading in the

Caribbean. These attacks began in 1797 and American losses mounted steadily. In response, and without actually declaring war, President John Adams ordered Benjamin Stoddert, the new secretary of the Navy, to provide armed escorts for American trading fleets. Thus began the undeclared Quasi-War with France, a conflict of more than two years' duration carried out entirely at sea.

Secretary Stoddert expanded the U.S. Navy well beyond the original six frigates in order to deal with the large scale of the crisis. At its height, the Navy employed more than forty warships, some of which were "subscription frigates" that had, in effect, been donated to the Navy in return for government bonds. Others were merchant ships that had been purchased into the Navy and converted to warships. The Navy's officer corps and enlisted ranks swelled as the ships were brought into service. Many of these men would remain in the Navy to become the core of its fighting strength as one war led to another.

No sooner had the Quasi-War with France ended with the Convention of Mortfontaine in 1800 than the United States was at war with Tripoli in a contest that was to last until 1805. The dispatching of four naval squadrons in succession between 1801 and 1805 indicates the difficulty of the conflict. Within another two years, the U.S. Navy and the British Royal Navy came into conflict over the issue of impressment, culminating in the *Chesapeake-Leopard* Affair of 1807. That event left a blemish on the reputation of the U.S. Navy that rankled its officers and many other American citizens until the outbreak of the War of 1812. That extended conflict is not a subject to be discussed here, but the struggle does provide a backdrop to some of the other maritime events that are the subject of this proceedings volume.

Readers will find a varied menu of maritime and naval issues served up in the following pages. Elizabeth Nuxoll provides interesting substance to the poorly understood transition from the Continental Navy to the establishment of the U.S. Navy. Joshua Smith tackles the thorny issue of smuggling between the United States and British subjects in Canada during the period of the Embargo and the War of 1812. Yes, both sides did engage in trading with the enemy. The scene then shifts, with Mary Gallagher's article, to the ingenuity of American merchants trading in the Far East in the closing years of the eighteenth century. James Mockford's article on the *Lady Washington* discloses fascinating results of his research into Japanese sources on the earliest American contacts with Japan in the 1790s. Richard Malley's article deals with a young Connecticut lad, Daniel Caulkins, who was caught up in the Quasi-War with France on a voyage to the Caribbean. Christine Hughes provides an enlightening account of the diplomatic difficulties that arose after Captain Lewis Warrington's *Peacock* took the last American naval prize of the War of 1812 in June 1815, well after the signing and ratification of the Treaty of Ghent. And Peter G. Fish provides an erudite discussion of how naval efforts to suppress the Atlantic slave trade fared in southern U.S. courts during the years leading up to the outbreak of the Civil War.

The final grouping of essays in this collection deals with the naval writings, both fiction and history, of James Fenimore Cooper. Cooper, of course, is best known in the United States for the novels of his Leatherstocking Tales. Among them *The Deerslayer* (1841) is perhaps the most popular. Yet, this author was a preeminent literary man of the sea. He had "run away to sea" in his teenage years as a way of escaping the obligations of a well-born youth. He chose to become a man of letters after his one year at sea in a merchantman and three as a midshipman in the U.S. Navy before the War of 1812. During the first decade of his literary career, he wrote three nautical novels that placed him firmly within the romantic movement. After a lengthy stay in Europe during the 1830s, Cooper turned from fiction and travel literature to writing the history of the U. S. Navy, which he capably accomplished in *History of the Navy of the United States.* He knew personally or had at least met many of the officers of the period. As a native New Yorker, from the Lake Otsego region, Cooper had been closely acquainted with the naval establishment at Oswego, where he supervised the building of the brig *Oneida.* He had a solid knowledge of the War of 1812 as it had played out between British and American squadrons on Lakes Ontario and Erie, as well as the ship-to-ship actions on the high seas.

In all, he was a man of firm opinions who did not hesitate to engage in literary polemics on subjects dear to his heart. In addition to his history of the Navy, Cooper wrote the biographies of several officers, including Commodore William Bainbridge, Lieutenant Richard

Somers, and Captain Richard Dale. He wrote a critique of British naval historian William James's multivolume history of the Royal Navy, *The Naval History of Great Britain*. He particularly attacked James's biased views of American naval officers as they are featured in the volumes treating the War of 1812. Following the sensational and infamous cruise of USS *Somers* in 1842, Cooper excoriated fellow naval writer Captain Alexander Slidell Mackenzie, USN, for his actions in the executions of three sailors accused of fomenting mutiny on board that ship. One of Cooper's most interesting nonfiction works is his *Ned Myers, or a Life before the Mast*, an as-told-to biography of a sailor Cooper had known as a shipmate during his cruise on board the merchantman *Stirling* in 1806–17.

Four leading American Cooper scholars participate in the essays that conclude this volume. Hugh Egan neatly dissects Cooper's attempt to write objectively about the political and literary feud that erupted between Commanders Oliver Hazard Perry and Jesse Duncan Elliott after the Battle of Lake Erie. From a textual perspective, Perry's account of the battle appears to slight Elliott's role in supporting his commodore. Elliott picked up on this slight and magnified it until it came to have great currency and was a severe embarrassment to Elliott himself. Perry had little further to do with the matter, because he died while on a mission to Venezuela. But Cooper, in his *History of the Navy of the United States*, chose to defend Elliott and for that reason earned the enmity of the Perry faction. Robert D. Madison analyzes Cooper's work in his "fleet" novel *The Two Admirals*, concerning two leading fictional British naval officers of the early eighteenth century drawn from Cooper's understanding of British naval history. Thomas Philbrick considers Cooper's maritime history sources as the basis for his sea fiction of the 1820s, 1830s, and early 1840s. Philbrick pays close attention to the development of Cooper's novel *Afloat and Ashore*, which he sees as containing the elements of a new realism based partly on Cooper's own experiences and those of others he had known. Wayne Franklin, in "Cooper as Passenger," gives the reader a cogent analysis of the circumstances under which Cooper came to make his first sea voyage at age sixteen. Each of these essays portrays a different aspect of James Fenimore Cooper's nautical writings during the period on which this volume focuses. They fit the subject perfectly and are appo-site companion pieces to the period essays that precede them.

The Early Republic and the Sea is a fitting tribute to the role played by seafaring in making possible the rapid expansion of the United States in the first seventy-five years of its existence. Until recently, many thought of the United States as an essentially maritime nation, with its roots deeply set in Great Britain's extensive maritime and naval control of the seas. With the fisheries and extensive merchant trading activities as the American "nursery for seamen," the development of a strong navy was probably an inevitable and necessary development. From these days emanated an American English language saturated with sea-faring terminology. Even though much of the American merchant marine has by now disappeared, we are still as a nation heavily depen-dent on imports and exports carried by ships, and we rely, for our nation's defense, on a navy continually called on to exercise forward presence and global control of the sea lanes of communication.

Yet, as has been observed in the annual conferences of the North American Society for Oceanic History (NASOH) and other maritime historical societies, there seems to be less and less national conscious-ness of our maritime dependence. Most of our schools and universities seem to ignore the need to inform students about the role that mar-itime and naval affairs have played in the formation of this and other nations. As this will likely remain the case, it will be up to societies like NASOH and the Canadian Society for Nautical Research, and mar-itime and naval museums of our linked nations to take on the task of teaching maritime history and the great traditions on which it is based. This volume of essays will certainly find its audience among the supporters, members, and staffs of these institutions and, it is hoped, among a wider public as well.

This volume is a collection of essays delivered as papers during the annual conferences of NASOH, during the years 1996, 1997, and 1998. In 1996 the conference organizers anticipated the two hundredth an-niversary of the Department of the Navy in 1998. We chose as a con-ference theme the early naval and maritime history of the United States. Contained in this volume are eight essays selected from among those presented at the Boston, Massachusetts, conference in 1996; one from the 1997 conference in Newport, Rhode Island; and two from the 1998 conference held in San Diego, California.

The director of the Naval Historical Center at the Washington Navy Yard, Washington, D.C., offered a prize for the best article on the early United States Navy published or accepted for publication between 1994 and 1998. The winner was Elizabeth Nuxoll's "The Naval Movement of the Confederation Era," and it is the lead essay of this proceedings volume.

William S. Dudley

Part One

Maritime Commerce and the Sea Services

Robert Morris

1

The Naval Movement of the Confederation Era

Elizabeth M. Nuxoll

Until Revenues for the Purpose can be obtained it is but vain to talk of Navy or Army or any thing else. We receive sounding Assurances from all Quarters and we receive scarce any thing else. Every good American must wish to see the United States possessed of a powerful fleet but perhaps the best way to obtain one is to make no Effort for the Purpose till the People are taught by their Feelings to call for and require it. They will now give money for Nothing.

— Robert Morris

This statement, written in July 1783 by Robert Morris in his capacity as agent of marine, the chief administrator of the Continental Navy, when he proposed to sell its last remaining ships, reflects the evolution of a nationalist naval policy at the end of the Revolutionary War that

1. looked forward to the creation of a new, stronger navy for the United States

2. recognized that current economic, political, and financial circumstances did not permit its creation at present

3. sought in various ways to create the conditions that would make a strong navy possible sometime in the future.

Within this consensus by most of the prominent leaders of the era, individual opinions varied considerably over the appropriate size and scope of the Navy, its purposes, the amount of political and constitutional change to create it, the economic conditions necessary for its development, and, finally, its rate of growth. Much of the historical analysis of the movement to create a United States Navy covers the Constitutional Convention, ratification struggle, and the first U.S. congresses. This paper reviews those events, but focuses on the earlier stages of the movement, grounding subsequent ideas and policies in the circumstances that led to the dissolution of the Continental Navy.

The naval experience of the revolutionary and particularly the Confederation era constituted the first factor shaping views regarding the peacetime Navy. The American Revolution, like most wars, encompassed not only a conflict of arms, but also a financial war in which the ability to obtain and to mobilize the economic resources needed to carry on the war strongly influenced the ultimate outcome. The Continental Navy was always linked to what Robert Morris called the "war of finance." Navies cost dearly, and the effort to create one from scratch that would be capable of contending with the world's greatest naval power threatened the limited funds of the revolutionary government. However, naval missions could also raise money through the sale of prizes and could facilitate the transportation of supplies and money. They could protect American trade, thus lowering the cost of war to the United States, and they could capture enemy shipping, thereby raising the cost of war for the British. The Navy could therefore help make or break the war effort. Such interaction between naval and financial affairs was personified in the career of Robert Morris when the Continental Congress assigned him the dual positions of superintendent of finance and agent of marine from 1781 to 1784.

Morris derived his maritime expertise from more than twenty years' service as active partner in the great Philadelphia mercantile firm of Willing and Morris. He had an adventurer's enthusiasm for naval operations and naval heroes, and, a patron of John Paul Jones, John Barry, and other great American naval captains, he has long been considered a founder of the American Navy.[1] Nevertheless, even in his most optimistic moments Morris had no illusions that the new nation could single-handedly protect American trade, much less defeat the British Navy. As a member of the Continental Congress from 1775 to 1778, he had been involved in efforts to secure French and Spanish participation in the war against England, in large part in order to obtain their naval assistance. He hoped to force the British Navy to spread its forces so thin as to preclude an effective blockade of the United States and the destruction of American trade. When he returned to national office in 1781, Morris was already quite familiar with the intricate linkage between naval operations, supply operations, diplomacy, and public finance. He viewed the Navy not in terms of battles and maneuvers, but in terms of its overall strategic contributions to the total war effort. His policies as superintendent of finance and agent of marine built upon his earlier practices. Since resources remained precarious throughout his administration, he always had to subordinate naval to financial considerations, giving top priority to policies that would preserve his credit and that of the government and "keep the money machine going."

Naval and military historians alike have criticized Morris for subordinating Navy and Army concerns to financial and commercial ones. William Fowler, for example, asserts in his *Rebels under Sail* that "In Morris's scheme of things the navy had a low priority, and indeed after Yorktown it is likely it had no priority at all." [2] The facts are to the contrary. After Yorktown, the British changed military strategies, hoping to win the war of finance by intensifying naval warfare along the American coast. They intended to crush American commerce and to drain off the specie supply, leaving the United States incapable of continuing the war. As losses mounted in 1782 and Morris's financial resources began drying up, he launched a drive to renew American naval strength, obtain increased French and Spanish naval assistance, and protect American trade.

He confronted numerous obstacles. His funds were minimal and the Navy was minuscule. Most of the ships built earlier in the revolution had been sunk, captured, or destroyed; only the frigates *Alliance* and *Deane* were operational. Consequently, Morris linked the Navy to his drive to obtain reliable revenues for the Continental government and sought financial support for rebuilding the Navy. [3] Using funds borrowed from the Bank of North America, he cooperated with other Philadelphia merchants in obtaining a ship for the defense of the Delaware. The widely publicized victory of that ship, the *General Washington* under the command of Joshua Barney, over the *General Monk* on 8 April 1782, lifted the spirits of the mercantile community and increased confidence that effective naval action could protect American trade. Morris sent Barney to the West Indies with dispatches to French and Spanish naval officials, requesting convoys for American trade, particularly the lucrative tobacco trade with the Chesapeake. The British naval victory in the West Indies known as the Battle of the Saints, which devastated the French Navy, undermined this plan. Nevertheless, part of the fleet under Vaudreuil did sail up the coast in August 1782 and remained in the United States in late 1782, providing limited protection.[4]

Morris next elicited the support of the French minister to the United States for rebuilding of the American Navy—largely through French loans. Chevalier Anne-César de La Luzerne passed on the proposals to his superiors, but by the time they reached France, they were disregarded because peace negotiations had opened. Meanwhile Morris publicized naval exploits in the effort to drum up public support, and La Luzerne promoted writings in newspapers advocating the rebuilding of the Navy and calling for the tax revenues necessary to finance it.[5]

In July 1782 Morris submitted to Congress two proposals with strong naval components. On 29 July he presented a plan for funding the national debt, which he suggested would not only strengthen the national government but would also restore public credit that the nation could borrow funds to develop the Navy.[6] Such a suggestion alarmed opponents of centralized power, who feared he sought a large, patronage-ridden military establishment that would saddle the country with a perpetual debt financed by permanent heavy taxation. When Congress finally adopted a funding plan in 1783, hostilities had ceased. Congress limited the funds to payment of prior wartime expenditures, allowing no room for their diversion to new naval expenses. Even in that limited form the plan failed to be ratified by the states.[7]

In his budget message of 30 July 1782, Morris highlighted the British change in the mode of warfare and outlined what he thought a revived navy could accomplish:

1. It could prevent the enemy from making predatory incursions.

2. It could force the enemy to keep its ships together, which would prevent them from injuring our commerce and obstructing our supplies.

3. If it forced the enemy to keep an equal or superior force in American waters, a navy would create a powerful diversion

in favor of our allies, affording them a naval superiority else-where.

4. If the enemy did not keep such a force, a navy, by cruising, would enable us to protect our own commerce, annoy theirs, and cut off supplies to their posts in America so as to distress their finances and relieve our own.

5. By economizing our funds and building six ships a year we could advance rapidly to maritime importance, so that the enemy would be convinced of the impossibility of subduing us.

6. We would recover full possession of our country without the expense of blood or treasure that would attend any other mode of operations.

Morris requested funding to man and supply properly the *Alliance* and the *Deane,* to complete the ships already under construction, and to build annually six new ships, each larger than the earlier frigates and modeled on the much-admired *South Carolina.* To accomplish this naval program he proposed a naval budget for 1783 of $2.5 million out of a total budget of $11 million. Congress dashed such hopes by approving a naval budget of $300,000.[8]

After these setbacks, Morris made some effort to acquire naval power, but primarily he began to cut back. He obtained a new ship, the *Duc de Lauzun,* in payment of a debt to the public.[9] He expended more than he could afford from the 1782 budget in an effort to complete the long-delayed construction of the *America* and the *Bourbon* but was hampered by shortages of supplies and funds. Consequently, at Morris's suggestion, Congress presented the *America* to France in September 1782, in part to cut expenses, but largely to soften the French up for another loan request and to interest them in American ship construction for the French Navy.[10] Morris's quest to acquire from the state of South Carolina Alexander Gillon's superb frigate *South Carolina* for John Paul Jones was frustrated in mid-1782 by the state's unfavorable terms and by Morris's failure to obtain the requisite funds from Congress. He and his associates had, however, seized the occasion to examine the ship for ideas on ship design and construction.[11] Having left Jones without a ship, Morris supported his request to train with the French fleet in the

West Indies. Jones thus spent the fall of 1782 studying fleet maneuvers and discussing naval affairs with French officers.[12]

Having failed to win support for a navy during wartime, Morris, after a brief burst of optimism at the onset of peace, gave up hope for a navy in the immediate future. Thus, it happened that, although Morris favored a peacetime navy to secure respect abroad and protect American trade, he presided over the dismantlement of the Continental Navy. By 10 July 1783, despairing of any increase in public revenue and anxious to obtain ships for private use in the China trade, Morris recommended selling the naval vessels. In proposing the sale of the *Hague,* he argued

> The public Wants and Distresses are so numerous and so urgent while the Means continue to be extremely feeble and defective that it becomes necessary to cut off every possible Source of Expence. It is in this View that I am to propose the Sale of the Ship Hague now lying at Boston. I do not expect she will sell for much but we should gain by giving her away. The Ship never was a good one and not being American Built is for that Reason also unworthy a Place in our Navy.

As indicated by the quotation opening this chapter, he then asserted that only after experiencing the consequences of doing without would the public be willing to vote the taxes needed to sustain an American navy.[13] Congress consented to the sale of the *Hague* and also the *Bourbon,* and Morris quickly arranged to auction the ships and related naval stores.[14]

The *Lauzun,* intended for sale in Europe, was sent to France transporting French officers.[15] John Barry's *Alliance* was fitted out to carry a cargo of tobacco to Europe to pay interest on a Dutch loan, but the ship sprang a leak and had to put back. After a committee of naval officers surveyed the ship, Morris proposed sale of the *Alliance:* "The heaving down and repairing of this Ship cannot but be expensive and after all which can be done she will still be an old Vessel which has endured hard service. Considering our situation in other Respects it might perhaps be wiser to Sell her even if we had funds to support a Marine," Morris urged. Repeating his request in March 1784, Morris asserted "this ship is now a mere Bill of Costs and I do not think we have the Means to fit her out were there even a Necessity for so doing. Prudence seems evidently to require that ... [the *Alliance* and *General Washington*] be sold. ... As to a Marine we must for the present give up the Idea and whenever the Situation of the American Finances will permit we can certainly build better Ships than any we have yet had." [16]

When Congress took up Morris's proposal, it asserted: "That the honour of the flag of the United States and the protection of its trade and coasts from the insults of pirates" required that the *Alliance* be retained and repaired. In 1784 Congress twice voted against her sale, but did agree to the sale of the *General Washington*. [17] Congressional resolve did not long survive Morris's retirement. Faced again with the need to cut costs in June 1785, Congress finally agreed to the sale, which took place in August 1785. Although there was no formal resolution or act to that effect, Congress had by selling its last ship terminated the Continental Navy. Morris subsequently acquired the *Alliance* from the purchasers and employed her first for a tobacco voyage and then for a landmark off-season voyage to China under the command of former naval officers Thomas Read and Richard Dale. The voyage bypassed adverse winds by employing a hitherto untried route around Australia that excited the interest of traditional China traders. [18]

The frustration of plans for rebuilding the Navy and finding cost-effective public uses for ships not on military assignment shaped the attitudes of both the Navy's supporters and detractors when they took up the issue of a peacetime military establishment in April 1783 shortly after Joshua Barney arrived with news of a preliminary peace treaty and the cessation of hostilities. A committee headed by Alexander Hamilton, after contacting General George Washington regarding recommendations for the Army establishment, approached Morris for his plans for the peacetime Navy. By that time Morris had submitted his resignation as superintendent of finance, effective 1 May, unless Congress came up with a workable funding plan. Although he did not consider the plan adopted on 18 April 1783 workable, Morris ultimately agreed in May to stay on in a limited capacity to pay the army and meet other financial obligations. But he was struggling to come up with Army pay and to get out of office with his public and private credit intact. Exasperated by mounting public criticism of his efforts, and exploring various private business opportunities, Morris became uncooperative with the committee. He noted in his diary on 9 April: "Colo. Hamilton informs me that he is of a Committee to Consult me respecting the Plan for reestablishing a navy. I replyed nothing would be more agreeable to me than to assist in that Business; but as I shall soon quit Public Office I recommend that Congress should appoint a minister of Marine who might now form the Plans he is to execute."[19]

Morris reiterated his stand in a letter to Hamilton of 16 April 1783: "I accepted the Marine Agency simply with a View to save the Expence of the Department but whenever a marine is to be established a previous Point would be (in my opinion) to nominate a Minister of marine and let his first work be the forming of those Plans and Systems which when adopted by Congress he would have to execute. For my own part were my abilities equal to the task my Leizure would not permit the attempt."[20] Yet, at the same time he was refusing to submit naval plans, Morris was apparently publicizing American intent to create a navy in letters intended for foreign consumption. Denying that the American war debt was heavy, he asserted on 10 April 1783: "If you consider the vast extent of the lands which Congress has at its disposition in our rear, and the rapidity with which it will dispose of them immediately in favor of emigrants who will come from Europe, do you think it will be so difficult a thing for us to get back on our feet? That is what will be our first object; the second, to establish immediately a respectable navy; to avoid war we propose to stand ready to wage one well."

In a letter to Congress of 3 May 1783, Morris complained "that the Affairs of the Marine Department occupy more time and attention than I can easily spare. This Department will now become important, and I hope extensive. I must therefore request that Congress will be pleased to appoint an Agent of Marine as soon as their Convenience would admit." However, Congress did not find it convenient to make an appointment, and Morris's supplementary duties as acting Agent of Marine remained substantial—but not because the Navy became either important or extensive.[21]

Hamilton's committee issued its report for a peacetime military establishment in June 1783, presenting a detailed plan for the Army but not for the Navy. The report refuted the idea advanced by some antinationalists that Congress had no power under the Articles of Confederation to raise an army or navy in peacetime.

> The distinction that this [the general security] is to be provided for in time of war, by the forces of the Union, in time of peace, by those of each state would involve, besides other inconveniences, this capital one, that when the forces of the Union should become necessary to defend its rights and repell any attacks upon them, the United States would be obliged to begin to create at the very moment they would have occasion to employ a fleet and army. They must wait for an actual commencement of hostilities before they would be authorized to prepare for defence, to raise a single regiment or to build a single ship. When it is considered what a length of time is requisite to levy and form an army and still more to build and equip a navy, which is evidently a work of leizure and of peace requiring a gradual preparation of the means, there cannot be presumed so improvident an intention in the Confederation as that of obliging the United States to suspend all provision for the common defence until a declaration of war or an invasion.

The report recommended that the articles should be interpreted in favor of a general power for defense, unless the states declared otherwise, but that Congress should submit any adopted military plan to the states for approval before its final execution. When Congress obtained sufficient attendance to take up the report in October 1783, it established a minimal peacetime army but made no decisions about the Navy.[22]

By October 1783 John Paul Jones approached Morris with suggestions regarding the naval establishment. A letter Jones wrote to his friend, Hector McNeill, on 26 April 1783 indicates that Jones had been collecting ideas on "the most prudent measures to be adopted for the first three years respecting the formation of our Marine, both as to Officers, Ships, and Regulations, as well as materials and building &c." while training with the French fleet in the West Indies. On his arrival in Philadelphia in May 1783, Jones visited the Office of Finance and offered to present a plan for reorganizing the Navy. Morris informed Jones of his intention to retire as agent of marine but offered to submit Jones's plan to Congress.

In his plan, only the draft of which survives, Jones called for "a proper fleet of evolution" for training the officer corps in tactics and recommended that each ship have "a little academy on board" and that each navy yard have a school where junior officers could be taught the "principles of mathematics and mechanics." He did not expect this could be done immediately, but invited Morris and Congress to reflect on the situation of Holland, which let her navy decline. "In time of Peace it is necessary to prepare, and be *always prepared*, for War by Sea," he argued. Applying lessons learned from his European naval experiences and his training mission with the French fleet, he reported on the deficiencies of the signaling system of the British fleet and the superior French system developed by the Chevalier du Pavillon.

It is not known how broadly Jones's proposals were circulated, but they were never formally submitted to Congress. Remarks in the Jones's draft letter suggest that Morris made Jones aware that the nation's dire financial state made funding of a naval establishment unlikely. Morris probably argued that it would be useless, perhaps even counterproductive, to raise the issue with Congress at that time. However, either Jones or Morris apparently suggested that the captain would have an opportunity to study European naval institutions if he asked Congress to appoint him agent to settle American prize claims in Europe. Jones made that request on 13 October, and Morris forwarded it to Congress on 15 October. Congress appointed Jones prize agent on 1 November 1783.[23]

Once in Europe, Jones did seek information on all aspects of naval affairs. In May 1784 he wrote French marine minister Castries: "On my arrival at Paris I had the honor to present a Letter from the Chevalier de La Luzerne mentioning that part of my business in Europe is to collect materials for forming a System for the future Marine of America. You had, My Lord, the goodness to promise me Copy's of every thing respecting the Government and manner of supplying the Marine of France and I shall, esteem it a great favor if you would now give your orders in consequence." Jones also wrote to Arthur Lee, a longtime opponent: "I am endeavouring to make myself better acquainted with Marine Affairs. I imagin I see faults in the Marine

Systems of Europe; but the Constitution of ours in America is too bad to be capable of being spoiled. If you should do me the Honor to communicate any thing on our prospects of forming a Navy, or if you think of any thing that can make my research useful for that purpose, I should esteem it a singular pleasure." Nevertheless, no evidence has been found that Jones ever presented further plans for a naval establishment.[24]

In 1785 Jones secured Thomas Jefferson's backing for a small fleet under his command to confront the Algerian pirate state. In the course of notifying Secretary for Foreign Affairs John Jay of the Algerian declaration of war against the United States, Jones echoed Morris's assertions that distresses might produce stronger government and perhaps a navy. He wrote, "This event may, I believe, surprise some of our fellow Citizens; but, for my part, I am rather surprised that it did not take place sooner. It will produce a good effect, if it unites the people of America in measures consistent with their national Honor and Interest, and rouses them from their ill-judged security which the intoxication of success has produced since the Revolution."[25]

Since the nation was not yet back on its feet, again no action was taken. In the meantime, with his customary mix of public and private interest, Morris had privatized the fleet and its finest seamen. He and his mercantile associates considered using the naval vessels to implement their plans for opening the China trade but abandoned that scheme when the ships were found unsuitable and their plans aroused public suspicion. Nevertheless, two vessels were sold to Morris's associates at low prices, raising charges of conflict of interest. Many of the naval officers had been in Morris's service before the war or had served in his ships during the war; they were quickly reassigned to his ships or those of his partners at war's end, and to some extent brought their former underlings with them. John Barry, John Green, James Nicholson, Thomas Read, and Richard Dale were among those working for Morris in the 1780s and 1790s.[26]

The first examples of the privatization process were the first American voyage to China and the subsidiary shipments associated with it, which included sending masts and naval stores to Europe to promote their sale to foreign navies. Morris and other merchants of his acquaintance had long sought to restore the shipbuilding, mast, and naval stores industries. Should they succeed, that development could lay the grounds for future shipbuilding for the American Navy as well.[27]

Morris saw little separation between public and private purposes in such endeavors. He depicted his China venture as designed both to open new trading opportunities for his nation and to lay the groundwork for an American navy. He did not specify how China voyages related to the Navy, but his intent probably included evaluating the merits of various ships, using them to display the flag in new areas of the world, and providing training to past and future naval officers in navigation and in undertaking long voyages. Morris's goals were achieved. The China trade provided some of his greatest postwar commercial successes. Naval officers remained prominent in the trade; and when the Navy was finally recreated, several of its top officers were among those active in it (for example, John Barry, Richard Dale, Thomas Truxtun). Truxtun employed his time on the long China voyages studying navigation techniques and incorporating them into a manual that he later presented for naval use.[28]

As noted above, it was Morris's hope that his dismantlement of the Navy would play a role in his quest for strengthening the government. Stephen T. Powers has argued that in adopting this strategy Morris played into the hands of antinaval forces and precipitated the extinction of the Continental Navy. This is true only from the short-range perspective. It was politically and constitutionally impossible to obtain funds for the continuance of a viable navy in the immediate postwar years. And the retention of the *Alliance* or one or two more ships would not have substantially overcome American weakness abroad or deterred North African corsairs. The perception of total vulnerability that followed did play some role in the adoption of the United States Constitution in 1787 and in obtaining the tax power necessary to finance an American navy.[29]

Morris, in 1783, clearly enunciated the link between a government that could raise solid funds—something possible only through constitutional reform—and naval revival. With the tide turning against centralization at war's end, he realized his pressing for a navy could and probably would be counterproductive—a fact demonstrated by efforts in Congress to deny disability pensions to amputees who had served under Jones in the *Bonhomme Richard.* It was alleged that certain congressmen had voted against the pensions merely because Morris backed them. Morris's efforts to support requests for depreciation pay for naval as well as Army personnel were similarly disregarded. Thus, just as they avoided recommending a specific commercial strategy until the states called for one, nationalists muted their support for the Navy and the claims of its personnel.[30] In 1787 the nationalists, now evolved into "Federalists," saw to it that the right of the central government to create a navy in peacetime was made explicit in the proposed new constitution and that the president's power as commander in chief was spelled out. Gouverneur Morris recommended creation of a separate naval department at the Constitutional Convention, but the idea was quickly dropped from inclusion in the Constitution. For the reasons discussed below, the importance of the Navy and the need for a stronger union to sustain it also occasionally played a role in the arguments for ratification.[31]

Three problems were identified in the 1780s as likely to produce the distresses that would inspire the public to call for a navy: First, a general need to protect commerce and to be able to negotiate commercial agreements from a position of strength. Second, the more specific need to protect American ships in the Mediterranean from the North African "piratical states" now that the United States was no longer protected by the British Navy or by British agreements with the Barbary powers. Third, the difficulty of maintaining neutral status for the nation's ships in the event of war between the naval powers of Europe—an event expected to occur soon.

Of these three issues, the commerce question had the greatest long-term importance. The pirate issue provided the immediate occasion for naval revival, and violations of neutrality produced a permanent United States Navy. The two most important pro-naval writings of the ratification debates of 1787–88 were Hamilton's *The Federalist,* No. 11, and Madison's *The Federalist,* No. 41. Neither of these emphasized the pirate question. Hamilton's piece focused on the commercial and neutrality issues, while Madison's raised the problems of self-defense and preserving peace or neutrality without a navy.

As previously noted, the threat from Barbary corsairs was given as the reason for Congress's reluctance to sell the *Alliance* in 1784. When American seamen were captured and held for ransom in 1785, Jefferson, influenced by John Paul Jones, backed creation of a small fleet to confront the corsairs. Appealing to national honor and the need to ensure respect for the flag, Jefferson gave a ringing call for naval action by a small squadron in the Mediterranean. Such an approach, he argued, would be cheaper and more effective in the long run than paying ransom and annual tributes. In any case, creation of a small naval force would be necessary sooner or later "even were we to buy peace from the Algerines," so part of the costs were already inevitable.[32] Secretary for Foreign Affairs John Jay also expressed his preference for naval action over ransom at this time.

John Adams had followed closely Morris's earlier plans for naval reconstruction and agreed on the necessity for a navy. In May 1783 he had exclaimed: "I wish I were in Congress that I might assist you in perswading our countrymen to pay taxes and build ships." Nevertheless, he declared Jefferson's naval plan impractical in 1785. Congress would not be willing or able to fund a fleet at this time, he pointed out. Nor could a fleet be a temporary measure. "We ought not to fight them [the Algerians] at all, unless we determine to fight them forever." Jefferson's proposals were not adopted. Negotiations were initiated but met with little success. Congress commissioned Jones to negotiate for release of the captives in 1794, but Jones died before learning of the assignment.[33]

Congress took up the issue of the Barbary corsairs, only occasionally cited during the ratification debates, in 1791. But the corsairs did not become the opening wedge for naval revival until 1794 when they signed a treaty with the Portuguese, who now no longer prevented them from sailing past Gibraltar to attack ships in the Atlantic. Opponents of big government charged with some truth that the corsair menace was exaggerated to justify naval rearmament. Nevertheless, the strong desire to revivify American trade with the Mediterranean and the sense of insult from attacks by corsairs were widely felt. If the corsairs could roam the Atlantic, they could in theory attack the American coast. The corsairs were a weaker foe than the British,

French, or Spanish navies and were perceived as what we would now call villains straight out of central casting. These circumstances no doubt made their enmity a good occasion for creating a small, but heroic and dramatic fleet to protect American interests, and to revive national pride and the national image abroad—just as Jones, Barry, Gustavus Conyngham, Henry Johnson, and others had done early in the Revolution. Although the corsairs made peace before the frigates approved by Congress in 1794 were completed, other issues convinced Congress to go forward with the rebuilding of the Navy.

In 1781 Silas Deane raised the problems of protecting American commerce under independence in the "intercepted letters" written for publication by the British. "Without a marine force, our commerce will be everywhere exposed to imposition and insult, and we shall probably not be able to support a marine. In truth neither our friends, nor our foes can wish to see us a maritime power," he proclaimed.[34] The subject came to the fore when peace and independence were in fact obtained in 1783. The United States then struggled to combat restrictions on American trade by the various colonial powers and campaigned to persuade these powers of the advantages of free trade. Robert and Gouverneur Morris played early and extensive roles in this process but many others involved in naval issues also participated in the commercial debates, including Jay, Adams, Jefferson, Jeremiah Wadsworth, Nathaniel Gorham, William Bingham, and Robert R. Livingston. The commercial debates helped define and clarify American views on the Navy and its relationship to commerce and to the merchant marine. In voting to close its West Indian ports to American shipping in July 1783, the British had, during debates in Parliament, and subsequently in Lord Sheffield's pamphlet "Observations on the Commerce of the United States," defended the importance of the navigation acts in preserving British shipping and thereby creating a nursery for seamen. In the course of countering that view, many Americans argued that it was not restrictive shipping measures but the promotion of commerce in general that provided the circumstances by which seamen were nurtured. So long as the United States expanded its commerce and provided employment opportunities, particularly for New England seamen, it would have the sailors it needed in wartime. This view did not preclude having a core group of naval ships and officers with more immediate and specific naval training around which a larger force could be developed when necessary. But both those who later favored and those who opposed a substantial peacetime force believed that the availability of commercially trained seamen would make naval expansion possible when war approached.[35]

Both Robert Morris and Gouverneur Morris were among those who argued in 1783 and 1784 that commerce was the source of marine strength and that whatever promoted commerce facilitated the development of the Navy. Free trade based on the principles of comparative advantage was the best way to promote navigation. The privatizing approach Morris took toward the Navy in the 1780s also drew some of its inspiration from such views. According to notes made by Jefferson of a letter to the Chevalier de Chastellux of 7 October 1783, Gouverneur Morris argued:

> The marine of a country depends on it's commerce. Commerce depends on 2 pillars. 1. Navigation, which forms seamen. 2. Wealth, which supplies taxes. To pursue a marine at the expence of commerce, is to destroy the foundation while the superstructure is erected. To dry up the channels of wealth in order to increase [the] number of seamen has precisely that effect. . . . Men will not go to sea while they find easy subsistence on shore.
>
> Therefore 1. Numerous seamen can only be drawn from populous countries.
>
> 2. The rewards of labor at sea must be greater than for labor on shore.
>
> Whatever then contributes to population tends to produce seamen. Wealth and commerce support numbers.
>
> The navigation act . . . does not increase either of [those] sources of a marine.

Gouverneur Morris then expostulated on the benefits of free trade, summarizing at the end, "More commodities are raised, more *carried,* more ships built, more *seamen* bred."[36]

Gouverneur Morris advanced similar claims in his "Ideas of an American on Commerce between the United States and French Islands" of October 1783. In this text, presented to La Luzerne, he argued that if France restricted commerce to increase the number of

French seamen, it would "defeat the very Purpose intended." If France allowed a free trade, "the Produce of the Islands will be so much encreased, that with every possible Deduction for what may be carried in American Bottoms, there must be a very great Increase of french Shipping to carry off that Produce." The benefits would be reciprocal. "Each Nation will derive an Addition of private wealth and of public Revenue, and the Number both of french and american Seamen will be encreased." Originally included but omitted in the final version was the following: "Which Circumstance ought to be a pleasing Consideration to both Countries, as the Time may not be far distant in which they may at Sea be joined under the same Banners as lately they were at Land." [37]

The same linkage between the commerce and Navy issues discussed in 1783 was further developed in 1788 in *The Federalist*, No. 11, wherein Hamilton warned

> that the adventurous spirit, which distinguishes the commercial character of America, has already excited uneasy sensations in several of the maritime powers of Europe. They seem to be apprehensive of our too great interference in that carrying trade, which is the support of their navigation and the foundation of their naval strength. Those of them which have colonies in America look forward to what this country is capable of becoming, with painful solicitude. They foresee the dangers that may threaten their American dominions from the neighborhood of States, which have all the dispositions, and would possess all the means, requisite to the creation of a powerful marine. Impressions of this kind will naturally indicate the policy of fostering divisions among us, and of depriving us, as far as possible, of an ACTIVE COMMERCE in our own bottoms. This would answer the threefold purpose of preventing our interference in their navigation, of monopolizing the profits of our trade, and of clipping the wings by which we might soar to a dangerous greatness.

After recommending a retaliatory policy of "prohibitory regulations" against foreign shipping, Hamilton argued that establishment of a federal navy would be a further resource for influencing the conduct of European nations toward us. "Continuance of the Union, under an efficient government," he predicted, "would put it in our power, at a period not very distant, to create a navy, which, if it could not vie with those of the great maritime powers, would at least be of respectable weight, if thrown into the scale of either of two contending parties." The contribution even a small navy could make would be especially important for operations in the West Indies where "a few ships of the line sent opportunely to the reinforcement of either side, would often be sufficient to decide the fate of a campaign, on the event of which interests of the greatest magnitude were suspended." Such a favorable situation "would enable us to bargain with great advantage for commercial privileges. A price would be set not only upon our friendship, but upon our neutrality. By a steady adherence to the Union we may hope, ere long to become the Arbiter of Europe in America; and to be able to incline the balance of European competitions in this part of the world as our interest may dictate."

Hamilton continued that "under a vigorous national government the natural strength and resources of the country, directed to a common interest, would baffle all the combinations of European jealousy to restrain our growth," resulting in an "active commerce, an extensive navigation, and a flourishing marine." After discussing the importance of the Navy to the fisheries—another nursery of seamen—Hamilton proclaimed that the "necessity of naval protection to external or maritime commerce does not require a particular elucidation, no more than the conduciveness of that species of commerce to the prosperity of a navy."[38]

Hamilton followed up the passage in *The Federalist*, No. 11, quoted above about unity enabling the United States to place a price on its neutrality with a warning of what would happen should the United States not mount a unified defense: "our commerce would be a prey to the wanton intermeddlings of all nations at war with each other; who, having nothing to fear from us, would with little scruple or remorse, supply their wants by depredations on our property, as often as it fell in their way. The rights of neutrality will only be respected when they are defended by an adequate power. A nation, despicable by its weakness, forfeits even the privilege of being neutral."[39]

In *The Federalist*, No. 41, James Madison further dramatized American vulnerability without union and a centralized peacetime defense.

The palpable necessity of the power to provide and maintain a navy has protected that part of the constitution against a spirit of censure, which has spared few other parts.... The inhabitants of the Atlantic frontier are all of them deeply interested in this provision for naval protection, and if they have hitherto been suffered to sleep quietly in their beds; if their property has remained safe against the predatory spirit of licentious adventurers; if their maritime towns have not yet been compelled to ransom themselves from the terrors of a conflagration, by yielding to the exactions of daring and sudden invaders, these instances of good fortune are not to be ascribed to the capacity of the existing government for the protection of those from whom it claims allegiance, but to causes that are fugitive and fallacious.

Madison emphasized the particular vulnerability of a state like New York.

The great emporium of its commerce, the great reservoir of its wealth, lies every moment at the mercy of events, and may almost be regarded as a hostage for ignominious compliances with the dictates of a foreign enemy, or even with the rapacious demands of pirates and barbarians. Should a war be the result of the precarious situation of European affairs, and all the unruly passions attending it, be let loose on the ocean, our escape from insults and depredations, not only on that element, but every part of the other bordering on it, will be truly miraculous.[40]

The Federalist effort to strengthen defense through the new Constitution received assistance from former naval officers who became involved as they campaigned for the claims of former naval personnel or sought to rebuild a navy in which they would have positions.[41] Many were members of the Society of the Cincinnati, though naval officers were not generally so conspicuous in political affairs as the army officers that dominated that organization.[42] Cincinnati member John Barry petitioned the Continental Congress on behalf of naval officers for naval depreciation pay, pensions, and land grants, only to be rebuffed. He ultimately facilitated a change in government by literally forcing members of the Pennsylvania legislature to attend so as to obtain the quorum necessary to vote for a state ratifying convention.[43] After such efforts were successful, naval officers participated in the elaborate procession held in Pennsylvania on 4 July 1788, celebrating ratification. John Green appeared as captain of the Federal Ship *Union*, a large, beautifully carved float that was a centerpiece of the procession. The procession also included strong representation of commercial and maritime professions, and ten decorated ships each representing a state that had already ratified the Constitution lined the harbor. Overall, the imagery of the procession was probably more that of the commercial and general maritime influences on ratification, but the Navy had a small but conspicuous role.[44]

The arguments for and against the Navy during the Confederation and Early National periods have been categorized by one scholar, Craig Symonds, as navalist or antinavalist, rather than pro- or anti-Navy. He documents adherence to concepts of navalism (the maritime equivalent of militarism) largely through the arguments advanced by Hamilton in *The Federalist*, No. 11, and to those he employed in 1783 in the committee report on the peacetime military establishment. Essentially, Symonds argues, navalism embodies adherence to a strong navy not for territorial and commercial protection, but for the diplomatic purposes of national prestige and respect abroad, deterrence, and, more ominously, for the purposes of influencing the balance of power in Europe, or for intervening in world affairs. He defines antinavalists, conversely, as limiting the size and cost of the Navy to what is necessary for current defense of territory and sometimes of commerce, but not for prestige and for broader diplomatic purposes.[45]

My appraisal of discussions of the Navy during the confederation reveals few who fully meet Symonds's definition of navalist. The nationalists surrounding Robert Morris and their successors, the Federalists, certainly believed in more than a defensive navy. They saw the nation as eventually becoming an empire, on sea as well as on land, and were concerned with issues of prestige, respect, and showing the flag abroad. Most advocated neutrality in European wars and expected American trade would benefit from such a role, but doubted neutrality would be respected without a credible deterrence. The question of an American role in the balance of power, however, came up only when Americans were attempting to persuade European powers to offer trade concessions in the West Indies. They implied that Americans would favor whatever countries offered concessions and that, in the event of a new war in the West Indies, American ships could play an important role in the outcome. A few hinted to Europeans that should their ships and goods be barred from the West Indies and Latin America, Americans would support the independence of those areas—exactly how that would be done was not spelled out. However, not even Hamilton held out the idea of a role for the Navy in the balance of power in Europe. Even the most extravagant expectations for future naval power presaged the ideas of the Monroe Doctrine and Manifest Destiny rather than American global interventionism or involvement in the affairs of Europe. In short, the notion that many nationalists/Federalists were navalists, in the sense that Symonds defines it, is exaggerated even for the Early National period, and applies to few, if any, in the Confederation era. Moreover, aside from the writings of John Paul Jones, although much information had been gathered, there was little specific planned in the Confederation era about the ultimate size, type of ships, training programs, and speed of development of the Navy. All that was considered premature.[46]

Few nationalists doubted that the nation would one day be a great maritime power—at least if the new central government under the constitution was created—but that day was still seen as far off, and the grandiose dreams attributed to "navalists" were subordinated to the practical realities confronting that generation of Americans. A navy was important, and should be begun, but other issues came first: the creation of national unity and a viable government; population growth and development of a larger and stronger economy, and through those means attainment of an adequate public income; and diminishment of the wartime national debt. Immediate threats could move the Navy up in the scale of priorities temporarily—but the priorities expressed in the Confederation era predominated well into the next century.

Furthermore, the specific responses of Congress to calls for naval revival in the 1790s were shaped by the Confederation experiences. Even the strongest supporters knew they had to wait until the government was established and finances improved. Thus, the congressional response in 1791 to Secretary of State Jefferson's irate report on corsair activity was merely a resolution acknowledging that trade could not be protected except by a navy, in another echo of Morris's statements of 1783–84, and a recommendation that a navy be created as soon as United States finances permitted.[47]

Despite the unreliability of protection by foreign navies in the past, the United States still was periodically forced to depend on them. When in 1794 the Portuguese made peace with the Algerians and freed them to capture American ships on the Atlantic rather than just in the Mediterranean, Congress, after discussions in committee and by a caucus that included Morris, Hamilton, and other holdovers from the 1783 discussions, voted to build six frigates, but with the stipulation that construction be halted if peace was obtained. Rather than quickly acquiring ships through purchase, Congress followed the lines that Morris suggested in 1783—building better ships in America than had previously been available.[48] Shipbuilder Joshua Humphreys forwarded designs to Senator Morris based on his diagrams of the *South Carolina*, which Morris and apparently Humphreys, among others, had examined in detail in 1783.[49] These diagrams became a basis for the designs of the *Constitution* and the *Constellation*.

Construction procedures for the first United States naval ships repeated many aspects of the Revolutionary and Confederation experience. The usual feuds and shortages, but particularly an effort to acquire southern live oak, delayed construction.[50] The policy of using southern wood, which Hamilton had mentioned in *The Federalist*, No. 11, was an outgrowth of many earlier attempts to develop the shipbuilding, naval stores, and timbers industries, such as plans to market oak from the estate of General Nathanael Greene on the Georgia coast. Following the long-established practice developed during the Revolution, the government distributed shipbuilding among various states and sections of the country, despite the fact that naval advisers like Thomas Truxtun warned against the inefficiencies involved, particularly in the south.[51] Washington, and members of Congress, had long ago learned the political necessity of distributing such patronage and tax monies if they wished to assure funding and support. Perhaps they also remembered the ease with which vessels under construction were blocked in or destroyed during the Revolution and chose not to have all their eggs in one basket.

In any case, peace was declared with the Algerians before the ships were completed and Congress had to wrestle with the question of continuing the construction of three of the vessels. Finally, the distresses derived from neutrality violations by both France and Britain and the breakout of the Quasi-War against France so stirred emotions that not only was the construction completed but also a full panoply of the earlier practices of buying and converting smaller ships and taking up subscriptions to finance them was quickly put into play.[52] When speed was needed, it was possible to employ it. The rapid naval expansion during the Quasi-War makes it likely that the 1794 naval construction was not seen as really urgent even by Navy backers, but was designed to send a message of deterrence and set the stage for future action. Acquisition of seamen and small ships could be done quickly and relatively cheaply; building the larger ships would take time and money.

During the 1790s, training programs similar to those suggested by Jones were proposed by Truxtun, John Swanwick, and Hamilton, but were not actually implemented on any scale until the nineteenth century.[53] While some new figures came on the scene, the chief backers of naval development in the 1790s were familiar Confederation figures or their protégés: Washington, Adams, and Hamilton of course, and in the Senate, Morris, who appears to have played a role largely behind the scenes, and, in the House of Representatives, his long-time associates. Thomas Fitzsimons in 1794, then John Swanwick in 1796–97 were among the foremost backers of pro-naval legislation—Swanwick despite the fact that he had switched to the Republican party.[54] Thus, the naval movement of the Confederation era—pro-Navy but mindful of limitations—both prefigured and continued to influence the ideas and actions of the 1790s.

Notes

This paper is based in part on research conducted for The Papers of Robert Morris, 1781–84, a documentary publications project supported by grants from the National Endowment for the Humanities and National Historical Publications and Records Commission and from various private funders. Citations to the published volumes (E. James

Ferguson, John Catanzariti, Elizabeth M. Nuxoll, Mary A. Y. Gallagher, et al., eds., *The Papers of Robert Morris*, 1781–1784, 9 volumes [Pittsburgh, Pa.: University of Pittsburgh Press, 1973–99]) are abbreviated as *RMP.* In citations, Robert Morris's initials RM are used.

1. Samuel Eliot Morison, *John Paul Jones: A Sailor's Biography* (Boston: Little, Brown, 1959), 59, 66–67, 87, 91, 180, 181, 297, 318; and Charles Oscar Paullin, *The Navy of the American Revolution: Its Administration, Its Policy, and Its Achievements* (1906; reprint, New York: Haskell House, 1971), 90, 173–76, 182–83.

2. William M. Fowler Jr., *Rebels under Sail: The American Navy during the Revolution* (New York: Charles Scribner's Sons, 1976), 85, 89–91. Stephen T. Powers gives the fullest discussion of Morris's handling of the Navy. He is somewhat critical of the Navy's subordination to finance but generally links it accurately to the failure of the "Nationalist" movement to obtain an independent revenue. Powers, "Decline and Extinction of American Naval Power" (Ph.D. diss., University of Notre Dame, 1965), 194–97. On the subordination of the Army's needs to finance, see William Johnson, *Sketches of the Life and Correspondence of Nathanael Greene, Major General of the Armies of the United States*, vol. 2 (Charleston, S.C., 1822), 253–56; and Wayne Carp, *To Starve the Army at Pleasure: Continental Army Administration and American Political Culture* (Chapel Hill, N.C.: University of North Carolina Press, 1984), 214–16.

3. On RM's effort to rebuild the Continental Navy in 1782, see *RMP,* 6:94–95, 101–3.

4. State of American Commerce and a Plan for Protecting It, May 1782, *RMP,* 5:145–57. The use of foreign convoys continued to be advocated, and sometimes practiced, during the 1790s.

5. For an example of RM's publicizing of naval exploits, see John Barry to RM, 18 Oct. 1782, *RMP,* 6:625. Writings by poet-polemicist-sea captain Philip Freneau also glorified American naval successes in 1782. Lewis Leary, *That Rascal Freneau: A Study in Literary Failure* (New Brunswick, N.J.: Rutgers University Press, 1941), 96, 428; and Morison, *Jones,* 317–18. On the press campaign for a new Navy, see also *RMP,* 5:101; and David Freeman Hawke, *Benjamin Rush: Revolutionary Gadfly* (Indianapolis and New York: Bobbs-Merrill, 1971), 255–59. For later press support for a navy, see Edward C. Carter II, "Matthew Carey, Advocate of American Naval Power, 1785–1814," *American Neptune* 26 (1966): 177–88. On the request for French assistance in rebuilding the Navy, see *RMP,* 6:95, 102–3.

6. On the Navy and RM's funding plan, see RM to the president of Congress, 29 July 1782, and notes, *RMP,* 6:, esp. 55, 65. For Hamilton's proposals to borrow for a Navy in 1799, see below at note 52. Gouverneur Morris

had suggested using a tax on exports and ships to finance a navy as early as 15 Apr. 1780, in an article signed "An American" printed in the *Pennsylvania Packet*. Drafts for this piece found in the Gouverneur Morris Papers at Columbia University reveal that the paragraph regarding the Navy was extensively reworked in an effort to find the right tone and to modify any phrasing that would suggest an aggressive or interventionist role for the future Navy.

7. On opposition to the funding plan, see *RMP,* 7:78–93.

8. For the budget request for $2.5 million, see *RMP,* 5:147–48, 6:95.

9. On the acquisition of the *Duc de Lauzun,* see *RMP,* 6:294, 295–96 n.

10. On the presentation of the *America* to France, see *RMP,* 6:302.

11. On the attempt to obtain the *South Carolina* (formerly *Indien*), see *RMP,* 5:105, 106 n., 148, 280, 507. Morison asserts that her design was probably studied at that time by Joshua Humphreys, architect of the first frigates built by the federal government, for in design she was the parent of USS *Constitution* and *Constellation.* Morison, *Jones,* 331.

12. For Jones's training in the West Indies, see *RMP,* 7:125–26, 134–35 n.

13. RM to the president of Congress, 10 July 1783, *RMP,* 8:265. For Morris's continued belief in the importance of the Navy, see also RM to —, 10 Apr., to the president of Congress, 3 May, and to John Jay, 27 Nov. 1783, *RMP,* 7:694–95, 790, 8:786. On the dismantlement of the Continental Navy, see Powers, "Decline and Extinction of American Naval Power," 162–87; and Fowler, *Rebels under Sail,* 84–86.

14. Accused of selling ships to cronies and rigging bids by allowing a shorter time for payment than usual, Morris did not succeed in warding off criticism despite taking precautions with regard to the sale of the *Hague.* See notes to RM's report to Congress of 22 July, James Read's memorandum of 20 Sept., and RM to Thomas Russell, 22 July, 12 and 19 Aug., and 9 Oct. 1783, and, for the context, the discussion of Morris's involvement in the China trade appearing in the appendix, *RMP,* 8:270, 325–27 n., 531, 415, 425–26, 442, 596–97, 857–82. Deputy Marine Agent Thomas Russell acquired the *Hague*—probably to ship masts or naval timber in conjunction with a plan for marketing such goods abroad discussed in Morris's letter to Russell and his partners of 2 Sept. 1783 (*RMP,* 8:486–87).

15. For the sale of the *Duc de Lauzun,* see *RMP,* 7:687, 708–10 n., 8:325, 326 n.

16. For Morris's recommendations on the sale of vessels, see also Report to Congress on the State of Vessels, 22 July 1783, and notes, and, for the *Alliance,* RM to the president of Congress, 1 Sept. 1783, and notes, *RMP,* 8:325–27 n., 480–81. For the sale of the *General Washington,* see RM to the president of Congress, 19 Mar., to Arthur Lee, 3 Apr., and to Joshua Barney, 11 May, and Advertisement Respecting the *General Washington,* 16 Apr. 1784, *RMP,* 9:194–95, 227, 258, 332–33.

17. For the survey of the *Alliance,* see John Barry, Benjamin G. Eyre, Joshua Humphreys Jr., Thomas Penrose, and Thomas Read to RM, 1 Nov. 1783, see *RMP,* 8:699. For the congressional actions on the question of selling the *Alliance,* see *RMP,* 8:481 n.

18. On the voyage of the *Alliance* to China, see *RMP,* 8:482 n.; Mary A. Y. Gallagher, "Charting a New Course for the China Trade: The Late Eighteenth-Century Model," below, in these *Essays;* and Martin I. J. Griffin, *Commodore John Barry* (Philadelphia: published by the author, 1903), 259.

19. *RMP,* 7:683, 684 n. On congressional efforts to acquire information for future naval endeavors, see also Jeremiah Wadsworth to John Paul Jones, 20 Jan. 1783, James C. Bradford, ed., *The Papers of John Paul Jones,* 10 reels (Alexandria, Va.: Chadwyck-Healey, 1986), 7:1445.

20. *RMP,* 7:712.

21. *RMP,* 7:790.

22. Harold C. Syrett and Jacob E. Cooke, eds., *Papers of Alexander Hamilton,* vol. 3 (New York: Columbia University Press, 1961–87), 378–97, especially, 378–79.

23. On Jones's proposals for a naval establishment and for an improved signaling system, see *Diary,* 22 May, and Jones to RM, 4 Oct. (second letter), and notes, *RMP,* 8:109, 575–76, 579–81; and Morison, *Jones,* 335. Thomas Truxtun later studied and proposed (1797) a signaling system, but unlike Jones's version, it was based on British rather than French practice. See Eugene S. Ferguson, *Truxtun of the Constellation: The Life of Commodore Thomas Truxtun, U.S. Navy, 1755–1822* (Baltimore, Md.: Johns Hopkins Press, 1956), 127–28.

24. Jones to Lee, 10 Feb., and to Castries, 25 May 1784, *Jones Papers,* 7:1500, 1515. On Jones's mission to Europe, see Jones to RM, 4 Oct. (second letter), and 13 Oct., and notes, *RMP,* 8:580, 583, 617–19.

25. Jones to Jay, 6 Aug. 1785, Mary A. Giunta, et al., eds., *The Emerging Nation: A Documentary History of the Foreign Relations of the United States under the Articles of Confederation, 1780–1789,* vol. 2 (Washington, D.C.: National Historical Publications and Records Commission, 1996), 734; and Morrison, *Jones,* 399.

26. For RM's hiring of naval officers, see *RMP,* 8:326 n., 482 n., 863 n., 865. Naval captains Thomas Read and James Nicholson sailed for Europe for Parker and Company in 1784 as commanders of the *Columbia* and the *Comte d'Artois.* Read subsequently sailed for Morris and for Constable, Rucker, and Company, his firm in New York. John Barry conducted some business for Willing, Morris, and Swanwick but apparently did not captain any of RM's ships. John Paul Jones was offered a cargo should he have gone forward with plans to acquire his own ship. Future naval officer Thomas Truxtun was sailing

for RM when he was appointed to the U.S. Navy in 1794. Besides Green, Barry, and Dale, other naval officers later in the China trade included Thomas Read, Thomas Bell, and James Josiah. On participation of naval officers in the China trade, see William Bell Clark, *Gallant John Barry 1745–1803: The Story of a Naval Hero of Two Wars* (New York: Macmillan, 1938), 330–31, 337–50; and, on Truxtun's role, Ferguson, *Truxtun*, 60–93, 103.

27. On the supply of foreign navies and shipbuilding for them, see *RMP,* 4:appendix, and 6:494, 8:326 n., 486–87, 566; Thomas J. Schaeper, *France and America in the Revolutionary Era: The Life of Jacques-Donatien Leray de Chaumont, 1725-1803* (Providence, R.I.: Berghahn Books, 1995), 212–14; Paul W. Bamford, "France and the American Market in Naval Timber and Masts, 1776–1786," *Journal of Economic History* 12 (1952): 21–34; and Mary Jo Kline, "Gouverneur Morris and the New Nation, 1775–1789" (Ph.D. diss, Columbia University, 1970), 218 n., and 234–35. On continued interest in restoring the shipbuilding, naval stores, and mast industries, see notes 50 and 54 below.

28. On the voyage of the *Empress of China,* see RM to John Jay, 27 Nov. 1783, and the documents and notes included in the appendix to *RMP,* 8:786, 857–82; and Philip Chadwick Foster Smith, The *Empress of China* (Philadelphia: Philadelphia Maritime Museum, 1984). Smith points out (p. 6) two of the ship's owners, Daniel Parker and Robert Morris, and five of the top officers, Green, Randall, Shaw, Johnston, and surgeon's mate Andrew Caldwell, were all members of the newly formed Society of the Cincinnati. (However, Morris's membership was an honorary one; and because there were several Daniel Parkers, it is not certain Parker was actually a member.)

29. On the perception of naval weakness and the adoption of the United States Constitution, see Frederick W. Marks III, *Independence on Trial: Foreign Affairs and the Making of the Constitution,* (Baton Rouge: Louisiana State University Press, 1973), 36–51; Powers, "Decline and Extinction of American Naval Power," 235–57; Marshall Smelser, *The Congress Founds the Navy, 1787–1798* (South Bend, Ind.: University of Notre Dame Press, 1959), 37, 44; Craig L. Symonds, *Navalists and Antinavalists: The Naval Policy Debate in the United States, 1785–1827* (Newark, Del.: University of Delaware Press, 1980), 23.

30. *RMP,* 8:247–49.

31. For naval issues at the Constitutional Convention, see Merrill Jensen, ed., *The Documentary History of the Ratification of the Constitution,* vol. 1 *[Constitutional Documents and Records, 1776–1787]* (Madison, Wis.: State Historical Society of Wisconsin, 1976), 238, 246, 247, 252, 254, 255, 264, 267, 268, 275, 280, 282, 289, 291, 293, 310, 311, 313; and John A. Rohr, "Constitutional Foundations of the United States Navy: Text and Context," *Naval War College Review* 45 (Winter 1992): 68–84. For Gouverneur

Morris's proposals during the Constitutional Convention for a separate navy department, see Max M. Mintz, *Gouverneur Morris and the American Revolution* (Norman: University of Oklahoma Press, 1970), 194.

32. For early writings on the threat of corsairs to American trade with the Mediterranean, see *RMP,* 8:548, 550 n., 558, 560 n.; Thomas Paine's "The American Crisis, XIII," 19 Apr. 1783, in Philip S. Foner, ed., vol. 1 *The Complete Writings of Thomas Paine* (New York: Citadel Press, 1945), 233; Benjamin Franklin to Robert R. Livingston, 2 July 1783, in Francis Wharton, ed., *The Revolutionary Diplomatic Correspondence of the United States,* vol. 6 (Washington, D.C.: Government Printing Office, 1889), 587; Marks, *Independence on Trial,* 36–45; Ray Watkins Irwin, *The Diplomatic Relations of the United States with The Barbary Powers, 1776–1816* (Chapel Hill: University of North Carolina Press, 1931), 1–54; James A. Field Jr., *America and the Mediterranean World, 1776–1882* (Princeton, N.J.: Princeton University Press, 1969), 27 67. On Jefferson's proposals for naval action against the Algerians, see Julian P. Boyd, ed., *The Papers of Thomas Jefferson,* vol. 8 (Princeton, N.J.: Princeton University Press, 1953), 426–27; Smelser, *Congress Founds the Navy,* 38–40; Symonds, *Navalists,* 19–29; and Marks, *Independence on Trial,* 42–44.

33. On John Adams's general support for a rebuilt navy, and his rejection of naval action at this time, see Adams to RM, 21 May 1783, *RMP,* 8:109; to Jones, 12 Aug. 1782, Jones Papers, 7:1419; and Symonds, *Navalists,* 19–20. For Jay's views, expressed in his report of 20 Oct. 1785, see Giunta et al., *Emerging Nation,* 2:868–70.

34. For Deane's predictions, see *RMP,* 1:137.

35. On Deane, British policy, and Sheffield's pamphlet, and the numerous American responses, see *RMP,* 8:603–13, especially 610–12.

36. *RMP,* 8:593–95. Robert Morris also denied that the Navigation Acts were the foundation of British naval superiority in his letter to Benjamin Franklin of 30 Sept. 1783 (*RMP,* 8:557–60, esp. 558).

37. *RMP,* 8:681–99.

38. See *The Federalist,* No. 11, *Hamilton Papers,* 4:339–46.

39. Ibid., 342.

40. See *The Federalist,* No. 41, in Robert A. Rutland, Charles F. Hobson, William M. E. Rachal, Frederika J. Teute, et al, eds., *The Papers of James Madison,* Congressional Series, vol. 10 (Chicago and London: University of Chicago Press, 1977), 390–98.

41. On John Barry and the naval officers' petitions for depreciation pay, pensions, and land grants similar to those given the army, see Clark, *Barry,* 325–26; and, for the background, *RMP,* 8:521–23 n. For the failure to obtain most such benefits even after the new government was formed, see Clark, *Barry,* 354–56.

42. On the membership of naval officers in the Society of the Cincinnati, see Minor Myers Jr., *Liberty without Anarchy: A History of the Society of the Cincinnati* (Charlottesville, Va.: University Press of Virginia, 1983), 114–15, 121, 212. Myers notes that of the six captains appointed to the Navy in 1794, five were already members of the society, while Thomas Truxtun was made an honorary member in 1800.

43. On Barry's enforced attendance for the vote in the Pennsylvania Assembly, see Clark, *Barry*, 331–34.

44. On the federal procession of 1788, see *Pennsylvania Gazette*, 9 July 1788, and Francis Hopkinson, *Account of the Grand Federal Procession, Philadelphia, July 4, 1788* (Philadelphia: Mathew Carey, 1788), reprinted in *The Miscellaneous Essays and Occasional Writings of Francis Hopkinson, Esq.*, vol. 2 (Philadelphia: T. Dobson, 1792).

45. Symonds, *Navalists*, 12–13, 24–25, 51–55. See also note 6 above.

46. *The Federalist*, No. 11; *RMP*, 8:476; *Hamilton Papers*, 23:227–28.

47. Members of the caucus discussing a solution to the Mediterranean crisis included Robert Morris, Ralph Izard, and Oliver Ellsworth (senators); Congressmen Fisher Ames, Theodore Sedgwick, and William Smith; and Secretaries Alexander Hamilton and Henry Knox. Of the group, Morris, Ellsworth, Hamilton, and Knox had all been part of the discussions of the peacetime military establishment in 1783. Symonds, *Navalists*, 28; and L. H. Bolander, "An Incident in the Founding of the American Navy," *United States Naval Institute Proceedings* 55 (June 1929), 491–94. On the committee report calling for naval protection in the Mediterranean as soon as "the state of public finances will admit," see Linda Grant De Pauw, Charlene Bangs Bickford, and LaVonne Marlene Siegel, eds., *Documentary History of the First Federal Congress, 1789–1791*, vol. 2 *[Senate Executive Journal and Related Documents]* (Baltimore, Md.: Johns Hopkins University Press, 1974), 114–15, 425–49. For an example of the opposition to stronger action at that time, see Maclay's Journal of 1 Feb. 1791 in Kenneth R. Bowling and Helen E. Veit, eds., *The Diary of William Maclay and Other Notes on Senate Debates, March 4, 1789–March 3, 1791* [*Documentary History of the First Federal Congress of the United States of America*, volume 9] (Baltimore, Md.: Johns Hopkins University Press, 1988), 77, 373.

48. For the new and better ships, see Ferguson, *Truxtun*, 109–11; Smelser, *Congress Founds the Navy*, 72–74.

49. See above at note 11. On the shipbuilders and naval officers who conferred in 1794 on the building of the six new frigates, most of whom had previously built for the Continental Navy or surveyed the ships when they were considered for sale, see Ferguson, *Truxtun*, 109; and Tyrone G. Martin, "The USS *Constitution:* A Design Confirmed," *American Neptune* 57 (1977): 257–65.

50. On the use of live oak, see Symonds, *Navalists*, 36; Ferguson, *Truxtun*, 114–19; and Virginia Steele Wood, *Live Oaking: Southern Timber for Tall Ships* (1981; reprint, Annapolis, Md.: Naval Institute Press, 1995). Morris was aware of stocks of naval timber remaining in Georgia after the Revolution and may have been the source of information given to Secretary at War Henry Knox about naval stores there. John Wereat to RM, 1 and 5 Nov. 1784 (Papers of the Continental Congress, 1774–1789, no. 20, vol. 2:448, Record Group 360, National Archives). For efforts to develop a market for ships' timber from General Greene's estates in the 1780s, see Theodore Thayer, *Nathanael Greene: Strategist of the Revolution* (New York: Twayne, 1960), 437, 443–44. For Hamilton's arguments on behalf of southern wood, see *Hamilton Papers*, 4:344.

51. For Truxtun's critique of the policy of widespread distribution of ship construction for the Navy, see Ferguson, *Truxtun*, 111–12; and Smelser, *Congress Founds the Navy*, 99.

52. On fund-raising and the acquisition of small ships, see Symonds, *Navalists*, 69–70, 79–80; Ferguson, *Truxtun*, 121; and Frederick C. Leiner, "The Subscription Warships of 1798," *American Neptune* 66 (1986): 141–58.

In 1799 Hamilton recommended the most grandiose naval plan of the Early National Period. See Hamilton to James McHenry, 27 June 1799, *Hamilton Papers*, 23:227–28. Part of this text is quoted in Symonds, *Navalists*, p. 24, as evidence of the imperialist, interventionist side of navalism, but the full text clearly refers to action in the American, not the European theater and primarily to army, not naval, activity.

53. For the plans for training programs, see *Hamilton Papers*, 24:308–11; Ferguson, *Truxtun*, 128; and Swanwick's policies cited below in note 54.

54. John Swanwick in the House of Representatives is depicted as a "navalist" in Symonds, *Navalists*, 40, 42–43. Fitzsimons is not mentioned as a "navalist" there, but other sources indicate it was he who proposed the bill for building frigates. According to Roland Baumann, Swanwick was a "realist" in foreign affairs, favoring a policy of preparedness, though not blind nationalism. As one of the principal supporters in the House of the plan to build six frigates, Swanwick argued that it was preferable to spend the money to support the domestic shipbuilding industry than to pay tribute to Algiers. Furthermore, not a cent should be spent, he declared, to purchase ships abroad. Swanwick eventually supported the establishment of a separate army and navy, each with an academy, as the only way to avoid waste and extravagance in naval affairs. Roland M. Baumann, "John Swanwick: Spokesman for 'Merchant-Republicanism' in Philadelphia, 1790–1798," *Pennsylvania Magazine of History and Biography* 97 (1973): 131–82, especially 144, 174–75.

Many aspects of Robert Morris's life in the 1790s gave further evidence of continuity with regard to support for revival of the Navy and of the related infrastructure. For example, Morris wrote Captain John Barry on 8 Aug. 1797, on behalf of a young man recommended by his old partner Benjamin Harrison Jr. "I am of the opinion," Morris proclaimed, "that the Frigates should take every young man that offers in order to bring up and breed both Seamen & Officers." (Feinstone Collection, American Philosophical Society). From his cell in debtor's prison, Morris wrote Secretary of the Navy Benjamin Stoddert on 20 June 1798, recommending another young man, Henry Kenyon, for a naval slot (Naval Department Records, 1794–1800, Applications for Appointments, Record Group 45, box 3, National Archives). Morris's son Charles joined the Navy in 1798–99, served under Truxtun, and ultimately died at sea. See RM to Marie Morris, June 1799, quoted in Eleanor Young, *Forgotten Patriot: Robert Morris* (New York: Macmillan, 1950), 245–47. Morris was also the principal backer and partner of Henry Foxall, whose Eagle Works provided technologically superior cannon for the U.S. Navy during the Quasi-War with France. Foxall subsequently moved to Washington, where he established the Columbia Works on the Potomac above Georgetown and continued as a major supplier of ordnance for the U.S. government. See Charles E. Peterson, "Morris, Foxall, and the Eagle Works: A Pioneer Steam Engine Boring Cannon," *Canal History and Technology Proceedings* 7 (1988): 207–40, esp. pp. 217–19, 226 n.–27 n.; RM to Thomas Jefferson, 6 May 1801, Jefferson Papers, Manuscript Division, Library of Congress.

Massachusetts, the first United States Revenue Cutter, commissioned in 1791

2

Patterns of Northern New England Smuggling 1789-1820

Joshua M. Smith

The period between 1789 and 1820 saw a persistent and trouble-some pattern of smuggling in northern New England that the fed-eral government, despite considerable effort, never succeeded in con-trolling. Large-scale illicit trade made a mockery of trade regulation by both the British and American governments. The how, why, and what of illicit trade in northern New England can provide some useful and surprising data concerning American seaborne commerce, especially that with the British possessions in North America and the Caribbean.

Smuggling was essentially a form of tax evasion. By avoiding gov-ernment customs officials, smugglers could gain substantial profits, both by avoiding the customs duties and by trafficking in proscribed goods. Contemporary accounts of smuggling generally disapproved of it. Dr. Johnson's definition of a smuggler, "a wretch who, in defiance of the laws, imports and exports goods without payment of the customs," is typical of feelings toward those engaged in the trade.[1] But even the most priggish observers had a difficult time strongly disapproving of smuggling. The following encounter with smugglers on the Nova Scotia coast is an excerpt from a missionary's journal. It being Sunday, the missionary disembarked from his ship to hear a sermon in the town. Finding none,

> after a solitary walk on the sea shore, we hailed the boat and returned on board, to read our bibles, and enjoy what conversation our circumstances afforded. Digby is given up to smuggling, and at night, when the smugglers came on board, to carry their contraband goods ashore, we were greatly disturbed with their profane and worldly conversation; they continued to grow worse, and at last we reproved them, but this brought upon us a flood of reproach and invective: one of them, to show his importance, quoted a scrap of latin, but upon my calmly telling him we did not deal in scraps, his fury became ungovernable; and I believe, had it not been for fear of the consequence, they would have murdered us both.[2]

The pedantic missionary's account reveals that he disapproved of profanity more than smuggling. Other contemporary accounts, especially from Americans, actually approve of smuggling. Fisher Ames in addressing Congress on the problem of smuggling put it nicely: "The habit of smuggling pervades our country. We were taught it when it was considered rather as meritorious than criminal."[3]

Smuggling in this period has received scant attention from historians. While a subject of great interest, it has been, in the words of one historian, "prejudiced from the outset by an aura of humor and romantic farce."[4] The problem is how to collect facts on a trade that depended on its ability not to be traced. This presents an interesting obstacle to the historian, but not one that is insurmountable. The easiest way to research smuggling is to go to the documentation left by federal law enforcement agencies. The records of customs collectors and revenue cutter officers, federal district and circuit courts, and U.S. district marshals (as well as military and naval officers) often contain valuable accounts of smuggling.

Government officials and those with an interest in maintaining order considered that smuggling defrauded the government's revenues, promoted disrespect for the government, and contributed to lawlessness in general.[5] Despite the approbation associated with smuggling, U.S. federal law did not consider smuggling a criminal offense until well into the nineteenth century. Heedful of the smuggling-associated problems with governmental authority before the American Revolution, the founding fathers considered smuggling to be a civil offense, punishable only by substantial fines, seizure of goods and ships involved, and forfeiture of bonds posted by merchants.[6]

The following incident illustrates graphically some of the problems the government had in curtailing smuggling, as well as some of the typical characteristics of smuggling. In the summer of 1800 the collector of Portland, Nathaniel Fosdick, seized a quantity of coffee brought illegally into that town by a merchant named Deering, the owner of the brig *Ranger*. The district attorney for Maine wrote the following account of what happened next:

> The Coffee for safe keeping was deposited <u>in the cellar of the Collectors dwelling house</u>. It was instantly reported that Deering and his friends had threatened to take his Coffee <u>by force</u> from the Collectors cellar. I made such inquiry into the origin of the report, as convinced me that it was not groundless; and I advised Mr. Fosdick to call for protection upon the Commanding officer of Fort Sumner; which he did; and a file of soldiers were quartered in his house for this purpose—The Marshal and myself passed the night in the Collectors house, armed in a proper manner for his assistance and protection. Not inclining to subject his family to such an inconvenience for any length of time he deposited the Coffee in that building of Fort Sumner in which were then stored the military apparatus and other property belonging to the United States. Lieutenant Leonard the then commanding officer of the fort, rec'd it into his custody, and placed over it a guard of soldiers; which Guard was continued over it, untill it was taken away in the outrageous manner which I shall now relate—
>
> Not many days after it was there deposited, the centinels <u>were bribed</u>; the building was violated and partly pulled down in the night time, and the coffee stolen and carried down to an Island in this harbour owned by the family of this same Deering; and there by the assistance of <u>his tenant</u>, and others whom he had seduced into this nefarious project, concealed in the woods. It was afterwards removed from this place, but where it was carried it was never in the power of any of us to ascertain.[7]

This incident over a few bags of coffee demonstrates several of the elements common to smuggling in northern New England. The involvement of one of Portland's leading merchants in smuggling reflects the *who* of smuggling, the illegal importation of coffee the *what*. The mention of islands and nighttime activity indicates the *where* and the *when* of smuggling. What is not mentioned is the *why* of smuggling.

The What and Why of Smuggling

One of the more surprising elements in studying smuggling is the commonplace nature of the goods involved. Smuggling in the early republic in northern New England was not about weapons, drugs, or other exotic contraband. Rather, it involved relatively mundane goods until the War of 1812, when Anglo-American trade was so badly disrupted that even delicate wares like ladies' silk gloves were passing through the rough and tumble settlements of Maine.[8] More commonly, smuggling involved the staples of life, unglamorous cargoes of flour, salt pork, plaster of paris, and even lumber. The size of this smuggling trade defied the best efforts of British and American policymakers to regulate it. The very basic nature of the commodities involved in the smuggling trade ensured that it would thrive. There are few commodities as basic as food, and both Maine and the Maritime Provinces were food importers.

Smuggling in northern New England followed a pattern of American agricultural goods flowing to British colonies in contravention of British (and occasionally American) law. This pattern was complemented by one of British and colonial goods entering the United States illicitly. The export of surplus American foodstuffs has long been a mainstay of this nation's maritime commerce. Even before the Revolution, American grain, fish, beef, and pork had been recognized as crucial supplies for both the British West Indies and the colonies in what is today Canada.[9] The British government after the Revolution attempted to create a new breadbasket for the colonies in the Canadas. This notably failed, despite repeated attempts by British administrators to shut Americans out of this trade and to foster food production in

British North America. Colonial consumers preferred American food-stuffs, and colonial governors, especially in the West Indies, persistently allowed American vessels to enter British colonial ports and to discharge cargoes of both food and lumber.[10] This drove some ambitious Royal Navy officers to exasperation, notably the young Horatio Nelson. In the mid to late 1780s, Nelson began what was virtually a one-man campaign against illegal commerce in the Caribbean.[11]

British colonial efforts in the Maritime Provinces were equally unsuccessful. American food was simply too needed to shut off. Restricting the flow of provisions was a highly sensitive issue that aroused the ire of the hungry populace. Until Jay's Treaty was approved in 1795, all American trade with British colonies was forbidden by the Navigation Acts, making most American merchants involved in the West India trade technically smugglers. Among their number were merchants from both New Hampshire and Maine.[12] British imperial policy fluctuated wildly concerning accepting American ships in colonial harbors throughout the period considered. This inconsistency often left British colonial and American merchants in the lurch as political decisions abruptly to halt or to open trade had considerable impact on markets and profitability.[13] The inconsistency of governmental trade policies is an important aspect of smuggling, perhaps even the definitive one. Smugglers followed natural patterns of trade, which had evolved over centuries to the contravention of laws that fluctuated. Smuggling can be seen as the constant; it was governmental policy that changed.

The primary American commodity smuggled to British colonies was flour, followed by salt beef, salt pork, and naval stores. These were also goods or produce that either could not be produced in British colonies or could not be produced in sufficient quantity to meet demand. These goods were often smuggled by northern New Englanders who had bought them in the southern or middle states. A degree of anonymity was guaranteed for the smugglers in that these were the very same goods that were required by the populace of Maine. The seemingly endless demand for flour in Maine during the embargo of 1807 (in reality headed for British markets in the Maritimes) drew wry comments and drastic actions from American policymakers.[14]

The primary goods smuggled from the Maritime Provinces into northern New England were plaster of paris (gypsum), millstones, and British manufactures, especially textiles. Plaster of paris and millstones were commonly illicitly brought into the United States from the Bay of Fundy, where the mining of plaster and the cutting of millstones formed an important part of the economy. Rather than pay the high duty charged for imported British goods, masters of small vessels brought the plaster and millstones surreptitiously to the American merchants and ships gathered on the uncertain boundary line that ran through Passamaquoddy Bay. American contraband (especially foodstuffs) was there traded for British. This practice thrived from the 1790s throughout the period considered and made the Passamaquoddy region on both sides of the border a hotbed of smuggling.[15] At least one British official observed that the only honest traders in New Brunswick were those who lived far away from the temptations of smuggling on Passamaquoddy Bay.[16]

The How and When of Smuggling

Smuggling is by definition a furtive process. It requires either stealth or subterfuge. Most smuggling was probably conducted by ships that relied on remote anchorages, surreptitious sailings, false paperwork, or in rare and extreme cases false names painted on their stern or the hiding of illegal cargoes under bulkier legal cargoes. Table 1 reveals that the majority of vessels involved in smuggling were open boats. Schooners, although fewer in number, possessed greater tonnage, and thus may be considered the most important of the smuggling vessels. Larger vessels, especially full-rigged ships, are a useful indicator of how desperate merchants were to trade. Full rigged ships were only apprehended four times in the period considered, and then only in the darkest years for American merchants as embargo and war took effect on normal, licit patterns of trade.

Open boats were mostly used in Passamaquoddy Bay to traverse the small distance of water between the British and American sides of the border. During the embargo, smuggling became a raging business.

Table 1. Numbers and Rigs of Vessels Involved in Successful
Prosecutions for Smuggling in the Federal District and
Circuit Courts of the District of Maine, 1790–1820

	Boats	Sloops	Schooners	Brigs	Ships	Total
1790			1			1
1791			1			1
1792						0
1793						0
1794		2	2			4
1795			2			2
1796		1				1
1797			1			1
1798			2			2
1799	1					1
1800	1		1	1		3
1801						0
1802	1					1
1803						0
1804						0
1805			1			1
1806						0
1807			1			1
1808	42	2	6	1	1	52
1809	2	3	8			13
1810			4			4
1811	1	1	1			3
1812	7	6	11	1		25
1813	9	3	10			22
1814	13	1	9	1	2	26
1815	5	2	8	1	1	17
1816	5	1	2			8
1817	7	1	4	1		13
1818	14	1	5			20
1819	1	3	4	1		9
1820	5	2	5			12
Total	114	29	89	7	4	243

SOURCE: *American State Papers* (20-2), H. doc. 146, no. 3, "Account of
Penalties and Forfeitures..."

Boats, rafts, skiffs, reach boats, and canoes were all used in the profitable contraband trade conducted during the embargo.[17] Small craft were also used to lighter goods ashore from larger vessels in remote harbors such as Deer Isle.[18] The commonplaceness of these craft allowed them to be used with a measure of impunity. For example, one customs collector discovered an open boat full of contraband English porcelain in the spring of 1814 anchored in Castine Harbor—virtually in front of his home![19]

Table 1 also indicates the *when* of smuggling. The number of vessels involved with the smuggling trade will probably never be established. But by using the numbers of vessels caught smuggling, we can establish a crude idea of when smuggling activity was greatest. After 1807 American restraints on trade imperiled the economic safety of many American merchants who were overextended. The result was a booming smuggling trade on the coast of Maine. This trade continued during the disputes between the United States and Great Britain until the 1820s. Even during the War of 1812 significant numbers of American vessels traded with the British. There appears to have been two distinct periods of smuggling activity. *Ordinary* smuggling occurred between 1789 and 1807. The American maritime economy was booming during that period, and while smuggling existed, it did not seriously threaten the functions of the federal government. *Extraordinary* smuggling began in 1808 and continued until 1820. American seaborne commerce experienced severe setbacks during this period owing to embargo, war, and a postwar economic slump. Extraordinary smuggling was a more diverse trade, involving more specie and manufactured goods than ordinary smuggling. It also involved far more violence and merchants from farther afield than the coast of Maine.

The Who and Where of Smuggling

The smugglers themselves were not cutthroats or pirates; generally they were ordinary merchants, farmers, and sailors. Merchants, of course, were very commonly named as smugglers. Small local merchants like Joseph Leavitt of Bangor were involved in smuggling, in his case to recoup losses inflicted by the War of 1812. Even William

King, the richest merchant in the district, was implicated in a smuggling scandal. Both merchants denied being smugglers.[20] In extraordinary smuggling times, merchants from as far away as New York came personally to the remote Passamaquoddy to take part in the illicit flour trade with Britain. John Clap was one such merchant. He attempted to smuggle a cargo of provisions across the border "in eight different boats, vessels, & rafts" but was found out and successfully prosecuted by federal authorities.[21] After the British army occupied the eastern third of Maine in the War of 1812, British merchants established themselves in Castine to engage in the contraband trade.[22] John Young was a Halifax, Nova Scotia, merchant who came to Castine to partake of the profitable trade with the enemy under the aegis of His Britannic Majesty's troops. Apparently he was not a man for half measures—not only did he buy smuggled goods from willing Americans, but he also avoided the 5 percent duty imposed by British customs officials. Among his methods of smuggling was to pack tobacco, soap, candles, and other American goods in barrels of codfish. His justification was of ancient vintage: "We are you know creatures of imitative habits & as all around me are smuggling I am beginning to smuggle too."[23]

Smuggling pervaded virtually all strata of Maine's coastal society. In the Penobscot collection district, the smuggling trade especially tempted physicians; two area doctors wound up in federal court on separate charges of smuggling. The failed attempt of one of the doctors to smuggle in a wagon with a false bottom prompted a newspaper editor to suggest he try smuggling in a hot air balloon next.[24] The only professionals seemingly immune to the temptations of smuggling were the clergy, whom to date I have not found mentioned in customhouse records.

Maine fishermen are often mentioned in legal records as smugglers. In this period, fishermen lived in the most remote of communities, often on islands. Their vocation frequently took them to the shores of the British provinces, where the temptation to sell relatively cheap American foodstuffs in return for scarce British manufactured goods was too great to resist. This was smuggling on a small scale: a bag of coffee, a few millstones, a barrel of salt pork. It was conducted in small fishing schooners like the *Morning Star*, which was found smuggling in Burnt Coat Harbor.[25] Fishing communities such as Penobscot, Deer Isle, Frenchman's Bay, Cranberry Islands, Fox Islands, Mt. Desert, Little River, and Passamaquoddy figured very large in smuggling, both in ordinary and extraordinary periods.

The timber industry was also often associated with smuggling, and with antisocial behavior in general. One English visitor to Maine commented that the lumbermen were "nurtured, not only in habits of idleness, intemperance, and dishonesty, but in the habits of an outlaw and desperado."[26] It was certainly an industry that relied almost entirely on the export trade. The embargo and War of 1812 were especially hard on Maine's many timber ports. Bucksport was one timber town often mentioned in connection with illicit trade, to the point where President Jefferson himself mentioned it as a community given to infractions of his embargo.[27]

In defense of the smugglers, it should be stated that Maine's ports were hardscrabble communities, newly settled, and overly reliant on exports to the British empire. It was difficult to make a living in these settlements, and local residents did what they had to in order to feed their families. Even in the long-settled town of York (established in the 1630s) times were hard enough to promote a thriving underground trade. Smuggling, except in extraordinary times, appears to be a last resort of impoverished men and their families, and it enriched few. That is to say, smuggling was not an act of greed, but of self-preservation.

There were some economic incentives to smuggle, however. The people of Passamaquoddy found it wise to assist both smugglers and law enforcement authorities. Smuggling flour across the border brought a rate as high as $3.00 per barrel; working for the customs collector brought $2.00 a day.[28] Locals thus took advantage of whatever opportunities came to hand. One wag commented: "So profitable was the boating business [smuggling], and the standing guard, that the poor people had suddenly become rich."[29]

During the War of 1812, smuggling again became a dominant factor in Maine's economy. The capture of Castine in September of 1814 by the British set off a flood of smuggling. The British garrison welcomed locals with foodstuffs and lumber, which they paid for in specie. British merchants also came to the town to trade with their American counterparts. The letters of one of these British merchants survive to detail the traffic and to give an impression of a community gone mad with commerce. British merchants jammed the town with manufactured goods and sold them to eager American merchants in return for fish, lumber, tobacco, provisions, shoes, and other goods. Few seemed bothered by the stigma of trading with the enemy.[30]

When stripped of romance, smuggling can largely be seen as a means of survival for those on the periphery of society, often at the behest of those better off than themselves. On rare occasions, when government regulation or policy threatened entire communities with loss of trade, it became a politically inspired, mainstream activity. On no occasion were the people happy to smuggle. If legitimate, profitable avenues of trade existed, people generally conformed to them, in Maine as elsewhere. There was little that was truly romantic about smuggling; it was merely an unsavory part of trying to survive in difficult times.

Lawlessness on the Coast of Maine

Smuggling represented a significant threat to the federal government, for it deprived the government of much-needed revenue. It should be no surprise then that the federal government directed considerable energy to curbing smuggling. The maritime nature of Maine's populace, the proximity of lucrative markets in the British provinces of New Brunswick and Nova Scotia, and the lawlessness endemic in any frontier society combined to make Maine the haven of large numbers of smugglers.

The key officials in the fight against smuggling were the customs collectors. These were men of some social standing, appointed by the president to regulate the nation's many ports and seaborne commerce. In Maine these officials often dedicated a large portion of their time to thwarting smuggling. It was an uphill battle; smugglers were numerous and often had the sympathy of the local populace. Moreover, the coast of Maine was extremely difficult to control. The collector of Frenchman's Bay, Melatiah Jordan, eloquently stated this in a letter to Secretary of the Treasury Alexander Hamilton, bemoaning his lack of a boat to patrol the coast adequately:

> The detached situation of the District interspersed with waters and abounding with a Number of Islands which afford commodious harbours and some of them as far distant as thirty miles from the Office will occasion my sending a Boat sometimes to visit the District throughout for I not only have reason to suspect that defrauding the Revenue is practised among the Island part of the District but have been informed of many little parcels of Goods landed on the Coast part of the District, it was impossible for me to prevent, all which difficulties a Boat will in great measure remedy.[31]

Jordan had neatly described the predicament of the Maine collectors. There were simply too many good harbors along the coast to patrol effectively, especially without the use of small craft.

The federal authorities charged with suppressing that illicit trade had never ruled out the chance that smugglers would resort to violence. As early as 1790, the federal government used armed vessels known as revenue cutters to intercept smugglers. These vessels patrolled the coast on a somewhat erratic schedule.[32] During time of crisis, the Navy's larger vessels joined the smaller revenue cutters in suppressing smuggling. A number of Jeffersonian gunboats patrolled Maine waters during the Embargo of 1807–9, as did ships as large as the frigate *Chesapeake*. The futility of using a vessel this large was proven by no less a naval personage than Stephen Decatur. Two smuggling vessels handily outsailed the frigate near Machias, causing the naval hero to write in disgust: "*Chesapeake* as a vessel of war sails uncommonly dull."[33]

Generally, the collectors were without the aid of naval vessels, or even of the revenue cutters. They were left to their own devices to enforce the commercial laws as best they could. In those times when smuggling was rampant, the collectors were obligated to arm their men and boats.[34] Running gun battles between officials and smugglers were common in the last few months of Jefferson's embargo.[35] The escalating violence so alarmed one junior customs official that he disarmed his revenue vessel. This act earned him a vote of thanks from the people of Castine in a town meeting. The reaction of the collector remains unknown.[36]

Josiah Hook, collector of Penobscot for much of the period considered, was burdened with an especially violent district. One of Hook's assistants was shot dead in a gunfight with smugglers on Deer Isle in 1808. Although Hook captured the perpetrators with the assistance of the revenue cutter *New Hampshire,* a mob subsequently freed them from the jail in Castine.[37] Another smuggler scuffled with one of Hook's men in Buckstown and received a $400 fine for his aggression.[38] And an assistant was viciously knifed in the streets of Belfast in 1815.[39] The presence of an armed British ship involved in smuggling led one sufficiently alarmed assistant to call on the U.S. Navy for help.[40] In addition, the collector's assistants were harassed with a variety of petty lawsuits intended to hamper their effectiveness.[41]

Perhaps the ultimate embarrassment occurred during the War of 1812, when Hook was chased out of Castine by a British invasion force, which occupied his home.[42] Hook was forced to retreat to a nearby settlement and watch a huge smuggling trade develop in Castine. This illicit trade not only supplied the enemy's troops with provisions, but also introduced British manufactured goods, such as linens and tinware, into the United States.[43] Overnight a fleet of allegedly "neutral" vessels with Swedish or Danish registers appeared in Penobscot Bay, quite legally bringing British goods from Castine to American territory.[44] This trade was substantial enough for the national press to comment on a drain of specie to Maine, and that in a year when the federal government was especially pressed for hard currency.[45] Collector Hook did his best to stop that trade, which occasioned hard words against him and violence upon his men.

The following journal entry of a local merchant in 1814 illustrates the hostility prevalent among the mercantile community toward the customs collector and his assistants:

I will here notice a circumstance singular Viz—that there have arrived a large quantity of English goods from Fredricton, in the British Province, said to be worth some thousands of dollars, bro't in birch canoes, except the carrying places—amongst them the trunks & packages are carried on men's shoulders, & from this place transported to Boston by land at the rate of $7 per cwt. Some of these goods are regularly entered and the duties paid—but many are

smuggled—and the customs house pimps & spies are vigilant &
watch for their part of the prey—now and then, make, what they
call, a good grab. I will here record their names—Joseph & James
Carr—Esq.—Saml. K. Whitting—Esq. are officers under Hook the
collector. With the under-officers, the whole, I can compare to
nothing better than a hungry set of wolves, prowling after, prey
upon the defenceless lamb. Thus we have here an exhibition of some
of the first of the Dem. administration. However, I will remark that
I do not approve of smuggling.[46]

This description of smugglers bringing goods from New Brunswick to
Bangor is a rare insight into overland smuggling. The merchant's identification of the customs house officers is noteworthy: Joseph Carr was a
Republican congressman recently turned out of office, and Samuel K.
Whiting was a future congressman. Most remarkable is the last sentence, for the author of this journal was at this time heavily involved
in illegal trade with the British. Yet he did not consider himself a
smuggler. This merchant was not alone in denying his role in the
trade, either publicly or privately.

Violence was the last resort of the smuggler and a distinguishing
feature of extraordinary smuggling. Bluff was more frequently used
than actual violence. For instance, antipathy to collectors was so great
downeast that threats were made to burn down the collector's home at
Passamaquoddy. This threat, and the prevalence of smuggling in that
area, were taken seriously by the federal government. In 1808 a company of soldiers was stationed there to support the beleaguered collector. The soldiers in turn were intimidated, bribed, and encouraged to
desert by a populace entirely in sympathy with the smugglers.[47] Not all
collectors were hated, however; some are remembered as pillars of the
community. It was a time of very personal government; an individual
officeholder's personality played a large role in his effectiveness. Some
collectors even sympathized with merchants who had to resort to smuggling. The collector of Waldoborough's name appeared on a petition to
Thomas Jefferson to end the embargo.[48] The collector of Frenchman's
Bay was willing to charge the duty for brown sugar on that of the more
valuable white sugar.[49] And the collector of York was summarily dis-
missed for colluding with smugglers.[50] Clearly even government officials had ambiguous feelings concerning the smuggling trade.

Conclusion

Smuggling, of course, persists to this day on the coast of Maine, a function of its position on a political boundary. The heyday of smuggling in that region was, during the difficult times of the embargo and War of 1812, a period when legitimate trade was denied to both British colonial and American merchants. Maritime historians can learn a great deal about seaborne commerce in the early republic by studying smuggling. A close look at this activity certainly reveals that trade closely linked northern New England and the Maritime Provinces and that no political boundary could stop these regions from trading. Greater effort on the behalf of governments in halting this commerce only resulted in greater resistance on the behalf of locals to commercial regulation.

Three major conclusions derive from the study of this region's smuggling trade.

First, the trade followed both ordinary and extraordinary patterns. Second, merchants were not the only ones involved in smuggling; fishermen and lumbermen also participated. Third, smuggling was the reaction of merchants to artificial constraints imposed on them by governments that were still struggling to catch up with modern ideas of commerce. This final conclusion may be the most important one. Smuggling, after all, only diminished with the advent of free trade and the industrial revolution.[51] Consider the instance of a Castine smuggler who had his son read Adam Smith's *The Wealth of Nations*.[52] It is possible that smuggling thus represented the creation of a new economic system as well as the death throes of mercantilism.

Notes

1. John O. Coote, *The Norton Book of the Sea* (New York: W. W. Norton & Co., 1989), 332.

2. Joshua Marsden, *The Narrative of a Mission to Nova Scotia, New Brunswick, and the Somers Islands* (Plymouth Dock, U.K.: J. Johns, 1816), 56–57.

3. *Annals*, vol. 1, 299 (9 May, 1789), quoted in Leonard D. White, *The Federalists* (New York: Macmillan, 1956), 460.

4. John D. Forbes, "Boston Smuggling, 1807–1815," *American Neptune* 10 (1950): 154.

5. See the article entitled "Smuggling" in the 12 June 1789 *Cumberland Gazette.*

6. William R. Castro, "The Origins of Federal Admiralty Jurisdiction in an Age of Privateers, Smugglers, and Pirates," *American Journal of Legal History* 37 (1993): 117–57.

7. Daniel Davis to Albert Gallatin, 5 Apr. 1803, Nathaniel Fosdick entry, National Archives Record Group 59, Letters of Application and Recommendation during the Administration of Thomas Jefferson, 1801–9.

8. *American State Papers* (20-2), H. doc. 146, no. 3, "Account of Penalties and Forfeitures. . . ."

9. John J. McCusker and Russell R. Menard, *The Economy of British North America 1607–1789* (Chapel Hill: University of North Carolina Press, 1991), 109, 114.

10. Gerald S. Graham, *Sea Power and British North America* (New York: Greenwood Press, 1968), 189.

11. Horatio Nelson, "Captain Nelson's Narrative of His Proceedings in Support of the Navigation Acts for the Suppression of Illicit Traffic in the West Indies," in *The Dispatches and Letters of Vice Admiral Lord Viscount Nelson,* ed. Nicholas Harris, vol. 1 (London: Henry Colburn Publisher, 1845), 171–85.

12. Ibid., 180–81.

13. Graham, *Sea Power,* 63.

14. Thomas Jefferson to Albert Gallatin, 4 Oct. 1808, in Carl E. Prince, ed., *The Microfilm Edition of the Papers of Albert Gallatin* (Philadelphia: Rhistoric Publications, 1970).

15. Graham, *Sea Power,* 168.

16. George Leonard to president of His Majesty's Council, 27 Sept. 1806, in Graham, *Sea Power,* 171.

17. The best account of smuggling at Passamaquoddy remains William H. Kilby, *Eastport and Passamaquoddy* (Eastport, Maine: Edward E. Shead, 1888).

18. Albert Gallatin to Robert Smith, 4 June 1808, in Carl E. Prince, ed., *The Microfilm Edition of the Papers of Albert Gallatin* (Philadelphia: Rhistoric Publications, 1970).

19. Portland, Maine, *Eastern Argus,* 5 May, 1814.

20. "Diary of Joseph Leavitt," typescript copy in Bangor Public Library, Bangor, Maine; William King and Mark L. Hill, *Remarks upon a Pamphlet*

Published at Bath, Maine, Relating to Alleged infractions of the Laws during the Embargo, Non-Intercourse, and War (Bath, Maine, 1825).

21. Records of the U.S. District Court, Maine, *United States vs. John Clap of New York*. Manuscript in New England Regional Branch of the National Archives, Waltham, Massachusetts.

22. See D. C. Harvey, "Pre-Agricola John Young, or a Compact Family in Search of Fortune," *Collections of the Nova Scotia Historical Society* 32 (1959): 125–59, for a detailed account of smuggling in Castine.

23. John Young to William Young, 6 Feb. 1815, in ibid., 135.

24. Records of the U.S. District Court, Maine, *United States vs. Andrew Webster* and *United States vs. a Waggon Load of Goods for Moses Adams*. Both Adams and Webster were physicians; Adams was later tried and acquitted of the murder of his wife in a state court. See the *Boston Patriot* of 9 Nov. 1814 for the comments on Adams's apprehension as a smuggler.

25. Ibid., *United States libel vs. Schr. Morning Star & Lading*.

26. E. A. Kendall, *Travels through the Northern Parts of the United States*, vol. 3 (New York, 1809), 75–76, quoted in Graeme Wynn, "Deplorably Dark and Demoralized Lumberers?" *Journal of Forest History* 24, no. 3 (Oct. 1980): 168.

27. Thomas Jefferson to Albert Gallatin, 13 Nov. 1808 in Prince, *Papers of Albert Gallatin*.

28. Lorenzo Sabine, "Moose Island," in *Eastport and Passamaquoddy*, ed., William Henry Kilby (Eastport, Maine: Edward E. Shead & Company, 1888), 145.

29. *Eastern Argus*, 16 Jun. 1808; Jamie H. Eves, "'The Poor Had Suddenly Become Rich' a Boom in Maine Wheat," *Maine Historical Society Quarterly* 27, no. 3 (Winter 1987): 130. This is an excellent article on Maine smuggling, although Eves labors under the misconception that the flour smuggled at Passamaquoddy came from New England. Almost all the flour at Passamaquoddy came from New York, Pennsylvania, the Chesapeake, and the Carolinas.

30. Harvey, "Pre-Agricola John Young," 125–42.

31. Melatiah Jordan to Alexander Hamilton, 1 July 1791, in Harold C. Syrett, ed., *The Papers of Alexander Hamilton*, vol. 8 (New York: Columbia University Press, 1965), 521–22.

32. John Foster Williams, "Log of the First U.S. Revenue Cutter *Massachusetts*," photocopy of original, U.S. Coast Guard Historians Office, Washington, D.C.

33. Stephen Decatur to Secretary of the Navy Robert Smith, 6 Sep. 1808, in National Archives Record Group 45, Captain's Letters.

34. *New York Evening Post*, 11 Feb. 1809.

35. Edward Trenchard to Secretary of the Navy Robert Smith, 9 Aug. 1808, in National Archives Record Group 45, Letters Received by the Secretary of the Navy from Officers Below the Rank of Commander.

36. Kilby, *Eastport and Passamaquoddy*, 145.

37. Harvey Strum, "Smuggling in Maine during the Embargo and War of 1812," *Colby College Quarterly* 19, no. 2 (June 1983): 92.

38. Records of the U.S. District Court, Maine, *United States vs. Eliakim Darling, jun.*, at New England Regional Branch of the National Archives, Waltham, Massachusetts.

39. Ibid., *United States vs. Thomas Cunningham*.

40. W. G. Pillsbury to the Commanders of the *Chesapeake, Wasp*, and *Argus*, 15 Nov. 1808, in National Archives Record Group 45, Letters Sent by the Secretary of the Navy to Officers.

41. David Perham to Josiah Hooke Jr., Esq. 25 Nov. 1823, in U.S. Congress. House. 1824. *Report of the Committee of Claims on the bill from the Senate, for the relief of Josiah Hook, jun.* 18th Cong., 1st sess., H. Doc. 46, 25.

42. George Augustus Wheeler, *History of Castine, Penobscot, and Brooksville, Maine* (Bangor, Maine: Burr & Robinson, 1875), 160.

43. See the Portland, Maine, *Eastern Argus* for all of 1814 for descriptions of smuggled British manufactured goods in U.S. Marshals' auctions.

44. Ronald F. Banks, *Maine Becomes a State* (Middletown, Conn.: Wesleyan University Press, 1970), 101–2.

45. *Eastern Argus*, 8 Dec. 1814.

46. August 1814 entry, "Diary of Joseph Leavitt," typescript copy in Bangor Public Library, Bangor, Maine.

47. Davis Zimmerman, *Coastal Fort* (Eastport, Maine: Border Historical Society, 1984), 21.

48. Jasper Jacob Stahl, *History of Old Broad Bay and Waldoborough* (Portland, Maine: Bond Wheelwright Company, 1956), 107.

49. Richard A. Savage, "The Collectors of Old Frenchman's Bay," *New England Galaxy* 14 (Winter 1973), 25–26.

50. Leonard D. White, *The Jeffersonians* (New York: Macmillan, 1951), 453–55.

51. Graham, *Sea Power*, 276.

52. Harvey, "Pre-Agricola John Young," 148.

The *Empress of China* in the South China Sea, 1784

3

Charting a New Course for the China Trade: The Late Eighteenth-Century American Model

Mary A. Y. Gallagher

The history of direct trade between the United States and China extends more than 200 years. Philip Chadwick Foster Smith's The *Empress of China,* the most comprehensive study of the first American voyage to Canton, formed an important part of this trade's bicentennial celebration in 1984. Where other historians of the North American China trade have produced overviews, reconstructed later voyages, or studied how the trade developed in different regions,[1] this chapter studies the patterns and events that shaped it from 1760 to 1790.

Independence brought with it economic hardship. The war destroyed assets and disrupted production. Specie was drained to pay for foreign imports. After the peace in 1783, Britain, France, and Spain imposed significant restrictions on American trade with their West Indian possessions, wrenching American commerce from its regular channels and forcing it to strike out in new directions. The *Empress* venture, a bold response to this crisis, was a signal triumph. It was also, however, a noteworthy failure: the *Empress's* owners proved unable to establish a concern that would dominate the trade as did the European East India companies. After this initial attempt, Americans improvised a successful small private enterprise model, snubbed their noses at established conventions, and developed the China trade into "the quintessential business innovation of the 1780s," which led inexorably to continental and extracontinental expansion.[2]

North American entrepreneurs habitually defied the British East India Company monopoly of trade with China and India before the colonies declared their independence. A centuries-old tradition called "captain's privilege" gave naval officers a certain amount of cargo space to transport goods on private account. Officers of East India Company vessels were generally allowed a privilege of about sixty tons of merchandise per voyage. American vessels met homebound Indiamen off the African coast, purchased East Asian products shipped by their officers, and brought them directly to America. They also smuggled East India contraband through St. Eustatius in the Dutch West Indies. These activities produced a pool of Americans with interest and some degree of experience in the procurement of East India goods. Robert Morris, half-owner of the *Empress*'s maiden voyage, was one of the "main" tea smugglers operating out of Philadelphia. After 1776, war disrupted these patterns.

The Continental Congress vacillated about its priorities with respect to East Asia. In September 1777 the Foreign Affairs Committee considered sending naval vessels to "intercept" British ships and to distress the "internal Trade of India." Some far-thinking delegates wondered whether France would allow American ships to put in at her islands in the Indian Ocean off the eastern coast of Africa. In 1779 Congress decided to allow its ministers to cede the right to trade in the East Indies in peace negotiations if the United States was adequately compensated. This decision was later reversed. In 1780 unnamed entrepreneurs asked François Barbé-Marbois, French consul in Philadelphia, whether American vessels could use Mauritius (Ile de France) and Réunion (Ile de Bourbon) as ports of call on voyages to East Asia. The request was most likely made by the future owners of the *Empress*. After the war, the application was renewed and France granted American vessels access to Mauritius.[3]

War did not destroy the American taste for tea. On the contrary, it opened a burgeoning market that encouraged entrepreneurs in both the United States and France to plan for direct trade with East Asia and to take initiatives to procure foreign assistance that would ensure the viability of their ventures. French trade with the East Indies had reached a watershed in 1769, when the French East India Company was dissolved. Some French commercial and financial interests quickly petitioned the government to reestablish it. They argued that individuals could not profitably trade with East Asia, that free trade could not adequately supply the French market with Asian merchandise, and that French firms that engaged in it would merely become fronts for foreigners. It was not clear, however, that the government would comply or to whom it might grant a new monopoly. This situation, combined with the war against Britain, created a window of opportunity for private ventures to Asia by French entrepreneurs and suggested the possibility of joint ventures with Americans.

Immediately after the war, the French government sponsored an expedition to China. On 2 February 1783, it authorized Grandclos-Meslé, a merchant from Saint-Malo associated with the former East India Company, to outfit four ships to China on the king's account. Shortly after, the crown attempted to broaden the base of the trade by forming an East India association of merchant-shareholders from six French ports (Marseilles, Bourdeaux, Nantes, Saint-Malo, Lorient, and Havre). On 21 July 1783 it empowered this association to finance and outfit an expedition of three ships (*Triton, Sagittaire,* and *Provence),* which the king supplied. One of the merchants most eager to participate was Thomas-Simon Bérard of Marseilles, who, with a group of friends, attempted to dominate the venture by purchasing a majority of the shares allotted to Marseilles. When the government responded to their attempted takeover by limiting the number of shares each individual could buy, Bérard and his confederates tried to kill the project by withdrawing their support. Enough capital was raised without them to send the three ships to China in February 1784.

These two incidents, however, convinced the French government that its objectives—an adequate supply of Asian goods, reestablishment of French power in India, and a working relationship with more entrepreneurial financial interests—could be achieved only through a new East Indies Company. This company, established in April 1785 and financed by the sale of stock, allowed the Bérards a major role, absorbed French resources, and put an end to incentives for French-American joint ventures.[4]

Among those who had been interested in a French-supported American venture to China was John Holker Jr., son of an émigré Englishman now prospering in Rouen. Holker and his father were politically connected with French Foreign Minister Vergennes, whose determination to use trade to gain leverage over foreign rivals led him to play an active role in the ministerial struggle to determine what form the new East India Company would take. The young Holker had come to America in 1778, where he served as agent of the French Marine and consul general at Philadelphia. He also engaged in private business on his own behalf and for a number of prestigious French clients, including the Paris banking firms of Le Couteulx and Company and Sabatier fils et Desprez, whose principals were interested in entering into the East Indies trade.

Soon after he arrived in Philadelphia, Holker established a close business relationship with Robert Morris, a leading local merchant and former member of Congress, who, as the dominant member of its Secret Committee of Trade, had managed many of its foreign procurement operations. In February 1781 Congress chose Morris to serve as superintendent of finance and appointed him to serve concurrently as agent of marine later that year. The combined appointments gave him control over all matters related to the public debt and expenditures, treasury and naval personnel, public vessels, naval stores and prizes. Holker, however, was forced to resign from all his public offices in September 1781 because he was so heavily involved in private trade.[5]

Holker and William Duer, a New York businessman and politician, discussed a China voyage with Morris in the fall of 1780, but Morris was not convinced that adequate resources were at hand. In the fall of 1781, Holker began actively planning a China voyage designed to take advantage of the wartime shortage of East Indies goods in the United States. He again tried to persuade Morris to participate. He also involved Matthew Ridley, a Baltimore merchant associated with both Morris and himself. Ridley left for France in October 1781 to negotiate loans and purchase supplies for Maryland. His carefully guarded letters to Holker and his partner, Mark Pringle, reveal that he was engaged in developing some important commercial prospects, including European support for the China venture. Ridley contacted both Sabatier and Desprez and the principals of Le Couteulx and Company of Paris, with whom Morris conducted both private and public business. Jacques, Louis, and Laurent Le Couteulx and Company, the latter firm's Cadiz branch, had close ties with the Bank of San Carlos, repository of the specie sent to Spain from America. Since silver was an important cargo component in most outbound China voyages, this connection was potentially very significant.[6]

Peace negotiations between the United States and Great Britain began in April 1782. Their success or failure was critically important to the nature and success of any commercial plans, especially for a China venture. Ridley, who was negotiating a loan for Maryland in Holland, was convinced by June that the time for a wartime China venture had already past. He predicted, however, that when peace came, American commerce would be much extended and that the first who settled "there" would realize very great advantages. By October Ridley was back in Paris and in contact with "one of the Bérards" and "our Friends Le Couteulx," both of whom were contemplating a China venture. The signing of the peace treaties and the exclusion of the Bérards from the first French postwar China expedition in 1783 may have prompted the firm's Lorient branch to consider sending a ship of 500 to 600 tons under the American flag to China, which would "return directly to you," and to invite Holker to participate in the venture.

In the meantime, Holker had persuaded Morris to invest with him in shipments of tobacco and a voyage to "Guinea" managed by Bérard and Company, profits from which could be used to fund a China venture. Holker and Morris probably combined their efforts to arrange for the *Romulus*, a French frigate then in the Chesapeake, to convoy their ships and other merchant vessels to Europe. Her commander, the Chevalier de Villebrune, was also interested in their project. Pringle reported that Villebrune was willing to ship ginseng, a root prized by the Chinese, on board the *Romulus* when it returned to France. He also noted that Villebrune was "sanguine" when his thoughts turned to the East, and that he planned to arrange for the *Romulus* to be used in the China trade. Unfortunately, *Romulus* was held in port first by the British blockade and then by ice, and the Bérards showed little interest in the American venture once they began maneuvering for control of the second French expedition to China.

Word of the first French expedition under Grandclos-Meslé reached the United States by early May 1783. Soon thereafter, Holker and Morris began to develop alternate resources for an American China venture. They now involved William Duer, who had served under Robert Clive in India, and Massachusetts merchant Daniel Parker, principals of Daniel Parker and Company, which held the contract to supply the Continental Army in New York and New Jersey. Holker was a silent partner in the firm. No business agreement between Morris and Parker and Company has been found, but it is probable that arrangements were concluded in mid-June—an understanding had clearly been reached by the time Parker acquired the *Empress of China* in the summer of 1783.[7]

The original plans called for Morris and Parker and Company to hold a third interest each, and for the final third to be purchased by merchants from Boston, including James Swan, and probably Joseph Barrell, Thomas Russell, and Samuel Breck. Morris was active in conceptualizing the venture. Daniel Parker assumed responsibility for overall management, procuring and outfitting vessels, obtaining commitments from the potential investors in Massachusetts, and operations in New York, where he came in frequent contact with British commander Guy Carleton. Turnbull, Marmie, and Company of Philadelphia, in which Holker and Morris held an interest, assembled the cargo, primarily ginseng. As early as May 1783, perhaps before Parker and Company became involved, Morris received a visit from John Ledyard, a Connecticut-born tar who had been on Captain James Cook's last voyage. Ledyard advocated sailing to China by way of the Northwest coast of North America where ships could trade for furs to be sold at Canton. He was eccentric, and his plan was unconventional and risky enough to be discounted by most prospective sponsors, but he persuaded Morris that it was feasible and potentially profitable. After several conferences, which probably extended into July, the two men were close to an understanding, and Ledyard expected to go to New England "to procure Seamen, or a ship, or both." Morris and his assistant, Gouverneur Morris were, he reported, "wrapt up in the Idea of Yanky Sailors."[8]

Morris announced his resignation as superintendent of finance on 24 January, effective at the end of May 1783. Shortly thereafter, he began engaging actively in private commerce, although he agreed to remain in office in a limited capacity at Congress's request. On 3 May 1783 he formally asked Congress to relieve him of his responsibilities for the Navy, but it did not. Morris was, thus, still in a position to manage naval personnel and to dispose of public resources in a manner favorable to the development of American commerce to China. He was, for instance, able to assign John Green to courts-martial held in Boston, where the *Empress of China* was being prepared for its voyage under his command. This service kept Green on the public payroll until the *Empress* was scheduled to depart for China. Other Army and Navy officers were hired for the China voyage or for related ventures. Morris endowed the project with both public and private character. He told John Jay, soon to be named secretary for foreign affairs, "I am sending some Ships to China in order to encourage others in the adventurous pursuits of Commerce and I wish to see a foundation laid for an American navy."[9] However self-serving, his analysis of the significance of the China trade was correct. Morris alone among government officers was able and willing to support it. Congress was weak, preoccupied with weightier issues, and not disposed to privilege any private enterprise, especially if Morris was involved.

Morris's group began to be referred to as the "East India service" or "American India Company." From August through October 1783, it made ambitious plans for several China voyages by different routes. Among the ships Parker considered for the China trade were naval vessels the superintendent put on the auction block. Complaints from his critics about their sale made Morris more discreet but no less determined to foster a commerce advantageous to himself and to the nation. By late summer, Parker had purchased the *Empress of China*, a proud new 360-ton ship designed by John Peck of Boston on the model of a famous American privateer, *Bellisarius*, which, after her capture by the British, gained a reputation as the fastest ship in the Royal Navy. The *Empress* proved an equally impressive sailer. Parker soon acquired three other ships: the 260-ton *Beaver*, purchased in New York City and renamed *Columbia*, the 800-ton *Bourbon*, a Continental frigate, and the 550-ton *Comte d'Artois*, a French Indiaman built "upon the Peck Construction," and being refitted at New London, Connecticut. He considered—but rejected—the *Hague* and the *Alliance*, both Continental vessels, and the *Angelica*, another Peck ship.

Guy Carleton, British Army commander headquartered in New York, was well informed about the evolution of the project. His first report on the plans for the China venture indicated that the primary focus would be the Ledyard voyage, although another ship, the *Hague*, would be fitted out at Boston for India and sail the traditional easterly route around the Cape of Good Hope. Another variant of the plan assigned the *Empress* to round Cape Horn, head northwest toward the Society Islands (French Polynesia), and then northward to Canton. The *Columbia* was to make a westerly voyage on the Ledyard plan; the *Bourbon* and the *Comte d'Artois* would sail east around the southern tip of Africa.[10]

The scope of these plans suggests that the "American India Company" expected to attract European as well as American investors. Ridley had negotiated a sizable loan in Amsterdam in 1782 for the state of Maryland, which regarded the terms as disadvantageous. Parker and Company then suggested that Ridley convert it into a private loan for which Holker and Morris would be security. Letters from Ridley, which arrived in September, probably reported both that the Dutch bankers would not accept this proposal and that the sale of shares in the new French expedition to China had attracted French investors who might otherwise have put their funds into the American venture. By October, the principals were quarreling among themselves. Duer, then slated to be supercargo on the Ledyard vessel, criticized plans for the westerly voyage, which Morris still strongly supported. He believed that Gouverneur Morris and Parker had "worked" to destroy Robert Morris's confidence in him. He also considered the compensation Morris offered him inadequate and was disgruntled at being subordinate to Parker and concerned that the diplomatic foundations for the trade had not been properly laid. By early December, he resigned as supercargo. The firm decided to send the *Bourbon* and the *Comte d'Artois* to Europe instead of to China. Repairs to the *Beaver/Columbia* had not strengthened her sufficiently, and Parker was unable to find a captain willing to take her around Cape Horn. Her voyage was canceled soon thereafter. Morris blamed Parker for the difficulties.[11] By January, the Company's expansive plans were foundering on harsh reality.

The struggle to finance the *Empress*'s voyage was even more tempestuous and divisive than the difficulties in locating ships and officers. Boston investors put in small amounts, but did not take a one-third share in the venture, thereby forcing Parker and Company and Morris to raise an extra $40,000. Parker claimed he had advanced large sums of his own money to cover the firm's expenses, continually asked his partners for funds, and begged Holker to persuade Morris to draw bills for this amount. Holker did not succeed. Duer believed that assets in Parker's hands should have been sufficient to meet the firm's obligations and suspected Parker of peculation. Holker drew on Le Couteulx for $60,000 to cover the full value of the firm's half share of the *Empress* and her cargo. Le Couteulx, however, refused to sell the bills or to market a loan for the sum with ship or cargo as security, and did not procure insurance. Prospective French insurers, the firm wrote, heaped scorn and criticism on the venture for "'novelty of the risk in every respect'"; a China voyage that began and ended in America, a crew and flag "making its debut in the trade," an outbound cargo of "very slender consumption," and insufficient specie to purchase a return cargo.[12]

Morris apparently juggled public and private assets to cover his $60,000 share. As superintendent of finance, he was able to draw either on Le Couteulx, which held funds belonging to the United States government and with which he also had a private account, or on the consortium of bankers administering a Dutch loan to the United States, against which he had already purchased bills worth $200,000 for his private account. He had already drawn bills for $23,000 to raise specie for the *Empress*'s cargo. On 13 January 1784, Morris instructed Le Couteulx to transfer government funds amounting to $37,000 into his private account (on the understanding that he would reimburse the government at home). The timing and the amount suggest that this transaction was used to cover the remainder of his share in the venture.

The struggle to raise money for the voyage may have fed tensions between Holker and Morris over settlement of accounts for earlier transactions. The acrimony between the two men was so acute by March 1784 that they completely severed all business connections. When Parker was pressed to pay his creditors, he could not. He fled to Europe in the summer of 1784, leaving Duer and Holker to face all demands against the firm.[13] The American India Company thus disintegrated completely before the venture was well under way.

The *Empress* sailed from New York for China on 24 February 1784 with instructions from her owners, letters of introduction from the French and Dutch ministers to the United States, sea letters from Congress and the governor of New York, and copies of the Declaration of Independence and the treaties with France and the United Provinces. Green met up with the *Triton,* one of the three ships forming part of the second French expedition to China, off the coast of Java. Its captain and several officers paid the *Empress* a visit, "offered their service in a polite manner," and invited Green and supercargoes Samuel Shaw and Thomas Randall to dine. The Americans discovered that one of the *Triton's* officers had served with Comte de Grasse in the American theater and this strengthened the bonds between the two groups.

The two ships kept company the remainder of the way to Canton, where the French introduced the Americans to the intricacies of trading. Shaw noted that even the English were not "behindhand" of the other nations, but believed they were motivated by "their jealousy of the French" and "their dislike of the good understanding we kept up with them, which would sometimes appear, in spite of their breeding." Several years later, however, he reported that British and Americans at Canton could "barely treat each other with civility."[14]

The *Empress* completed her return cargo and began her homeward voyage in December 1784 in the company of a Dutch vessel, the *General de Klerk.* Randall remained at Canton and arranged with Captain John O'Donnell to ship the supercargoes' private cargo of teas and nankeens on the *Pallas,* one of the many "country ships," owned by British merchants but restricted by East India Company regulations to trade between the Cape of Good Hope and Canton. At the Cape of Good Hope, the *Empress* met up with another American ship owned by Elias Hasket Derby of Salem, Massachusetts, the *Grand Turk*. Her captain, Jonathan Ingersoll, planned to take on East Asian goods at the Cape and then stop in the West Indies to sell tea and take on sugar and cotton for Salem.

The *Empress* left the Cape on 14 March 1785 and put in at New York harbor on 10 May. Her cargo was disbursed and sold, and the profits were divided among her owners. French chargé d'affaires Guillaume Otto, reporting from New York, did not consider her voyage exceptional, but profitable enough to encourage others in New York to form companies and plan new ventures. Otto was closely monitoring the trade and predicted that, once Americans were established in it, the French would be able to sell them only those goods that they absolutely could not import for themselves.[15]

In their initial venture, Morris and Daniel Parker and Company patched together enough capital to acquire four vessels for the China trade, but were able to outfit only one. Their resources were inadequate to create an American India Company, and the United States government could neither restrain nor organize the American urge to trade with East Asia. The *Empress's* maiden voyage was based on the India Company model, which sent large vessels on the traditional route with no other trading stops on the outbound or homeward voyages. It put a premium on reaching each destination ahead of competitors as well as on market control.[16] Ownership was generally restricted to men with substantial personal fortunes who were able to invest large amounts of capital over a long period of time and to raise funds from conservative European sources of credit. More indigenous American models based on variations of the prewar trade were, however, already emerging.

By the summer of 1785, Morris was worried that trade with China might be "overdone." Nevertheless, he planned the *Empress's* second China voyage with assistance from his new firms, Constable, Rucker, and Company of New York and Tench Tilghman and Company of Baltimore. William Constable, a merchant with connections in

Canada and England, was managing partner of the first firm, and directed the outfitting of China voyages from New York. He and a partner, William Edgar, had already sent out the 150-ton *Betsey* from New York for Bombay, Madras, Batavia, and Canton on 5 April 1784, a route designed after consultation with an employee of the British East India Company. No details of her voyage have been discovered to date, but she returned in 1785 with a cargo of teas, fabrics, and porcelain. Constable's papers contain a memorandum on the China trade, dated 10 May 1784, the day he signed the agreement with Robert and Gouverneur Morris establishing William Constable and Company. Both its date and its content testify to the preeminent role the China trade played in the establishment of this firm, later enlarged to include London-born John Rucker, a member of a mercantile family active in England, Germany, and France. Tench Tilghman, managing partner of Tilghman and Company, was a former aide to George Washington. His firm supervised the purchasing of ginseng for the outbound cargoes.

The *Empress's* second voyage was capitalized at $100,000, divided into $1,000 shares. Shareholders included Morris, Tilghman, Constable, Edgar, Isaac Sears, owner of the *Harriet* mentioned below, Affouke, a contact in Canton who held a one-fifth share in the venture, and William Duer, now secretary to the Board of Treasury, who invested $20,000 by advancing that amount in *public* funds to Constable, Rucker, and Company on a contract that firm held to repay the public debt. Morris had originally tried to engage Shaw and Randall to participate in a more "extensive" plan, but could not agree on terms with them. The *Empress's* cargo included specie, ginseng, wine, brandy, tobacco, tar, logwood, sassafras, anchors, and lumber. Her voyage plan allowed for stops at Madeira, Cape of Good Hope, Madras, and Batavia.[17]

The second venture resembled the first in that, although it was under new management, it was relatively conservative and relied on major players. It incorporated some new elements, such as intermediate trading stops and Asian financing. Some of the new items in the *Empress's* cargo—logwood, sassafras, anchors, and lumber—proved unsuitable for the Chinese market. The venture also suffered from competition from an inexperienced rival, the *Experiment,* which reached Canton ahead of the *Empress, Canton,* and *Hope,* all of which were expected from the United States. Affouke reported that her captain, Stewart Dean, had been so determined to sell his ginseng before these vessels arrived that he let it go for $150 per picul, an Oriental weight equivalent to 133.3 pounds. This capped the price for the season—the *Empress's* best ginseng brought only $142 per picul. The *Experiment* was almost certainly the same sloop that transported tea, nankins, and cotton from the *Empress's* first cargo from New York to Philadelphia in the summer of 1785. Peter Schermerhorn and Ten Eyck & Seaman, two of the investors in the *Experiment,* had put a small sum into the first voyage of the *Empress,* and Peter Schermerhorn had sailed out of New York harbor with her on her maiden voyage as far as Sandy Hook. On 18 December 1785, the *Experiment* began her own voyage to China. Her burden was only eighty-five tons—the Chinese reportedly mistook her for a tender vessel. Her cargo of ginseng, specie, furs, turpentine, tobacco, and wine was valued at £8,860. Nineteen shares worth £600 were sold to eleven individuals and seven partnerships, realizing a return sufficient to entice several of the original investors to plan a second venture.[18]

Scrappy, underfinanced figures operating on the periphery of the mercantile world were developing radically different voyage plans that imitated the prewar and the "country ship" models. Outfitters like the *Experiment's* owners used smaller vessels, designed outbound cargoes to satisfy European needs in East Asian establishments as well as the Chinese market, and allowed for different destinations and routes and stops along the way. They took on shark fins, bird nests, sandalwood, rhinoceros horns, and other exotic products that found a good market at Canton. They invested smaller sums and used different sources to finance their ventures. Captains sold outbound and inbound cargoes wherever they could find an outlet, and defied mercantilist regulations whenever they felt the need.

One such voyage began in Boston in December 1783, as the *Empress* was coming down to pick up her first cargo in New York. Isaac Sears, owner of the fifty-ton *Harriet,* Captain Hallet, had originally intended to send her to Europe to sell ginseng to vessels bound for China but had not been able to get her off in time. He ordered her instead to the Cape of Good Hope, where, it was reported, officers of outbound Indiamen bought her ginseng for double its value in Hyson tea to prevent her from competing with British sales at Canton—a story no doubt intended to put a favorable face on the same kind of irregular trade American vessels had conducted before the Revolution. The *Harriet*'s exclusion from St. Helena on her homeward voyage suggests this as well. Her six-month voyage earned Sears a tidy profit and may have encouraged him to invest in the second voyage of the *Empress.*[19]

Americans, including Morris, were quite willing to forego the expense and risk of complete voyages to India and China if they could find desirable cargoes at some intermediate point. Only a few days after entering into partnership with William Constable, Robert and Gouverneur Morris suggested to their French friends that the crown open Mauritius or Réunion to American trade. Gouverneur Morris offered a plan of trade reminiscent of a controversial proposal by Bertrand-François Mahé de La Bourdonnais in the 1740s. La Bourdonnais, who had captured Madras from the British, argued that France should abandon the idea of establishing an empire in India and concentrate instead on developing a few strongholds, such as Mauritius, which would be emporiums for trade in East India goods and which could serve as bases for naval operations during war.

Gouverneur Morris's plan was designed to suit both French and American circumstances and make a new French East India Company superfluous. He recommended that the French trade should be divided into two separate legs, the first from France to the islands, and then from the islands to East Asia, with two separate sets of vessels. The islands would, thus, be the final destination for ships from France and America, not merely a way station. "Assorted cargoes" both for East Asia and for home ports in France and the United States, would be available there, and the trade could be carried on "in smaller vessels, smaller expence, shorter time." He also expected that officers of other East India companies would carry on their private trade at the islands because they could more easily conceal it from their employers and would get a quicker return on their investments. He predicted that this trade would produce the traditional list of benefits mercantilists aspired to: increased numbers of French seamen; greater revenue for the crown; decreased expenditures for defense and for East India establishments; increases in population, revenue, mercantile wealth, and consumption of French manufactures; and military preparedness at a strategic location. He suggested that it would strengthen bonds between France and the United States, and that France's rivals would be weakened by their continued support of "cumbersome establishments" in the East Indies.

Robert Morris made essentially the same arguments in a letter written shortly after, but he added calculations that France would stand to gain five to ten million livres in revenue annually by allowing free trade at the islands. French authorities had, in fact, already decided to open Mauritius as a way station for American vessels and gave them limited rights to trade. The *Grand Turk,* Captain Ebenezer West, was the first American vessel known to have taken advantage of the privilege. Once the French East India Company was reestablished, monopolistic restrictions severely limited the amount and variety of East Indies merchandise available there. A decree issued in 1787 improved conditions somewhat, but the trade Gouverneur Morris envisioned failed to develop until after the French monopoly ended in 1790. Then it flourished briefly until the outbreak of European war in 1793.

The opening of Mauritius was, nevertheless, significant. Stephen Higginson, former congressman from Massachusetts, saw that it allowed "common traders of small Capitals" to engage in the East India Trade. He continued: "To have that or any other branch of trade so circumstanced that none but wealthy Individuals, or companies can pursue is not to be desired upon public principles." Higginson also stressed the strategic location of the two islands, which he considered "peculiarly favourable" to allow the French "to annoy the British trade to India and China and to protect their own," and argued that "if a free trade is permitted to us, they certainly will have every Supply, and every advantage for cruising upon the British from thence."[20]

The East India trade was also democratized when it was demonstrated conclusively that small ships could profitably engage in it. The ninety-ton *Lady Washington* sailed in company of the *Columbia* on the first American voyage to the Northwest Coast (1787). Six owners expended $49,000 to outfit the two ships. In August 1788, Phineas Bond, British consul in Philadelphia, mentioned the arrival of two 150-ton brigantines, one from Canton, the other from Madras, whose cargoes were "valuable, tho' their burden is not great." In 1790 the seventy-ton *Hope* left Boston for the Northwest Coast, where it took on 1,400 otter skins and proceeded to China. She was a two-masted, square-rigged brigantine registered to Thomas H. Perkins, James Magee, and Russell Sturgis. She carried a crew of fourteen and sailed the westerly route to Hawaii, then to the Pacific northwest, and then to China. The ship's smith, who forged iron collars to trade to the Indians, was responsible for the great success of the fur-trading leg of the voyage.

In 1794 the eighty-nine-ton sloop *Union* sailed out of Boston on the same route with a nineteen-year-old captain, John Boit. Probably smallest of all was the twenty-six-ton *Fair American*, whose ability to traverse "Such an immense tract of Boisterous Ocean as she had done" amazed a British observer. These voyages defied the common wisdom that only large vessels could trade profitably since the Chinese taxed all ships equally, whatever their size.[21]

One of the largest ships known to have been sent to China during this period, the 800-ton *Massachusetts*, owned by Samuel Shaw and Thomas Randall, had a disastrous outbound voyage and never returned. She was to have exchanged her cargo at Batavia for goods suitable for China, but Dutch authorities refused her permission to trade. By the time she reached Canton, her hold was covered with mold an inch thick, and her goods rendered all the more useless. Shaw accepted an offer to sell her to the Danish East India Company for $65,000. William Constable discussed plans to build a China ship of 900 tons modeled on the *Massachusetts* with shipbuilder Thomas Robison of Portland, Maine, in 1790, at an estimated cost of $40,000, which Constable believed would be recouped in one voyage. He canceled his order, however, when he learned that the market for cotton, which the ship was to carry from Bombay to China, had collapsed.[22]

Entrepreneurs reduced the total amount they invested in outbound cargoes by loading a variety of goods for sale along the way and by varying destinations. The voyage of the *United States*, Captain Thomas Bell, which left Philadelphia on 24 March 1784, is a prime example. The ship was owned by Philip Moore, Mark Bird, James

Wilson, Joseph Harrison, James Hood, John Redman, and Joshua Humphreys, the shipbuilder who would design frigates for the United States Navy after 1794. She carried silver, lead, tobacco, ginseng, wine, turpentine, naval stores, and other goods, and was instructed to stop at Mauritius on both the outbound and homeward voyages. Bell ignored these orders and went directly to Pondichéry to sell the wines. There the supercargo absconded with the silver. Bell managed to take on a return cargo and headed home by way of the British West Indies. On the pretext that his crew was ill with scurvy, he put in at Jamaica, no doubt hoping to sell goods there in defiance of British trade restrictions. A vigilant governor however, forced him to depart after only two days.[23]

Bell's disappointment was not typical. Other vessels regularly sold their teas, silks, and porcelains wherever they could find a market along the way. Sales in the Caribbean were common by 1787. Phineas Bond reported from Philadelphia that Americans not only stopped in the West Indies on their homebound voyages, but there reshipped, in casks covered with Indian corn, teas that they could not market in the United States. He also expected that the practice would, "no doubt, . . . thro' some other medium of deception be extended to Gt. Britain and Ireland particularly to the latter."

After her second voyage to China, the *Empress*, renamed the *Edgar*, was reassigned to European duty and made at least one trip between New York and Belfast, Ireland. Whether she had East India goods in her hold has not been determined, but Morris's firm, Constable, Rucker, and Company, is said to have reexported East India goods on a "vast" scale both to the West Indies and to the British Isles, and even to have sold tea to the British East India Company. Americans trampled on British sensibilities in yet another way. To Bond's great chagrin, the *Asia*, which sailed for China in 1788, carried British as well as American commodities to sell at Canton. He remarked that most of the British goods had been "intrusted" by the "too liberal faith of British merchants" to American dealers "who are now speculating and sporting with the property of their creditors and screening themselves under a most relaxed system of laws."[24]

Shaw's journal of the first voyage of the *Empress* pointed to yet another possibility interested Americans would exploit. "British subjects in India, who wish to remit their property to Europe," he noted, "will find means of doing it through other channels than that of the company's treasury. They get a penny, and sometimes twopence, more on a dollar, and bills at a shorter sight. Besides, the credit of the English company is not now so good with their subjects in India as formerly." Bottomry or respondentia loans, in which the vessel or its cargo served as collateral, gave Americans financing for return cargoes that was so difficult to raise elsewhere. This was, no doubt, how the *United States* was able to acquire a return cargo after the supercargo ran off with the silver. Within months, these loans were a regular feature of American voyage plans. The *Canton's* several voyages provide an example. A French observer, describing her first voyage, noted in April 1786 that it was an expedition characterized by the "greatest economy"—the cargo of goods and silver worth no more than 20,000 piastres. He had heard, however, that outfitters were counting on investment from East India company officers to make up their return cargo.

After the *Canton's* arrival in Philadelphia, Bond passed on a report "that a large sum was advanced at Canton at a moderate premium upon Bottomry on the ship *Canton,* Captain [Thomas] Truxton, lately arrived here." He also noted how general this practice had become. "European factors," he said, had given "considerable credit and made great advances" to American traders, who now "look with a certainty of support." Bond also described the return of the *Commerce* from Madras with a cargo, three-fifths of which was owned by Americans and the remainder by "various persons in Madras who adopt this circuitous mode of getting their property to England, in preference to the more expensive one of a direct remittance."

Even worse than the assistance Americans had found "from the very quarter from whence they expected opposition" was their boasting "of the civility and kindness they had experienced." Bond felt constrained to recommend that "an early check or restraint" should be "thrown in their way, either by thwarting their credit, or by withholding the articles suitable to their commerce." Truxtun experienced no such check during his voyage of 1790–1. One half of this venture was "owned in India and China by people whose names will not appear but who will furnish the principle part of the funds." Truxtun was received in Calcutta by none other than Charles Cornwallis, whose surrender at Yorktown was prelude to his new career as governor general there. India Company rules made no difference to Cornwallis, who reportedly said he would *welcome* a hundred American ships a year, because they drove down the prices British captains charged on their goods.

Americans depended heavily on foreign funds to finance their China ventures. Bond was well aware of the importance of specie for the China trade and fingered illicit commerce between the United States and Cuba as a major source. He reported that "Spaniards" came secretly into American ports and brought an "enormous" amount of specie ($500,000 in 1786, $60,000 lodged in the Bank of North America within a few weeks recently) in return for which they exported a variety of commodities. He parried Gouverneur Morris's recommendation to the French about Mauritius by suggesting that Britain should make the Bahamas a free port "under proper regulations from whence the Spaniards could draw the supplies they want," as a way of diverting this commerce into British channels.[25]

Americans also strove to best their competitors by developing or using nontraditional routes. Two voyages in 1787 illustrate this trend. The *Alliance,* Captain Thomas Read, now a Morris vessel, approached China from the east, but sailed south of Australia, around New Guinea and then north to Canton through the Solomon Islands. Her off-season (December 23) arrival allowed her supercargo, George Harrison, to make a very profitable sale of her cargo ("upwards of two hundred and fifty piculs of ginseng"), and the novelty of her route attracted considerable attention. On 30 September 1787, the *Columbia,* Captain John Kendrick, and the *Lady Washington,* Captain Robert Gray, left Boston, rounded Cape Horn, and headed for the Pacific Northwest Coast, the first of many such ventures on the Ledyard plan that became a New England specialty. Like the *Empress,* the two vessels also obtained letters of introduction from French and Dutch consuls. After taking a cargo of furs to Canton, the *Columbia,* now commanded by Gray, sailed home by Africa and became the first American flag vessel to circumnavigate the world. By the 1790s, American captains were ranging freely all over the Pacific, north and south of the equator.[26]

Bond listed a number of factors that militated against the success of early American ventures, "the delays of the voyage, the necessary expense of the outfit, the difficulty of making suitable remittances to obtain the proper investments," even the inferior teas American ships brought home. Awed by the power of private enterprize and American determination, he reported, however: "if one may judge from the present rage, it should seem as if new sources of profit appeared, and that the means of investment were facilitated so as to secure the future extension of the trade." Two months later he noted that Americans were "using every possible endeavour to render this trade as productive as possible; and to extend it to more valuable articles, than they have hitherto dealt in."[27] The creativity he described minimized chances that the American China trade would founder.

There were sixteen American vessels at Canton in 1789, by which time Americans were second only to the British there. Eight of the vessels were from Massachusetts, four from New York, two from Philadelphia, and two listed as from Mauritius. Higginson estimated that at least twenty American vessels annually went to Mauritius, India, and China. Soon after the American Constitution was ratified, Americans active in the China trade, including William Constable, petitioned the government to impose an additional duty on China goods imported into the United States in foreign bottoms.[28] U.S. mariners and merchants had demonstrated that trade with East Asia would flourish more under "independency" than it had under British rule. American seafarers had negotiated successfully for unofficial complicity, cooperation, and companionship with sailors and officials from every European nation represented in East Asia and won the grudging admiration of their rivals for their unorthodox, free-trading methods. They explored every avenue that might enable them to win against the odds recited by conservative European mercantilists who shrank from financing their ventures. The "American India Company's" inability to survive the *Empress*'s maiden voyage was a loud sermon in favor of innovation based on more indigenous models: smaller ships, new routes, varied cargoes, shorter or circuitous voyages, jerry-rigged financing, defiance of mercantilist regulations, and daring. Its openness, lack of discipline and organization, its willingness to improvise, and the superior quality of its officers, crews, and vessels were, in fact, the source of its strength and resilience.

Acknowledgments

I would like to thank Elizabeth M. Nuxoll and Philip F. Gallagher for their comments and suggestions on this article, which derives in part from research undertaken for *The Papers of Robert Morris,* a project sponsored by Queens College, CUNY, and funded by the National Endowment for the Humanities, the National Historical Publications and Records Commission, and the private contributors listed in its volumes.

Notes

1. On the *Empress,* see Philip Chadwick Foster Smith, *The Empress of China* (Philadelphia: Philadelphia Maritime Museum, 1984); Samuel Shaw, *The Journals of Major Samuel Shaw, the First American Consul at Canton with a Life of the Author,* eds. Joseph Quincy, William Crosby, and H. P. Nichols (Boston: W. Crosby and H. P. Nichols, 1847); Clarence L. Ver Steeg, "Financing and Outfitting the First United States Ship to China," *Pacific Historical Review* 22 (1953): 1–12; and E. James Ferguson, John Catanzariti, et al., eds., *The Papers of Robert Morris,* vol. 8 (Pittsburgh, Pa.: University of Pittsburgh Press, 1995), 857–82 (volume series hereafter *RMP*).

For general accounts of the trade, see Foster Rhea Dulles, *The Old China Trade* (Boston: Houghton Mifflin, 1930), 1–64; Louis Dermigny, *La Chine et L'Occident: Le Commerce à Canton au XVIIIe Siècle, 1719–1833* (Paris: SEVPEN, 1964); and Alfred Tamarin and Shirley Glubok, *Voyaging to Cathay, Americans in the China Trade* (New York: Viking Press, 1976). Regional histories of the trade include: Samuel Eliot Morison, *The Maritime History of Massachusetts, 1783–1860* (Boston: Houghton Mifflin, 1923), 27–118; Carl Seaburg and Stanley Paterson, *Merchant Prince of Boston: Colonel T. H. Perkins, 1764–1854* (Cambridge, Mass.: Harvard University Press, 1971), 49–71; Conrad Edick Wright, "Merchants and Mandarins: New York and the Early China Trade," in David Sanctuary Howard, *New York and the China Trade* (New York: New York Historical Society, 1984); and Jonathan Goldstein, *Philadelphia and the China Trade, 1682–1846: Commercial, Cultural and Attitudinal Effects* (University Park: Pennysylvania State University, 1978); and the sources on the northwest coast trade cited at note 26 below.

2. See John J. McCusker and Russell R. Menard, *The Economy of British America, 1607–1789* (Chapel Hill: University of North Carolina Press, 1991), 351–77; and Thomas M. Doerflinger, *A Vigorous Spirit of Enterprise:*

Merchants and Economic Development in Revolutionary Philadelphia (Chapel Hill: University of North Carolina Press, 1986), 283–96.

3. On the smuggling, see François Barbé-Marbois, Memoire sur le Commerce entre la France et les Etats-Unis, Chapter 3, Commerce entre les Etablissemens françois aux Indes et les Etats-Unis, Affaires Etrangères, Sous-Série B III 442, Archives Nationales, Paris; and Goldstein, *Philadelphia and the China Trade,* 18. On the congressional deliberations, see Paul H. Smith, et al., eds. *Letters of Delegates to Congress, 1774–1789,* vol. 8 (Washington, D.C.: Library of Congress, 1981), 366–67; and Worthington C. Ford, et al., eds., *Journals of the Continental Congress, 1774–1789,* vol. 13 (Washington, D.C.: U.S. Government Printing Office, 1909–37), 242. On the request to Barbé-Marbois, see his letter to Charles Eugène Gabriel de La Croix, Marquis de Castries, 10 Oct. 1781, Affaires Etrangères, B I 945 (Correspondence Consulaire, Philadelphia, I) 135, Archives Nationales, Paris.

4. See Frederick L. Nussbaum, "The Formation of the New East India Company of Calonne," *American Historical Review* 38 (1933): 475–97; and Dermigny, *La Chine,* 3:1021–32, 1072–81.

5. See *RMP,* 1:3–4, 30, 2:214–19, 7:272–77; and Elizabeth Miles Nuxoll, *Congress and the Munitions Merchants: The Secret Committee of Trade during the American Revolution, 1775–1777* (New York: Garland, 1985).

6. See Robert A. East, *Business Enterprise in the American Revolutionary Era* (New York: Columbia University Press, 1938), 111, 112–13; Holker to Matthew Ridley, 28 May 1783, quoted in Clarence L. Ver Steeg, "First U.S. Ship to China," 8; *RMP,* 2:33, 3:519, 4:245, and Dermigny, *La Chine,* 3:1081.

7. See *RMP,* 7:250–51, 263, 8:858, 880; Ridley to Holker, 22 June and 14 Oct. 1782, Pringle to Holker, 19 Oct. and 14 Dec. 1782, 16 and 22 Feb., and 3 and 6 May 1783, [Holker] to [Ridley] 21 Nov. 1782, and Bérard and Company to Holker, 16 Feb. 1783, Holker Papers, vol. 18, 2982, 3406, 3462, 3526, 3564, vol. 19, 3776, 3780–81, 3789, vol. 20, 3975, 3987, Library of Congress, Washington, D.C.; and [Holker] to Ridley, n.d. [1783], Ridley Papers, Massachusetts Historical Society, Boston, Mass. On Daniel Parker and Company, see Ver Steeg, "First U. S. Ship to China," 2–5.

8. On the early phase of the China venture, see *RMP,* 8:184, 185, 858–59, 866; Carleton to North, 29 Aug. 1783, Colonial Office, Class 5/Volume 110, fols. 280–81, Public Record Office, London, U.K.; James Swan to Parker, 4 Oct. 1783, Holker Papers, vol. 22, 4289, Library of Congress, Washington, D.C.; and Smith, *Empress,* 23, 36–42. On Turnbull and Turnbull, Marmie, and Company, see *RMP,* 1:89, 8:873, and Robert Morris to Turnbull, Marmie, and Company, 31 Mar. 1784, 9:221.

9. See *RMP,* 7:361–71, 767–81, 789–90, 8:407–8, 786, 860.

10. On the "American India Company" and its plans, see Information respecting two American Ships intended for the East Indies, 27 Aug. 1783,

enclosed in Carleton to Lord North, 29 Aug. 1783, Carleton to North, 6 and 25 Oct. 1783, Colonial Office, Class 5/Volume 110, fols 280–81, 304–5, and Volume 111, fols. 51–52, 120–21, Public Record Office, London, U.K.; and James Maury to Turnbull, Marmie and Company, 21 Oct. and 9 Dec. 1783, Holker Papers, vol. 22, 4336, vol. 23, 4493, Library of Congress, Washington, D.C. On the *Empress,* see Smith, *Empress,* 25–28, 138, 143. On the other ships, see *RMP,* 8:265–66, 270, 325–27, 384–85, 859–61, 862, 875, 878, and James Nicholson to Robert Morris, 11 Mar. 1784, and notes, *RMP,* 9:181–82. For a comparison of American and European navigation, see Harold C. Syrett, Jacob E. Cooke et al., eds., *The Papers of Alexander Hamilton,* vol. 5 (New York: Columbia University Press, 1962), 466–69.

11. On the Ridley loan and Holker's proposal, see his letters to Ridley, [ca. January], 1 and 10 Feb. 1783, Ridley Papers, Massachusetts Historical Society, Boston, Mass.; and *RMP,* 8:508, 509, 510, 729. On the internal dissension, see *RMP,* 8:865–71, 880, and Parker to Robert Morris, 10 Feb. 1784, and Robert Morris to Parker, 14 Feb. 1784, 9:98–99, 119–20.

12. See Smith, *Empress,* 43, 84–88, 104, 115–21, 129–33; Duer to Holker, 4 Mar. 1783, and Parker to Holker, 8 and 10 Feb. 1784, Holker Papers, vol. 20, 3810, vol. 24, 4727–30, 4731, Library of Congress, Washington, D.C.

13. On Morris's funds, see *RMP,* 8:390, 646, 808, 850–53; Robert Morris to Le Couteulx and Company, 13 Jan., and to the Dutch consortium, 12 Feb. 1784, and notes, Robert Morris, Accounts (1785) (No. 11) *RMP,* 9:24, 110, 867–68; and Parker to Holker, 18 Feb. 1784, Holker Papers, vol. 24, 4744, Library of Congress, Washington, D.C. On the quarrel between Holker and Morris, see Robert Morris to John Rucker, 18 June, and notes, *RMP,* 9:407–19. On the collapse of Parker and Company and the flight of Parker, see Smith, *Empress,* 115–21.

14. See Smith, *Empress,* 64–71, 138, 141–45, 184–85; Ver Steeg, "First U.S. Ship to China," 11; *Hamilton Papers,* 9:39–42; and Quincy, *Shaw,* 354.

15. On the "country ships," see Quincy, *Shaw,* 342–44; and *Hamilton Papers,* 9:45. On the *Grand Turk's* voyage plan, see Smith, *Empress,* 218. On the return of the *Empress* and the Pallas, see ibid., 220–34, 312–13; and Otto to Vergennes, 26 Aug. 1785, Correspondence politique, Etats-Unis, vol. 30, 248, Archives du Ministère des Affaires Etrangères, Paris, France; Quincy, *Shaw,* 218; and *RMP,* 8:878.

16. See Green's orders in Smith, *Empress,* 67–69.

17. On the arrangements for the *Empress's* second China voyage, see Tench Tilghman and Company, Constable, Rucker, and Company, the articles of partnership and the memorandum of 10 May 1784, see *RMP,* 8:796–97, 880–81, and 9:325–31; Robert Morris to Tilghman, 28 June and 6 July 1785, Robert Morris Papers, New York Public Library, New York,

N.Y.; the Tilghman Papers, Maryland Historical Society, Baltimore, Md., which contain Tilghman's outgoing correspondence, and Affouke to Constable, Rucker, and Company, 11 Dec. 1786, Constable-Pierrepont Collection, New York Public Library, New York, N.Y.; Quincy, *Shaw*, 218–19; Donald G. Tailby, "Chapters from the Business Career of William Constable: A Merchant of Post-Revolutionary New York" (Ph.D. diss., Rutgers University, 1961), 210–12, 222–24, 227; and William A. Davis, "William Constable, New York Merchant and Land Speculator, 1772–1803" (Ph.D. diss., Harvard University, 1955), 130–31. On the *Betsey*, see ibid., 72, 85, 122–26.

18. See Smith, *Empress*, 5, 78, 269, 283–84; Constable to Thomas Fitzsimons, 30 Nov. 1785, Holker Papers, vol. 30, 5880, Library of Congress, Washington, D.C.; Affouke's letter of 11 Dec. 1786, cited above; Paul E. Fontenoy, "An 'Experimental' Voyage to China 1785–1787," *American Neptune* 55 (1995): 289–300; East, *Business Enterprise*, 255; and Wright, "Merchants and Mandarins," 24–25. Wright considers the voyage more profitable than do Fontenoy and East.

19. On the *Harriet*, see the *South Carolina Gazette* and *Weekly Advertiser*, 29–31 July 1784; Smith, *Empress*, 23–24, 205; *RMP*, 8:875; and Parker to Robert Morris, 10 Feb. 1784, and notes, *RMP*, 9:98–99. Subsequent voyages on the *Harriet*'s plan, like the initial voyage of the *Grand Turk*, were less successful.

20. See Gouverneur Morris to Chastellux, 14 May, and notes, Robert Morris to Lafayette, 19 May, 1784, *RMP*, 9:336–43, 351–52; Auguste Toussaint, ed., *Early American Trade with Mauritius* (Port Louis, Mauritius; Esclapon, 1954), 4; and "Letters of Stephen Higginson," in the *Annual Report of the American Historical Association for the Year 1896* 1 (1897): 760–61, 762–65.

21. On the *Hope*, see "Letters of Phineas Bond, British consul at Philadelphia, to the Foreign Office of Great Britain, 1787, 1788, 1789," in the *Annual Report of the American Historical Association for the Year 1896* 1 (1897): 545; Seaburg/Paterson, *Merchant Prince*, 58–61, 65–71, 73–76, 81–82, 90, 91, 100, 101. On the *Union*, see Morison, *Maritime History*, 74–76. On the *Fair American*, see James R. Gibson, *Otter Skins, Boston Ships, and China Goods: The Maritime Fur Trade of the Northwest Coast, 1785–1841* (Seattle: University of Washington Press, 1992), 39. On the duties, see Ridley to Holker, 9 Oct. 1783, Holker Papers, vol. 22, 4301, Library of Congress, Washington, D.C.; Dulles, *Old China Trade*, 19; Eugene S. Ferguson, *The Life of Commodore Thomas Truxtun, U.S. Navy 1755–1822* (Baltimore, Md.: Johns Hopkins Press, 1956), 75–76; and *Hamilton Papers*, 9:44, 52.

22. See Morison, *Maritime History*, 52; Smith, *Empress*, 249; and Quincy, *Shaw*, 356–360. On Constable's plan, see Davis, "Constable," 156–59.

23. See *RMP,* 8:876; and Guillaume Otto to Vergennes, 24 Sept. 1785, Correspondence politique, Etats-Unis, vol. 30, 310, Archives du Ministère des Affaires Etrangères, Paris, France.

24. See Bond, *AHA Report,* 535, 542, 554, 555–56; Smith, *Empress,* 249–50, 315; Davis, "Constable," 151–52.

25. See Smith, *Empress,* 177; Pierre François Barbé-Marbois to Castries, 28 May 1786, Affaires Etrangères B I 946 (Correspondence consulaire, Philadelphia,) 304, Archives Nationales, Paris, France; Bond, *AHA Report,* 541, 542, 556, 566–67; and Constable to A. Ellice, 7 Nov., and to Robert Morris, 1 and 12 Dec. 1789, Constable Letterbook and Shipping Papers, Constable Pierrepont Collection, New York Public Library, New York, N.Y.; Ferguson, *Truxtun,* 89–90.

26. On the voyage of the *Alliance,* rated by Shaw at 1,000 tons, see Quincy, *Shaw,* 254; "Robert Morris," in John Sanderson, Robert Waln Jr., and Henry D. Gilpin, eds., *Biography of the Signers to the Declaration of Independence,* vol. 5 (Philadelphia: R. W. Pomeroy, 1823), 370; and Bond, *AHA Report,* 540. On the *Columbia* and the trade on the Northwest Coast, see Abraham P. Nasatir and Gary E. Monell, *French Consuls in the United States: A Calendar of Their Correspondence in the Archives Nationales* (Washington, D.C.: Library of Congress, 1967), 49; Gibson, *Otter Skins;* Frederic W. Howay, ed., *Voyages of the Columbia to the Northwest Coast, 1787–1790 and 1790–1793* (Boston: Massachusetts Historical Society, 1941; reprint, Portland: Oregon Historical Society Press, 1990); Frederic W. Howay, *A List of Trading Vessels in the Maritime Fur Trade, 1785–1825,* ed., Richard A. Pierce (Kingston, Ont.: Limestone Press, 1973); J. Richard Nokes, *Columbia's River: The Voyages of Robert Gray, 1787–1793* (Tacoma: Washington State Historical Society, 1991); Briton C. Busch and Barry M. Gough, eds. *Fur Traders from New England: The Boston Men in the North Pacific, 1787–1800, The Narratives of William Dane Phelps, William Sturgis, and James Gilchrist Swan* (Spokane, Wash.: Arthur H. Clark, 1996); Barry M. Gough, *The Northwest Coast: British Navigation, Trade, and Discoveries to 1812* (Vancouver: UBC Press, 1992); *Hamilton Papers,* 9:45–49; Kenneth S. Latourette, *The History of Early Relations between the United States and China, 1784–1844* (New Haven, Conn.: Yale University Press, 1917), 31–33; and Morison, *Maritime History of Massachusetts,* 46–47.

27. See Bond, *AHA Report,* 540, 545.

28. See "American Ships at Canton in China December 1789," in Constable's Shipping Papers, Constable-Pierrepont Collection, New York Public Library, New York, N.Y.; and *Hamilton Papers,* 5:469. For lists of American voyages to China, see Rhys Richards, "United States Trade with China 1784–1814," *American Neptune,* Special Supplement to Volume 54

(1994); and Kenneth Scott Latourette, "Voyages of American Ships to China, 1784–1844," *Transactions of the Connecticut Academy of Arts and Sciences* 28 (1927): 237–71. On the request for a duty, see *Hamilton Papers,* 8:20–21; and Davis, "Constable," 140–41, 160. For the Impost Act passed 4 July 1789, see Linda Grant DePauw et al., eds., *Documentary History of the First Federal Congress of the United States of America* (Baltimore, Md.: Johns Hopkins University Press, 1972), 5:940–83, passim.

The modern reconstruction of the *Lady Washington* operates out of Grays Harbor Historical Seaport in Washington State.

4

The *Lady Washington* at Kushimoto, Japan, in 1791

Jim Mockford

Robert Gray, age thirty-two, commanded the sloop *Lady Washington* when it sailed from Boston for the Pacific in 1787. The *Lady Washington* was part of a two-ship commercial expedition headed by Captain John Kendrick, age forty-seven, who sailed on the ship *Columbia Rediviva*, and was sponsored by a group of investors led by Joseph Barrell. The adventurers planned to acquire furs along the Pacific Northwest coast of America and transport them across the Pacific to Canton, China, where members of Captain Cook's third expedition to the Pacific had reported that a fortune could be made in the fur trade.

American merchants did not expect opportunities to trade with Japanese, for they knew Japan to be closed to all foreign interchange except for a small trading concession operated by the Dutch at Nagasaki. Nevertheless, in his instructions to Robert Gray before his second voyage to the northwest coast in September of 1790, Joseph Barrell wrote, "When you leave the coast in the ship, we advise your trying what can be done on the coast of Japan and Pekin, where, if you find safety in anchoring, and can dispose of furs to advantage, we would advise you by all means to do it."[1]

Robert Gray, having become the first American to circumnavigate the world in 1790, was already famous at the time he received the above instructions. By the time Gray reached the Pacific Northwest coast in the summer of 1791, John Kendrick had already anchored at Kushimoto, Japan. The two men had exchanged commands of their ships in 1789 while in the Northwest, so it had been on the *Columbia Rediviva* that Gray had circumnavigated, and it was on the *Lady Washington* that Kendrick arrived in Japan.

By the late eighteenth century, the coast of Japan remained among the portions of the Pacific rim that had not been explored by Europeans. James Cook and George Vancouver had led British expeditions that meticulously charted the west coast of the American continent. Russian, Spanish, French, and Dutch captains had also made extensive contributions to geographic knowledge of the Pacific. But the Japanese feudal government had closed Japan to trade and communication with the outside world for nearly 150 years before Captain Kendrick's arrival. The Tokugawa shogunate regarded any contact between Japanese subjects and foreigners, whom it regarded as barbarians, as a punishable offense. Edicts reminded subjects of the need to expel any alien violators and prescribed scrutinizing the Japanese who had limited dealings with the Dutch trading concession at Nagasaki. If authorities determined that any breach of the seclusion, or *sakoku*, laws had been violated, it was likely that the accused would face exile or even death. Japanese coastal fishermen and mariners mostly avoided contact with foreign ships, and Japanese rarely attempted to sail away from the home islands of Japan. The exceptions included hapless castaways; Japanese pirates, outlaws anyway, who ventured south toward China; participants in a few military expeditions to Korea in previous centuries; and during the Tokugawa period (1600–1868), a few authorized explorers of the northern islands, Hokkaido, the Kuriles, and Sakhalin.

But I must return to the voyage of Captain Cook to tell the story of maritime explorations of Japan's coast in the late eighteenth century because it is a little known fact that, while his ships the *Resolution* and the *Discovery* made their passage home from the north Pacific in June of 1779, Lt. James King charted a portion of the coast to fulfill a last remaining objective of the Cook expedition, to complete the maritime exploration of Japan and the northeast coast of Asia. Captain Cook's instructions for the third voyage included a return to Tahiti from where he would sail north for New Albion and chart the waters between 45 degrees north latitude to about 65 degrees north along the North American shore in search of a Northwest Passage. If he found no inlets leading toward Hudson or Baffin Bay, he was to sail west for Kamchatka and winter for the purpose of continuing his search the next spring, "either east or west," a choice between the Asian and American continents, and as far north as he considered prudent.[2] It was en route from Tahiti north for New Albion that, by his discovery of the Hawaiian Islands, Cook changed the history of the north Pacific. Had it not been for his death in Hawaii in February 1779, it is quite possible that this chapter regarding maritime exploration of the coast of Japan in the late eighteenth century would be about the expedition of Captain Cook. But Cook's death changed everything, and the return expedition under the command of John Gore had little interest in anything but heading home as they faced gale winds and rain while heading south from Petropavlosk, Kamchatka, and the Kurile Islands, and then along the east coast of Japan.

The brief lifting of clouds along the northeast coast of the Mutsu province, now called the Iwate region of Honshu Island, on 26 October 1779, allowed Lt. James King to draw a chart from 40 degrees 5 minutes latitude and 142 degrees 28 minutes longitude, as the ships moved south under the watchful eye of Sailing Master William Bligh. So it is with Captain Cook's voyage that my story begins, because a chart of a small portion of the Japanese coast added to the Royal Navy's geographic knowledge of the Pacific and reminded the Admiralty that there still remained a geographic task undone in the effort to complete the exploration of the Pacific.

William Bligh, as we know, would return to the Pacific as commander of the infamous *Bounty* and later in command of the *Providence*. A midshipman named George Vancouver was also on board the *Resolution*. He would later return to the Pacific in command of an exploring expedition in 1791. Mutineers destroyed the *Bounty* at Pitcairns Island in January 1790, and the *Providence* wrecked in 1796 off Miyako Island in the chain of Japanese islands that stretch south of Okinawa.

Bligh completed a successful mission in the south Pacific in 1792 on board the *Providence,* a story that is less well known than the mutiny he encountered on the *Bounty* in 1789. Meanwhile, the British had left the exploration of the coast of Japan unattended; but a French expedition under the command of Jean François Galoup de La Perouse examined the east coast of Asia in a voyage from 1785 to 1788.

La Perouse visited Kamchatka in 1787, having sailed along the coast of Hokkaido and through a strait to which his name was given. Having added to Western knowledge of Japanese seas, La Perouse disappeared in 1788 after sailing south in search of the Solomon Islands. Later his ship was found at the bottom of the ocean. Geographers recognized his cartographic work in naming the Straits of La Perouse between Hokkaido and Sakhalin. La Perouse was unable to determine whether or not Sakhalin was a peninsula or an island, but others were soon to pursue this task.

Having briefly noted the British and French visits to the coast of Japan in the 1770s and 1780s, I would like to summarize the state of Japanese geographic efforts at exploring and mapping the islands of Japan during this period. For some 150 years before the Cook expedition arrived off the coast of Iwate, the Tokugawa shoguns had ruled Japan in a feudal system they controlled from Edo (Tokyo). The Tokugawa shoguns allowed a small concession held by the Dutch at Nagasaki, the sole place for a limited access to trade with the West. They forbade Japanese to travel abroad on the threat of death. Occasional castaways from foreign ships were immediately sent to Nagasaki and confined on Dejima Island until their repatriation or expulsion could be arranged on the Dutch transport or occasional passing ship. The strict isolationist outlook not only limited Japanese knowledge of the outside world but also prevented a clear assessment of the geography of their own archipelago. However, during the reign of the tenth shogun, Ieharu, from 1760 to 1786, and particularly because of the views of his chief councillor, Tanuma Okitsugu (1719–88), some signs indicated a potential for change in the Japanese policy on international trade and communication.

Grand Chamberlain Tanuma, historians say, dominated Shogun Tokugawa Ieharu. Tanuma encouraged commercial expansion at

Nagasaki and elsewhere, including the promotion of dried sea products from the Hokkaido frontier. He considered plans to colonize the north and even opening trade with the Russians, who had become ever more present in Kamchatka, Sakhalin, and the Kuriles. Tanuma relaxed sakoku seclusion policies and encouraged "Dutch Studies," or *rangaku,* allowing the importation of clocks and scientific books and instruments. Japanese scholars translated Western medical journals, and some writers such as Hayashi Shihei, who had traveled to Nagasaki in 1775, memorialized the government on such issues as colonization of Hokkaido, strengthening of national defenses, improvement of geographic and military education, and the need to study the West.

In 1785 Hayashi wrote a treatise, *Sangoku Tsuran Zusetsu (Illustrated Survey of Three Countries),* about the geography of the region just beyond the main Japanese islands, including Korea, the Ryukyu Island chain, and Hokkaido, which was still regarded as a frontier.[3] In 1786 Hayashi completed another book, *Kaikoku Heidan (Discussion of the Military Problems of a Maritime Nation),* in which he forecast the imminent encroachment by the Europeans from the north. It would take him five years to obtain the funding to see his treatise on naval defense published. But the foreign ships that arrived in Japan in 1791 were not Russians, and they did not arrive at the northern island. Rather, the ships were the American brig *Lady Washington* and sloop *Grace,* under the commands of Captain John Kendrick and William Douglas, and they arrived at the main island of Honshu and in the domain of a collateral family of the Tokugawa shogun, at Kushimoto, Wakayama.

Village headmen documented the incident well, immediately sending reports of a crisis to military authorities at Wakayama City. Delivering the reports required a journey of several days, from the tip of the remote and mountainous Kii Peninsula, where Cape Shionomisaki and Oshima Island create a sheltered bay at Kushimoto.

Accompanied by the sloop *Grace* under William Douglas, Captain John Kendrick sailed from Lark's Bay in south China in March 1791, having decided that fur prices were too low and the opportunity to explore trading in Asia outside the control of Hong merchants and Chinese mandarin authorities might yield better profit. He had spent the previous six months refurbishing the *Lady Washington,* converting the ship from a sloop to a brig and adding an impressive masthead carving of a woman, which drew comments from later observers. The Americans met Japanese fishing boats off the coast before making landfall in early April. The northeasterly current known as the *Kuroshio,* or Black Current, which sweeps along the east coast of Japan, brings a warm stream north from the tropics and makes the Kumano Sea off the Kii Peninsula a productive fishery. The Kuroshio had pushed the *Lady Washington* and the *Grace* north from the Chinese coast. The Cape Shionomi projection toward the Kuroshio makes it a visible point for sailing ships to mark. From the sea, the mountains of the Kii Peninsula that rise dramatically behind the cape leave no doubt that the sailor has reached the major island of the Japanese chain. The mountainous region also isolates the villages along the southern areas of the peninsula, which are already distant from the nearest large cities of Kyoto, Osaka, and Nagoya and the regional capital and daimyo's castle at Wakayama City.

Heading toward land, the Americans found just to the east of the protruding peninsula a sheltered cove behind a small island. As they drew in to anchor between the island and shore, their arrival caught the attention of local villagers. The first report came from the town of Koza, situated on the Honshu mainland and sheltered from the Pacific by Cape Shiomonoseki to its southwest and Oshima Island across the bay directly south. A narrow passage between the island and the cape makes rounding the island possible for fishing boats, but rock outcroppings, including the scenic Hashikui rocks, would have made Kendrick careful about where he was to anchor and move his ships during his visit. Nakanishi Riezaemon, town headman of Koza village, sent out a report crafted with words of deference to authorities, humbly requesting their consideration of the urgency of his alert that foreign ships had arrived in the bay between Oshima Island and Koza. His warning reached neighboring villages up and down the coast and was echoed by several other reports written during the eleven-day stay by the American vessels.[4]

The local reports were combined in the Tokugawa archive as part of the Nanki Tokugawa Shi, and the accounts have recently been published in the *Kushimoto Cho Shi (History of the City of Kushimoto),* 1996.[5] In

1991 Hisayasu Hatanaka and Mitsanori Hamano translated into English a portion of the record taken from Kinan Younou, a report by Samurai Sakamoto Tenzan, for an article by Mary Malloy in *Quarterdeck* (newsletter of the Columbia River Maritime Museum).[6] Japanese author Kazuo Sayama has written a biography of Captain Kendrick, entitled *Waga Na wa Kendorikku (My Name Is Kendrick)*, 1991.[7] Another alert, penned by Kimoto headman Nishikawa Matsuzo, and also forwarded along the coast, confirmed Nakanishi's initial report. The Japanese writers testified to the violation of the law of seclusion, but they had yet to determine by what nation and in whose command these outlaw vessels were held and for what purposes the ships had arrived in the waters off Kushimoto. Meanwhile, the inhabitants of Oshima Island were even more anxious than those on Honshu, because the foreign ships had anchored directly between the islanders and the neighboring villages. On the island village of Sugariura, the village headman, Kichigo, discussed the situation with his son Komataro, whom he prodded into a closer observation of the unwelcome visitors. The vessels shifted to a better anchorage near "Kaneyama," indicating their intention for a longer stay. Komataro ventured out toward the ships and, as his account has it, "heard Dutch words being spoken" but "couldn't understand" anything.[8] The ships appeared to be fully laden with cargo and carrying guns and an ample amount of gunpowder. The foreign sailors began to pass the time firing at seabirds and, it seemed, to prepare a landing party.

However, the ship's boat that was lowered into Japanese waters was assigned the task of taking soundings. An American exploration of the coast of Japan was under way. No logbook or chart remain of Captain Kendrick's documentation of his visit to Japan. Kendrick was killed in Hawaii in 1794, and the *Lady Washington* was lost in a storm at the entrance of the Cavayan River in the Philippines in 1797. But the visit of the Americans to Kushimoto would have an effect on the Japanese effort to improve coastal defenses along the Kii Peninsula. Japanese recording the American visit viewed the intrusion as a disgrace to the Japanese nation, and the villagers in the area were embarrassed that they could do nothing to prevent the first step of an American sailor on Japanese soil.

In spite of the fact that it was the middle of the night, embarrassed village headmen recorded Komataro's report and sent a message to the next village. The reports by the village headmen were forwarded from village to village along both sides of the Kii Peninsula, but it would take several days for the message to reach military authorities at the daimyo's capital of Wakayama and as much time or longer for them to respond with a military force to expel the barbarians. Meanwhile, the ships sent out a boat to Oshima Island with five men to scout for wood and water. They would begin to supply their ship with what they could find by cutting down trees and assembling an unusual system for transporting water, which the reporters described as "carried water in cotton bags to the ships."[9]

Everyone involved realized that the next communications would need to be an exchange between the Japanese and the foreigners. And it turned out that both sides had some resources to assist this effort. At nearby Takamimura lived Dr. Date Rishun, who as a learned man might understand something of the "Dutch" being spoken by the foreign men. Some gathered at his home to request his assistance, and the doctor took up his writing brush and paper and set out for the waterfront. A boat carried him out to the *Lady Washington,* where sailors waved it off at first but then permitted a villager to climb up a ladder to the ship's rail. The villager was about to board the *Lady Washington* but was met by a guard dog at the rail and turned away as the dog snapped at his sleeve. Dr. Date drafted a message that was delivered aboard, and he received a reply written in Chinese characters. He returned with the first communication from an American sea captain to a Japanese official. This document is preserved in the record of the Tokugawa House of Kii (Nanki Tokugawa Shi).[10]

Captain Kendrick had hired at least three Chinese men while in south China for the purpose of working as shipwrights on the Northwest coast of North America, where fur traders were building additional ships for commerce. Their utility as translators and scribes in communications with the Japanese was to be tested at Kushimoto. The nationality of the foreign ships and the identity of the commander were finally established in the message Kendrick drafted and sent to Dr. Date. Date later reported his experience to a traveling samurai named Sakamoto Tenzan, who published the account in his book *Kinan Younou* in 1799. The American message to the Japanese began as follows: "This ship belongs to the Red Hairs from a land called America. Its cargo includes copper, iron and fifty guns."[11]

The letter noted that the ship had "drifted here under stress of wind and wave" and that "we shall not stay here more than three or five days" or "as long as the wind continues to be adverse." These remarks were probably meant to mollify local officials and at the same time offer an opportunity for potential trade should the locals want to obtain copper, iron, or guns. The mention that "there are about 100 persons aboard" may have been included to show the strength of the American force and prevent any attempt at capture. It is unlikely that there were so many people unless a much larger Chinese contingent was being transported to the northwest. Kendrick was known to have saved a crew of Chinese sailors from a sinking junk during a typhoon on one occasion, but the number in this message seems more likely to have been inflated to deter a local militia from considering a boarding party. Finally the message concluded with the statement, "The captain's name is Kendrick."[12]

Sakamoto Tenzan's account based on his interview with Dr. Date provides other details, including a description of the finely made and realistic statue of a lady on the figurehead, which measured about eight feet tall and had flowing hair and a long gown that almost touched the sea. The *Lady Washington* may have presented an appealing image among the fishermen in the area, as the figure also carried a fishing rod and seemed to beckon the resources of the sea. This sea goddess also had a jade ornament in her hair and must have been protected by the image on the consort vessel, the *Grace*, which is reported to have on its bow a statue of a man wearing armor and carrying a half-drawn sword.[13]

As the visit of the American ships extended beyond the three or five days referred to in the message, their presence increasingly annoyed some local villagers. The ships had arrived and sailors landed without permission of Japanese authorities. The sailors had cut trees and taken wood and water without consent of local headmen or residents. The sailors' constant firing of cannon blanks and muskets was noisy, and the shooting of seabirds for no purpose other than amusement offended observers. The ship's dog had nearly bitten a villager and a landholder named Chiuemon had attempted to complain to the foreigners directly but was chased away with shouts and musket fire. Chiuemon was not injured, but the proximity of passing bullets was unnerving and the audacity of the foreigners insulting.

The only communication that had been obtained was in Chinese and could be read only by Dr. Date. Yet the document in Chinese was archived by Tokugawa authorities and remains the first evidence of an attempt at communication between Americans and Japanese. The document is also one of the few letters from Captain Kendrick that survived his expedition in the Pacific.

As previously noted, Kendrick was killed in an exchange of cannon fire in Hawaii in 1794, and the *Lady Washington* never returned to Boston, having continued Pacific and Asian trading under John Howell after Kendrick's death until it met with disaster in the Philippines in 1797. Daniel Paine, who joined the vessel at Macao and noted in his journal entry for 4 July 1797 its departure for a voyage to Manila, recorded an account of its final voyage.[14] Arriving off the Cavayan River bar on 20 July, the ship proceeded to enter but soon hit ground and the "swell of the sea counteracted all of our endeavors."[15] During the next day, the crew attempted efforts to save the ship, despite wind and rain, but eventually decided to abandon ship. All hands except the mate swam ashore, leaving the steward who refused to leave the ship and thereupon lost his life. When the heavy rains subsided, the crew of the *Lady Washington* made their way to Bigan City, where Captain Howell began a search for a new ship to purchase.

Before these events brought a dramatic end to the story of the *Lady Washington,* the ship had returned to the Pacific Northwest coast in 1791 and during the next few years encountered many other trading and exploring vessels during its voyages along the Northwest coast and to Hawaii. Kendrick's attempt to trade in Japan would have been a story to pass on to other fur traders and Spanish and British explorers who in the 1790s were positioning themselves for strategic and commercial objectives as well as scientific exploration.

If the Americans could so quickly respond to the opportunities of the fur trade and open their own trade with China, might they not also be the first to open trade with Japan? Such a possibility must have been considered by the British. Their explorers George Vancouver and William Robert Broughton had met the Americans along the northwest coast only to find that Robert Gray had indeed made a discovery of great importance. Gray had entered the mouth of the "Great River of the West," naming it "Columbia's River" after his own ship.[16] In time the discovery would strengthen an American claim to the region the British called New Albion, where Cook had first arrived in 1778. It took less than a decade for American ships to compete with the British in the trans-Pacific trade, and the persistent efforts of the American captains made their maritime explorations a potential challenge to British strategic interests in the Pacific. An American success in Japan might eventually present a challenge to British commercial interests in Asia. It was not long before the Admiralty decided to commission another expedition to the Pacific, and this time a maritime exploration of the islands of Japan would be an objective of the commander, William Robert Broughton, in HMS *Providence*.

Although Kendrick had spent only eleven days at Kushimoto, his timing was good on this occasion. Two days after he sailed from Japan, military troops arrived from Wakayama to expel the barbarians. But Kendrick had departed because no commercial opportunity presented itself and perhaps his Chinese translators had managed to convey the unlikelihood of any other port in Japan offering much of a potential for trade either. In any case, the Americans had left an impression on the Japanese in Kushimoto, who conveyed their distress to the military contingent that arrived too late to take credit for defending the Japanese coast.

It was apparent that foreign ships from any country in the world could arrive at most any part of the coast of Japan, and defenseless villages would be without protection. In response to the visit of the *Lady Washington,* the village headmen determined to improve the watch towers and crisis mobilization effort. They initiated a system of lookouts and response team members or militiamen who would wear special "happi coats," or jackets with special markings indicating the responsibility of each team member. Individuals were assigned the tasks of being lookouts, setting signal fires, carrying a firearm, raising banners, and mobilizing villagers and fishermen who would be sent out in all available boats, including fishing boats, whaling boats, and transport vessels, to deter another arrival of any foreign ships along the coast of the Kii domain.[17]

The same year the *Lady Washington* arrived at Kushimoto and triggered a local reassessment of coastal defenses in the Kii domain the writer Hayashi Shihei finally published his book *Kaikoku Heidan* in an effort to bring attention to the Tokugawa government of the need to change its policies toward the northern island and improve the national defense. It is ironic that within eight months after publication of *Kaikoku Heidan*, Hayashi was arrested and placed in confinement for criticizing without permission the official policy of the shogunate and "disseminating false information." Printed copies of his book were destroyed and the printing blocks confiscated. He wrote a poem stating, "I have no parents, no wife, no children, no printing blocks, no money, no desire to die." However, Hayashi died in 1793, and the significance of his books would be recognized by other Japanese writers who began to turn their interest toward mapping and defending the Japanese coast.[18]

Even before Hayashi's death, a Russian effort to establish trade at Hokkaido took place in 1792, when Adam Laxam arrived at Nemuro on the brig *Ekatarina*. Laxman repatriated several Japanese castaways and was sent away with a paper document, which he thought was a "trading permit." The Russians did not attempt to use the permit until 1804, when Nicolai Resanov made a voyage to Nagasaki to repatriate other Japanese castaways and unsuccessfully attempted to initiate the discussion about trade. By this time, the Japanese attitude toward sakoku or seclusion had returned vigorously, and the shogun Ienari had adopted the views of his chamberlain Matsudaira Sadanobu (1758–1829), who had opposed Tanuma's view on commercial and international policies. Although Sadanobu served the shogun as chamberlain only from 1787 to 1793, Sadanobu's views shaped the fifty-year reign of Ienari. So the Japanese government returned to a policy of suppression as well as seclusion. Scholars such as Hayashi Shihei found that publishing views that advocated change would result in a shogunal denial of the need for change, even though it was obvious that changes were taking place in the world, because outsiders in sailing ships were increasing their visits to the waters around Japan.

The shogunate recognized that in order to prevent foreign invaders from breaking the laws of seclusion, a better system of monitoring the coast was needed and that an extensive mapping of the islands would be useful. Scholars such as Honda Toshiaki (1744–1821), known for his school for mathematics and astronomy in Edo, founded in 1758, began to study Dutch and carefully turned his attention toward the issue raised by Hayashi Shihei. One of Honda's students, Mogami Tokunai, visited Hokkaido in 1785 and reported he had met a Russian on Etorofu Island, confirming the fear that foreigners were making their way down from Sakhalin and the Kuriles to Japan proper. Honda captained a ship to Hokkaido in 1801 and returned with the conviction that Japan needed to abandon isolationism and emulate Western models.[19] Honda's emphasis on British examples is intriguing, and it would be interesting to know to what extent Honda was familiar with the visit of British exploring vessels under the command of William Robert Broughton, which arrived in Japan in 1796 and 1797.

While Japanese traveler-writers such as Hayashi Shihei and Honda Toshiaki, who was also a navigator, contributed to the discussion of Japanese maritime geography and coastal defense, a few Japanese were explorers in their own right during this period. Honda's student, Mogami Tokunai (1755–1836), first went to Hokkaido in 1785, apparently as a substitute for his teacher, during a shogunal surveying expedition. In 1786 Mogami returned north and continued the Japanese survey to southern Sakhalin and the southern Kuriles. He is said to have made the earliest recorded visit by a Japanese to Etorofu and Uruppu Islands. Mogami shares a legacy with Mamiya Rinzo as one of the great Japanese explorers of the northern regions. Mamiya continued the work of Mogami and in 1808–9 established the insularity of Sakhalin Island, which had evaded previous explorations by Europeans.[20] Mamiya Rinzo is also known for his part in a political intrigue that involved some of Japan's leading geographers.

The preeminent Japanese geographer of the Tokugawa era was Ino Tadataka (1745–1818). He was the first one of Japanese origin to use Western geographic methods for mapmaking. His coastal survey maps, covering the entire country, became known as Ino maps. Ino waited to make his mark on history until the age of 49 in 1794, when he decided go to Edo (Tokyo) and study astronomy under Takahashi Yoshitoki the following year.[21] Takahashi, a shogunal astronomer, shared with Ino his knowledge of scientific methods, which he had acquired through Chinese texts. Thus developed the use of astronomical observations as a basis for Japanese surveys. The primary work of a shogunal astronomer was related to creating an accurate calendar, and Takahashi used this task as a means for sending a survey team to Hokkaido to take observations for calculating the size of the earth. The expedition ended up undertaking a 180-day survey of Hokkaido in 1800, during which Ino Tadataka's work on the project so impressed his superiors that they asked him to continue making maps of Japan's islands. He continued his work to the age of seventy and covered over 43,700 kilometers of travel just within Japan. A complete publication of his work, which was not produced until after his death, appeared in 1821 as *Dai Nihon Enkai Jissoku Zensu (Records of an Actual Survey of the Japanese Coast)*.[22]

The Ino maps were so accurate that they were used for the next 100 years. An intrigue developed when Phillip Franz von Siebold, a physician employed by the Dutch in Nagasaki, obtained copies of Ino maps, which the Tokugawa government regarded as a state secret. In 1828 Takahashi was imprisoned when it was found out that, in an apparent exchange for maps, he had obtained Western books, which he hoped to translate into Japanese. Siebold was found in possession of the maps and ejected from Japan. After Takahashi died in prison, his corpse was "formally executed." Siebold suspected that Mamiya Rinzo may have been a ringleader in the effort to discredit Takahashi.[23] Whatever the details of the intrigue and tragedy of Takahashi, the story shows how unfavorably the Tokugawa authorities viewed collaboration between Japanese and foreigners in the field of geographic and maritime exploration.

Western attitudes toward the sharing of scientific knowledge and maritime exploration were quite different, as can be seen in the gift of a set of Captain Cook's maps to Japanese authorities by William Robert Broughton during his exploration of Japan in 1796–97. Broughton's log, "A Voyage of Discovery to the North Pacific Ocean," is relatively uneventful until he arrives in Japan, where he began charting the coastline of Hokkaido and had a series of encounters with aboriginal Ainu tribesmen and communications with a few Japanese officials.[24] Then, while the *Providence* was off the coast of Hokkaido, a death occurred on board. A Danish sailor named Hans Oldson died on the last day of September and Broughton anchored near a small island to hold burial services. Broughton's chart bears the name Hans Oldson Island after this man. At the nearby city of Muroran, a granite statue of the *Providence* was erected in 1996 to commemorate the bicentennial of the visit by the British maritime expedition. Today a monument to Hans Oldson marks the grave site on Daikoku Island. The Broughton expedition provided the Royal Navy with information about the coast of Japan and northeast Asia, including portions of the coast of Korea and Sakhalin. There were still some omissions, but the geography of the north Pacific Rim was almost complete by the end of the eighteenth century. During the nineteenth century, American maritime power would demonstrate the growth of its trans-Pacific reach with the Perry mission, which opened Japan to trade and communication with the world. But research continues to show that there was a greater variety and impact of interchange between Japan and the Western world before Commodore Matthew Perry's arrival in 1853. Even though Japan was officially closed to international trade, the arrival of maritime explorers and traders such as the *Lady Washington* in the late eighteenth century marked the beginning of the great changes that occurred in the nineteenth century when Japan officially opened to the world.

Acknowledgments

I want to acknowledge and express my gratitude to Dr. William Dudley and the NASOH committee for the invitation to participate in the 1998 NASOH conference. Mayor Noboru Kishitani and Mr. Yorio Hamaguchi of Kushimoto Town provided historical materials relating to Kushimoto, Japan, where the *Lady Washington,* first American flag vessel to arrive in Japan, anchored in the spring of 1791. It has been my pleasure to have sailed with these gentlemen aboard the historic replica tall ship the *Lady Washington* on the occasion of their visit to Washington State to commemorate the bicentennial of the U.S.-Japan connection at Kushimoto.

I must also acknowledge the assistance provided by Les Bolton and Grays Harbor Historic Seaport Authority for information on the historic tall ship and replica vessel the *Lady Washington*, which was built in 1989 in Aberdeen, Washington.

Notes

1. J. R. Nokes, *Columbia's River: The Voyages of Robert Gray, 1787–1793* (Tacoma: Washington State Historical Society, 1991), 290.

2. John C. Beaglehole, *The Exploration of the Pacific*, 3d ed. (Stanford, Calif.: Stanford University Press, 1966), 289.

3. Hayashi Shihei, *Ezo: Sangoku Tsuran Zusetsu* (Illustrated Survey of Three Countries), (Japan: S.n., [1785–1850]). This was reprinted in *Shinpen Hayashi Shihei zenshu*, 5 vols. (Tokyo: Daiichi Shobo, 1978–80), vol. 2, *Chiri* (Geography).

4. Kushimoto Cho Shi, Editorial Committee for Kushimoto History, *Kushimoto Cho Shi—Tsu Shi Shu* (A Compendium of Kushimoto City History) (Kushimoto, 1995).

5. Ibid.

6. Malloy, Mary, "The *Lady Washington* at Oshima Island, Japan 1791," *Quarterdeck* 18(Fall 1991): 10.

7. Kazuo Sayama, *Waga na wa Kendorikku (My Name Is Kendrick)*, (Tokyo: Kodansha, 1991).

8. *Kushimoto Cho Shi—Tsu Shi Shu*, 340.

9. Ibid., 367.

10. Ibid., 328–44.

11. Sayama, *Waga na wa Kendorikku*, 13.

12. Ibid.

13. Malloy, "The *Lady Washington* at Oshima Island," 10.

14. Daniel Paine, *The Journal of Daniel Paine, 1794–1797*, edited by R. J. B. Knight and Alan Frost (Greenwich, U.K.: National Maritime Museum, 1983), 59.

15. Ibid.

16. Nokes, *Columbia's River*, 189.

17. *Kushimoto Cho Shi—Tsu Shi Shu*, 331–32.

18. Katagiri Kazuo, "Hayashi Shihei," *Kodansha Encyclopedia of Japan,* vol. 3 (New York: Kodansha, 1983), 118.

19. John J. Stephan, "Honda Toshiaki," ibid., 3:219–20.

20. Ian R. Stone, "W. R. Broughton and the Insularity of Sakhalin," *Mariner's Mirror* 82 (1996): 76–81.

21. Hoyanagi Mutsumi, "Ino Tadataka," *Kodansha Encylopedia of Japan,* 3:309.

22. Ibid.

23. John J. Stephan, "Takahashi Kageyasu," ibid. 7:312.

24. William R. Broughton, *A Voyage of Discovery to the North Pacific Ocean* (London: T. Cadell and W. Davies, 1804).

Daniel Caulkins in his later years as a successful farmer and innkeeper in East Lyme, Connecticut

5

Daniel Caulkins's Voyage: An Incident of the Quasi-War

Richard C. Malley

"I am resolved to try my luck at sea," so wrote Daniel Huxham Caulkins (1780–1851) in a letter to a friend, recorded in his journal, 9 June 1799.

The nineteen-year-old Caulkins was the eldest son of physician Daniel Caulkins, whose early death some years before had been, in the words of the Vital Records of Lyme, Connecticut, "ocationed by the kick of a Horse."[1] The newly widowed Elisabeth Caulkins took over the running of the family inn and tavern, the "Rising Sun," located in the Flander's section of what is now East Lyme,[2] while Daniel was eventually given charge of the family's extensive farm.

It seems likely that some of the surplus grains, fruits, vegetables, and livestock from the Caulkinses' farm found their way to the nearby port of New London and from there to the expanding markets in the West Indies. Shortly Daniel himself would follow a similar course.

Daniel Caulkins's journal for 1799, in the collection of The Connecticut Historical Society, recounts in numbing detail the myriad tasks required to make a farm simply break even. It was drudgery, pure and simple, compounded this particular year by an unseasonably cold, wet spring that wreaked havoc with the grain crops. Little wonder that the lure of the sea, seemingly well planted in Daniel's mind, prevailed in spite of his mother's continuous opposition.

Despite the close connection between the port of New London and the Caribbean that had developed since the late seventeenth century, Caulkins had considered other possible destinations. In ongoing correspondence with several friends, he broached the possibility of sailing to Europe, the Mediterranean—even the East Indies.[3] In the end, his acquaintance with a local shipmaster, Enoch Lee, brought him to the West Indies as a bit player in the international imbroglio known as the Quasi-War.

The young man who comes through in this journal seems quite well educated for his years, certainly well enough to know that if he wanted to make a life as something other than a hand before the mast, he needed some basic navigational training. He did not have to look far for this, as his entry for 25 May noted, "went to Groton & concluded to go to school to N. Daboll to learn navigation." A mathematician and instructor in navigation, "Master" Nathan Daboll (1750–1818), as he was known locally, trained the majority of southeastern Connecticut's shipmasters of the late eighteenth and early nineteenth centuries.[4] Following completion of ten days of study, Caulkins recorded in his journal on 8 June:

> I this day came from Groton, have been at school to Mr. Nathan Daboll, boarded at Mr. Barber's—I went for the purpose of learning Navigation—Began with finding the diff. of Lat. & Long. between places—from there to Plain Sailing—Traverse Sailing & Mercator Sailing—finding the variation of the Compass. Next I kept a Journal from New London to Martinico & back again, & then a Journal from New London to Madiera.

Caulkins was quick to add that "while I staid I paid good attention to my business studied about 12 or 14 hours a day." For this instruction he paid a little over a pound.

On 4 July Caulkins joined with his militia company in observing patriotic celebrations at New London. The conclusion of the exercises almost certainly found the militiamen at a local tavern, as Caulkins noted that "it being Ind. day the[y] felt pretty merry." Caulkins's patriotic feelings may have prompted him to consider pursuing a naval career, for on 6 July he wrote, "I have an idea of going out in the ship Connecticut if I can get a midshipman's birth. she is shortly expected at N. London." The 492-ton, twenty-four-gun ship *Connecticut*, recently completed at Middletown, was experiencing difficulty in crossing the troublesome bar at the mouth of the Connecticut River. Ironically for Caulkins, by early November this ship would be patrolling on the Guadeloupe station, not far from his own location.[5]

Over the next few days Caulkins made his final decision to sail with Captain Enoch Lee. He wrote to an acquaintance in New York on 16 July, "Capt. E. Lee is going down to N. York in about 8 or 10 days & I expect to go down with him." Thirty-one-year-old Enoch Lee of Lyme was experienced in the coasting and West Indies trades. Although Caulkins never mentioned the fact, it appears that he had married Daniel's half sister Hester in 1793.[6] Enoch's younger brother, George Washington Lee, whose career as a shipmaster would one day eclipse that of Enoch's,[7] completed what would become a close threesome on the coming voyage. The Lee brothers, especially Enoch, would figure closely in Daniel Caulkins's sea education.

On 25 July Caulkins sent his chest and other belongings ahead into New London, noting, "Went into N. London with Capt. E. Lee expecting to get a passage to N. York but we were disappointed & returned home." Three days later Caulkins wrote:

> [T]his morning Capt. E. Lee & myself went into N. London & went on board Capt. Chappels for N. York, we found him waiting for us therefore we just saved our distance. Mamma gave me in cash before I came away 58 dolls. This evening at sunset we went into N. Haven harbour.

Captain Edward Chappels's sloop, *Betsy*, was one of several packets that provided year-round connections between New London and New York.

Caulkins quickly learned that time and tide wait for no man as, according to his journal, at two the next morning, 29 July:

I turned out & assisted in getting under way. we have a light wind & fair breezes. P.M. came to anchor below Hell Gate, 7 miles from N. York & I went ashore with Capt. Lee & Mr. Nat. Ledyard. we went to the tavern & drank a bowl of milk punch, took a walk in the fields & got a few pairs.

This journey ended the following day as, Caulkins related,

At about 8 this morn we weighed anchor & set sail, in going thro' Hell Gate we had but little wind & that a head we were obliged to row as hard as we could. at 12 O'Clock we landed at Beekman's slip & I went up to cherry street & concluded to board with Capt. Lee at Jacob Van Nostrand's. In going up I called at Messrs. Wm. & S. Robinson's & delivered a letter.

Sylvester Robinson, a commission merchant, originally hailed from Stonington, Connecticut, and Daniel was well acquainted with his sister, a Mrs. Taber, in New London. She had written to Sylvester asking him to help Daniel find a berth if he was not able to go with Captain Lee.

Enoch and George Lee began the search for a vessel to purchase, with Daniel tagging along. After a fruitless day's effort, the threesome sought relaxation. Caulkins wrote on 2 August, "Last evening Capt. E. Lee, his brother George & myself went into a tavern & played a game, called the rocks of Scilly, we play'd for a mug of beer, I lost it." The search for a vessel continued another week, and Caulkins was getting nervous as time slipped away. Finally on 10 August Caulkins was able to write, "this day Capt. Lee has bought a vessel, & Mr. Sylvester Robinson advises me to go with him, he thinks after a short voyage I shall stand on a better footing to get into business." Here we see that Caulkins had given up on any idea of a naval calling and was really more interested in gaining experience for a future mercantile career.

Caulkins's real education began two days later, 12 August, as he wrote, "this morning went on board the schooner Harmony owned by Enoch & George W. Lee & went to work, but before night made 2 blisters on my hands." On 17 August he noted, "I signed the shipping bill. I am to have 10 dollars per month & the privilege of carrying what I please as an adventurer."

Lee registered the eighty-one-ton topsail schooner *Harmony* on 13 August. Built in 1791 at Duxbury, Massachusetts,[8] she was similar to many other American vessels in the West Indies trade. A certain amount of work was required to put her in order and Caulkins noted in his journal on 25 August, "the week past we have been pretty busy rigging & loading the vessel." While we do not know what the cargo consisted of, it was likely a mixture of agricultural produce, wood products such as barrel staves, and perhaps some light manufactures like spermacetti candles and tow cloth. There is no mention of large livestock being transported as cargo. We have a better idea what the young adventurer brought for private sale, as he noted, "I have bo't last week 4 doz fowl @ 4-½ dolls. per doz. & 2 hund. bunches onions @ 5-½ dolls. per C." (Note: C. stands for "100"). He later added several barrels of apples to his private manifest.[9]

Last-minute preparations for the voyage included a trip to the customhouse on 29 August where, he noted, "got me a protection." A protection, a document issued by federal customs collectors stating that the bearer is a citizen of the United States, was intended to give a sailor some protection against impressment into service on foreign, in particular British, warships. The vessel officially cleared the customhouse that same day[10] but did not actually sail until 31 August, when, Caulkins related, "This morn at ½ past 10 the pilot came on board, we cast off & set sail for Martinico. at 6 came to anchor near the lighthouse & the pilot left us."

On Sunday, 1 September, the voyage began in earnest. Wrote Caulkins: "At about 7 O'Clock in the morning we weighed anchor & set sail again, but the wind not being fair, we make but slow way a head." Caulkins's brief cruise down Long Island Sound did not prepare him for the experience of blue water sailing. On 3 September he wrote, "having been very seasick yesterday & today I have not eat anything for 24 hours, but by persuasions I drink a glass of Madeira wine & water & eat a piece of toasted bread dipped in it & feel better." This remedy seemed to work at first, as he reported the following day, "have gain'd my appetite in some measure & feel much better. evening being in the cabin with an English gentleman, he insisted on my drinking toast—To our Sweethearts—." But Caulkins's optimism was short-lived, as the next day he lamented, "not having had anything pass thro' me since I sail'd & feel somewhat indisposed I take on going to bed one of Lee's bilious pills." The pill seemed to do the trick, as he confided the next day, 6 September, "This morn I have a passage & feel better. Today noon we were in Lat. of 35 & a little more."

Fortunately Caulkins's stomach was much improved by Sunday, 8 September, when, he reported:

This day we have in the cabin a very good dinner consisting of a fricasee made of ducks, a soup made of fowls &c & corned beef & potatoes, but the people before the mast took an opportunity & stole the beef & potatoes which provoked the captain very much.

This breach of shipboard discipline brought retaliation at dinner the following day. Caulkins recorded the events of 9 September as follows:

The captain orders for the people's dinner meat & bread only, without any grog, not refusing them water. P.M. the people get intoxicated with liquor which they have of their own & they act so bad that the mate gets from the people 2 car bottles of rum which provokes them so much that in the evening they came forward & demanded their rum, which being refused them one of them viz. Jno. Williams swore he would have it & if the Capt. did not deliver it up he would go into the cabin & get it. then the Capt. ordered him forward to keep a look out which he refused to do. Jesse Sealy came forward likewise & talked so saucy to the mate, he standing on the quarter deck, that he pushed him back then Jesse clinched him, the mate got the better of him & they soon parted. Thos. Evans was likewise very saucy. John Smith said not so much, he standing at the helm. They went on in this manner till sometime in the evening, they all turned in except Jno. Smith not being able to do their duty, & Jno. Williams I understand did not get up until morning.

Captain Lee, who up to now had taken a fairly low-key approach, decided to put an end to this nonsense the next day, 10 September. As Caulkins related:

[T]his morning the people are pretty peaceable, at noon when the people eat dinner Jno. Smith asked for some grog & the mate turned out ½ pint for them, he asked if it was some of theirs, he told them yes, & refused to take it, & the mate bro't the 2 bottles upon deck & the Capt. threw them overboard with the liquor.

By 15 September the *Harmony* was in the latitude of the Bahamas. Caulkins wrote, "There are in sight 2 sail; the people on board are very much afraid they are privateers." This was Caulkins's first mention of the depredations of the French. Clearly he had to be aware of French seizures of American vessels in Caribbean waters. French outrage over the ratification of Jay's Treaty several years earlier had left little doubt about their willingness to savage the commerce of their erstwhile American ally. Frequent articles in many East Coast newspapers, including the *Connecticut Gazette*, published at New London, detailed the constant losses to both French naval forces and especially the privateers.

Privateers from Guadeloupe, acting under orders of the island's military commander, General Edme-Etienne Borne Desfourneaux, were particularly active in taking American merchantmen.[11] The supercargo of an American schooner who had fallen prey to privateers from that island described the vessels as "generally well-armed carrying from 14 to 20 guns, and full of men, the most desperate and relentless in the world when they meet with resistance."[12]

A week passed and concerns over French privateers were put aside as a bit of shipboard fun ensued. Caulkins's entry for 22 September related:

Our Cook has a barrel of apples & the passengers conclude to hustle for it. I put in a dollar with them there being 5 besides me, but Mr. Gerard wins it. I then set up one of my barrels for 5 dolls. we hustle & I win it. I set up another we hustle & Mr. Gerard wins it. I then have one left I hustle with Mr. Gerard who shall have the two, he wins them. & then he opens one barrel & find they are almost all rotten. I think I have done well with them having gained on the 3 barrels 5-1/2 dollars.

The following day found the *Harmony* passing St. Thomas. Caulkins's last entry for the month was dated 28 September and noted the vessel's position as Latitude 21.42 North, placing them northeast of Hispaniola.

The next entry heading told all: "In Guadaloupe prison Thursday 17th of October 1799." Wrote Caulkins:

I shall now undertake to write a little concerning what I have suffered, & what has happened since the 28th ultimo. On Wednesday the 2nd day of October at about 3 O'Clock P.M., the crew discovered to the leeward 2 sails in sight, which proved to be a french privateer of 12 guns—6 pounders—& a sloop (I believe English) taken the day before. when she was observed we kept as close to the wind as possible, but all in vain she gain'd upon us very fast, & about 7 O'Clock in the evening she came within gun shot of us, & she fired a gun over us, Capt. Lee said it was in vain for us to try any longer to keep out of her way he immediately rounded her too & ordered a lantern to be hung upon the shroud but they would not be content when we had struck for they immediately fired a number of muskets at us, (I believe as many as 20 or 30) & then came pretty near & hoisted their boat out & several came on board of us, armed with knives, cutlasses, &c. & immediately ordered all into the boat except G. W. Lee the mate, & myself. They then took charge of the vessel & the next morning the mate was taken out & myself & put on board the privateer, but before we went the Capt. of the privateer Resolution, (whose name is Ross) came on board the Harmony & examined every chest (except mine he overlook'd) & took out all the papers. he likewise took some provisions & put on board the privateer, our 3 passengers were then put on board the Harmony & he proceeded to Guadaloupe.

The *Resolution,* with Caulkins on board, captured a Dutch brig that evening. The ferocity of the French privateers in the face of any potential resistance was clearly demonstrated following the capture of the brig. As Caulkins related it:

[S]everal of her crew were put on board the privateer together with the Supercargo, with whom Capt. Lee exchanged a few words, & asking him to where he was from, for saying which Capt. Ross struck him over the head & ordered him to be put in irons where he remained for about 12 or 14 hours.

Caulkins continued:

When we went on board the privateer we carried nothing with us except what we wore & were obliged to lie on deck or in the hold which was much worse. A day or two after the brig was taken the privateer took an Eng. schooner & then he steered for Guadaloupe keeping company with the last prize & on Sunday the 13th day of October 1799 at about 7 O'Clock in the evening we came to anchor in Guadaloupe.

Captain Lee's experience in the West Indies trade paid an unexpected dividend when, a rather incredulous Caulkins wrote:

> The Capt. of the marines on board Capt. Lee was somewhat acquainted with & indeed knew his father & thinking he might confide in him (his name is Gabriel Boughed) he advised the mate & myself to put our money into his hands for protection. we accordingly did, we put in $17 cash & the mate his watch likewise.
>
> After we came to anchor the Capt. of the privateer went ashore, & then two young fellows, they being the highest in office then on board, took the mate & myself into the cabin & searched us in every pocket, & indeed pulled off my boots thinking to find some money, but not a farthing did they get. the same night they stole from Capt. Lee out of the cabin a good Brd cloth coat & other clothes & an elegant silver watch.

Had Caulkins been able to read the account of an American recently released by the French at Guadeloupe, published in the *Connecticut Gazette*'s 2 October edition, he would have been prepared for the next step in his captivity. The account read in part:

> Americans, who are captured and carried into Guadaloupe, on their arrival on shore, are received by a guard of eight black soldiers, who conduct them to what they call the Government house—and there orders are given for their commitment to prison. There is no difference between officer and seaman, good and bad. Those who have ability to pay 14 dolls. per week for board are the only exempts. Such may obtain security for their parole and then are permitted to promenade the town.[13]

Clearly the Guadeloupeans had fashioned an orderly and financially rewarding system to handle this steady influx of unwilling visitors. In Caulkins's own words:

> The next morning we were all put into a boat, sent ashore (the sailors having been in irons ever since they came on board) & conducted to prison by a guard, consisting of negroes, where we found our four passengers, viz, Mr. Gerard an Englishman, Mr. Loe an american, Mr. Renodanz & Mr. St. Felix, frenchmen & about 50 other prisoners. in the Goal there is board to be had for 2 dolls. a day & at noon (having not eat since we ate our supper) we sat down

to dinner, & indeed I think it was as good a dinner as I have ate of, there was at the table I believe about 20, our supper was likewise very good, we had beds of our own to lie upon, our breakfast consisted of Coffee & bread only, a part of us then removed to the other prison, where we had ½ lb. of beef & 1 lb. of bread a day allowed us. with about ½ dollar apiece more laid out in provisions daily we could live comfortably, then on Wednesday Capt. Lee & the mate went back to the other prison. When came to this prison the Captain's considering there must be some regulations, the people were then divided into 15 parts, & 8 in a mess. Capt. Lee was chosen presidt. & Capt. Giles Starr Vice presidt. & there were at the same time other officers made. On thursday Capt. sent for me to come to the prison where he is, I accordingly take my bed on my back & gives a negro half a dollar to bring my chest where I am now writing this, inclosed in a building, the walls of which are 2 feet in thickness & the windows iron grates.

Once reunited with his mentor, Caulkins had more time to consider his situation. "I have the greatest reason to speak well of Capt. Lee, for since we were taken he has been very friendly & kind to me, calling me his brother & treating me as such." But despite his relative good fortune, he allowed himself a bit of self-pity, writing, "I am almost ready to curse the day I was born here in prison now & God only knows when I shall be at liberty again."

Almost without pause, however, he began an accounting of his losses, which included a greatcoat, two pairs of shoes, a jacket and trousers, plus the onions and fowl, for a total value of $69. He would continue to press for full restitution for decades.[14]

Shortly after his capture several events occurred that had a bearing on his imprisonment. On 19 October he noted that General Desfourneaux was arrested and sent back to France. It turned out that while the general had been urging the seizure of American vessels, he was apparently in contact with the British about possibly turning over the island to their control. Of more immediate importance for Caulkins, however, was the fact that Capt. Boughed's father, with whom Capt. Lee was acquainted, posted bond for Caulkins and the Lees. Once paroled, they could move about the town quite freely and without fear of harassment.

By 25 October they had all settled their debts for board with their jailer, Mons. Denocuse, and were able to recover some money through the courts for belongings seized. Caulkins and the Lees found a less expensive place to lodge, but the next day he and George Lee called on Mons. Denocuse again. We do not need to read between the lines of Caulkins's journal very deeply to fathom the reason.

> At about 10 this morning Geo. W. Lee & myself called at our old lodgings, Mr. Denocuse gave us a cut of cold mutton & a glass of wine. Mons. Denocuse has a daughter which used to dine & sup with us daily (Mariette by name) who is the most agreeable of her sex of any I have form'd an acquaintance with since I have been upon this island.

The men took the opportunity of their newly bought freedom to move about the town of Basse Terre. Among their stops was a watering spot called Bushong's Tavern, whose owner, recently deceased, was married to a woman from Norfolk, Connecticut. This seemed to have become a popular meeting place for paroled American shipmasters. Meanwhile, Caulkins and several companions paid another visit to the Denocuse house, enjoying a glass of gin with Mariette.

By mid-November, Caulkins and friends were awaiting permission to board a recently arrived cartel ship but, owing to confusion following the arrest of General Desfourneaux, they were unable to secure their passports from the authorities. Finally on Sunday, 17 November, Caulkins was able to write:

> This morn at about 10 A.M. we go on board the Cartel with about 12 American prisoners, & about 11 P.M. the guard came on board, consisting of 3 white men & 3 negroes armed with cutlasses & muskets & we set sail with a light breeze.

They dropped off the armed guard at another port on the island next day and then proceeded to St. Barts, St. Maarten, and finally St. Kitts, where, on 21 November, they boarded a schooner bound to Charleston. On the same day they departed for home, the first word of their capture appeared in the New York papers.[15] The very next day, Caulkins wrote:

Our Capt. spoke a brig in the fleet which consists of 27 sail to be convoyed to Lat. 25 by the brig Eagle. The brig he spoke is bound to Philadelphia or New York & Capt. Lee asked him if he would give us passage there & he consented without reluctance, we then took our effects into the boat & went on board him.

The English brig *Perseverance,* Hillary B. Marlton, commander, became Caulkins's home for the next three and a half weeks until, on 18 December he noted, "At about 12 O'Clock we came up N. York harbour & the Doct. came on board, then we were permitted to go ashore." The next day a grateful Captain Lee invited Captain Marlton to dine with them, with Marlton returning the favor the following day.

On 21 December, the day word of George Washington's death reached New York, Caulkins recorded that he and the Lees

went to the Custom house & made out a bill of our baggage & got a permit to land it. I saw there an elegant piece of painting—Gen'l Washington's portrait. We likewise went to a notary Public where Capt. Lee made a protest & G. W. Lee & myself signed it.

The day before Christmas, the three men boarded Captain William Harris's packet sloop *David & Jott* and sailed for New London, arriving the following evening. Caulkins ended his account of his journey with the following Christmas Day entry: "at 6 P.M. we went ashore at N. London & then went home on foot where we arrived at about 8 P.M."

As for Daniel Caulkins, following this adventure there is no evidence that he ever seriously attempted further to make a life as a mariner or merchant, and when he died in 1851 at age seventy his lasting legacy would be that of a successful Connecticut farmer.

Notes

1. Verne M. Hall and Elizabeth B. Plimpton, eds., *Vital Records of Lyme, Connecticut to the End of the Year 1850* (Lyme, Conn.: American Revolution Bicentennial Commission of Lyme, Connecticut, 1976), 111. While these records list the death date as 1792, other sources say 1790 or 1792.

2. James Lawrence Chew, "Famous Old Taverns of New London," in *Records and Papers of the New London County Historical Society,* part 1, vol. 2, (New London, Conn., 1895), 72. The tavern sign from the Rising Sun is in the collection of The Connecticut Historical Society, Hartford, Conn.

3. Journal of Daniel H. Caulkins, 17 Apr. 1799 and 31 July 1799, The Connecticut Historical Society.

4. Telephone conversation with Groton town historian Carol Kimball, 15 Feb. 1996.

5. U. S. Navy Department, *Dictionary of American Naval Fighting Ships,* vol. 2 (Washington, D.C.: U.S. Navy, Naval History Division, 1963), 165.

6. Reuben H. Walworth, *Hyde Genealogy,* vol. 2 (Albany, N.Y.: J. Munsell, 1864), 956.

7. George W. Lee Papers, Coll. 23, G. W. Blunt White Library, Mystic Seaport Museum, Mystic, Conn.

8. Forrest R. Holdcamper, *List of American Flag Vessels that Received Certificates of Enrollment or Registry at the Port of New York, 1789–1867,* vol. 1 (Washington, D.C.: National Archives, 1968), 302.

9. Journal of Daniel H. Caulkins, 22 Sept. 1799, The Connecticut Historical Society.

10. New York, *Commercial Advertiser,* 29 Aug. 1799, 3.

11. Letter published in the *Connecticut Gazette,* 6 Nov. 1799, 3.

12. Letter from John Moore published in ibid., 13 Nov. 1799, 3.

13. Letter from Joseph Clark published in ibid., 2 Oct. 1799, 3.

14. Listing kept by Daniel H. Caulkins, "French Spoliations 1799," 1832, The Connecticut Historical Society.

15. New York, *Commercial Advertiser,* 21 Nov. 1799, 3.

USS *Peacock* captures HMS *Epervier*, 29 April 1814

6

Lewis Warrington and the USS *Peacock* in the Sunda Strait, June 1815

Christine F. Hughes

L ewis Warrington had a long naval career spanning over fifty-one years from 1800 to 1851. He rose in service gradually but steadily, attaining in 1814 the rank of captain, the highest grade achievable in the Navy before the Civil War. He garnered this captaincy after winning a forty-two minute battle between his ship, the U.S. sloop of war *Peacock,* and H.M. brig *Epervier* on 29 April 1814. Fourteen months later, Warrington and the *Peacock* would fight the last engagement of the War of 1812 against the British East India Company brig *Nautilus* in the Sunda Strait off Java. The *Peacock* again triumphed, but a diplomatic controversy developed over Warrington's actions. Did the American captain know or suspect that Great Britain and the United States had ratified a treaty of peace? Was his attack on the brig an act of "wanton violence," or was it acceptable conduct during war? Just what happened in the Sunda Strait in June 1815 and what were the ramifications for Anglo-American diplomatic relations?

Lewis Warrington

In one of his last official duties before resigning as secretary of the Navy on 1 December 1814, William Jones directed Commodore Stephen Decatur to lead a four-ship squadron composed of the frigate *President*, sloops of war *Peacock* and *Hornet*, and the storeship *Tom Bowline* on a commerce-raiding cruise in the East Indies. On 14 January 1815, under the cover of a snowstorm, the *President* sortied from New York harbor. Nine days later the *President*'s consorts stood to sea, heading for their appointed rendezvous at Tristan da Cunha, not knowing that a British blockading squadron had captured the *President* on 15 January. The *Peacock* and the *Tom Bowline* lost sight of the *Hornet* on 26 January in squally weather, and the latter sailed on alone until the three rendez-voused at Tristan da Cunha two months later.[1]

Bringing the war to the British economy was the purpose of this commerce-raiding cruise. The *Peacock*'s crew eagerly sought out each approaching sail as a potential prize. One of the *Peacock*'s midshipmen, William Tennent Rodgers, diligently recorded the daily occurrences of the cruise, and his spirited remarks relating to sighting strange sails no doubt reflected the crew's enthusiasm. Little success, however, marked the first five months of cruising for the *Peacock*, as the ships she pursued proved to be American or neutral vessels, or were lost in the dark.[2]

As the *Peacock* sailed to her rendezvous in the South Atlantic, the war with Great Britain was coming to a speedy conclusion. A peace had been signed at Ghent on 24 December 1814, the news of which did not reach America until February—well after Warrington had departed on his cruise. The Senate ratified and confirmed the Treaty of Peace and Amity on 17 February 1815. The *Peacock* was in the South Atlantic just west of Ascension Island when peace was pro-claimed. The treaty's second article stipulated a specific time limitation for captures made in different latitudes after the ratification. Peace commissioners recognized that notifying the ships of two navies already at sea about peace would take some time. Therefore, they determined that a prize captured in the Atlantic Ocean, south of the equator, and as far east as the latitude of the Cape of Good Hope would have to be restored if taken sixty days after ratification. The limitation was ninety days for every other part of the world south of the equator. As the *Peacock* continued sailing eastward, this latter restriction applied to her and 18 May became the cutoff date for Warrington to take prizes legally.[3]

The *Peacock* arrived at Tristan da Cunha on 21 March and sighted the *Hornet* there four days later. The latter had succeeded in capturing H.M. brig *Penguin* on 23 March, and no doubt the *Peacock*'s crew was envious. The *Peacock* and the *Hornet* left the rendezvous to continue on their cruise without the *Tom Bowline*, having sent her as a cartel with the *Penguin*'s prisoners to San Salvador. As the Americans had heard reports of the *President*'s capture, there was no point in tarrying any longer at the rendezvous.[4]

On 25 April excitement soared because the *Peacock*'s crew spotted their first sail after a barren period of forty-four days. Losing sight of the vessel after only forty minutes dashed the momentary elation. But two days later off southeastern Africa Midshipman Rodgers recorded sighting and pursuing a very large ship—"probabley a <u>fat</u> East India Man—a good recompense for all our lost time (<u>if taken</u>)." The *Peacock* lost track of her in the darkness, but the next day the chase continued and Rodgers's initial exhilaration was only slightly tempered by trepidation. At a distance of six and a half miles, Rodgers wrote that she "showed two tier of guns—still our anxiety to finger English <u>dollars</u> & English <u>goods</u> under the supposition of her being an East India Man, induced us to run over to her."[5]

Captain Warrington and his crew were anxious for a capture, but soon they determined that the chase was an English line of battle ship. Rodgers noted in his journal that "not being so solicitous of further acquaintance we hauled our Wind to the NW—having chased her for thirty-two hours and she in her turn gave <u>us</u> chase—." The *Peacock* and the *Hornet*, which were cruising together up to this point, separated, and Warrington feared that the seventy-four had captured his consort.[6]

Indeed, all that remained of the squadron was the *Peacock*, because the *Hornet*'s captain, James Biddle, in attempting to escape H.M. ship of the line *Cornwallis*, discarded most of the *Hornet*'s guns, thus effectively ending her ability to cruise and forcing her to return home. On board the *Peacock*, the initial thrill of the voyage was waning. A squadron of four ships had dwindled to one. The *Peacock* was alone in the Indian Ocean just off the southeastern coast of Africa. Perhaps

Midshipman Rodgers's musings exemplified those of many of the crew when he wrote on 30 April: "Ninety seven days out—no prizes—short allowance—poor fare—but still have strong hopes and good spirits natural & artificial."[7]

Warrington, unaware of the *Hornet*'s fate, continued on, reaching the squadron's second rendezvous at the islands of St. Paul and Amsterdam in the Indian Ocean in the middle of May. Here Warrington saw no sign of the *Hornet* but learned of Decatur's fate in a letter left by the captain of the merchant brig *Macedonian.* Warrington proceeded on alone to the East Indies. Boredom no doubt settled over the crew, which must have become enervated by the hot, sultry weather. Warrington tried to relieve the monotony by practice drills and exercising the guns. Certainly the sight of logs and bamboo heralded the approach of land and raised spirits. The *Peacock* made the Island of Java on 8 June.[8]

After almost five months of cruising, Warrington still had not learned that the war had ended. Anticipation was high among the crew on 13 June after sighting a sail off Java. Midshipman Rodgers remarked, "thus are our hopes again raised. May fortune favor us!" The *Peacock* had struck gold literally, as she captured the English East India Company Ship *Union,* six guns, carrying a cargo of peppers, opium, raw silk, saffron, piece goods, wine, and $5,000 worth of gold.[9]

The *Peacock*'s crew labored hard during the following week to transfer the captured goods and then burned the merchant vessel. The American sloop cruised at the entrance to the Sunda Strait, searching for more victims. A midshipman's logbook entry for 21 June noted that the *Peacock*'s sailors observed a peacock strutting along the shore of Mew Island and pronounced it a "happy omen." Perhaps it was auspicious, as later that day the crew saw a sail standing up between Mew and Princes Island. By 6:00 P.M. the Americans had captured another English ship, the *Venus,* which was traveling from Mauritius to Batavia in ballast. Besides carrying some rather mundane but useful articles, such as shoes, stockings, handkerchiefs, razors, and combs, the *Venus* had $6,000 stowed in her pork barrels.[10]

Warrington did not burn the *Venus* as he had the *Union,* because he needed her as a cartel to transport all the prisoners he had captured.

He kept the *Peacock* at anchor for several days off the northwestern coast of Java, giving liberty on shore to his crew and making necessary repairs. The Americans weighed their kedge anchor on 28 June and ordered the cartel not to set sail until the next afternoon. While standing up the strait on the 29th, the *Peacock* chased and captured another English merchantman, the *Brio de Mar,* in ballast, but carrying a few casks of wine and about $9,500. The *Venus* conveniently appeared on the scene, permitting Warrington to burn the *Brio de Mar* and transfer her crew to the cartel.[11]

On the morning of 30 June, the *Peacock* stood up the strait for Anjier Point. The logbooks and a journal kept by three midshipmen on the *Peacock* all record about the same information relating to that fateful afternoon. Between 1:45 and 2:30 in the afternoon, the *Peacock,* flying British colors, sighted three vessels at anchor in Anjier Roads. About 2:30 a brig, flying no colors, stood out and approached the *Peacock.* At 5:15 the brig sent out a boat with two officers and at 5:20 another boat, with R. B. Macgregor, the master intendant (a civilian administrator) from Anjier, advanced toward the *Peacock.* The midshipmen's accounts imply that the three visitors thought that the Americans were British. The British messengers were taken below almost immediately upon boarding the sloop.[12]

At 5:30, when the two vessels were within hailing distance, the *Peacock* hoisted her own colors and Lt. Charles Boyce, the captain of the brig *Nautilus,* fourteen guns, declared that their two countries were at peace. Warrington ordered Boyce to haul down his colors as a token if peace really did exist. Boyce refused. The Americans shot first. The *Nautilus* fired a broadside, and *Peacock* responded in kind. The *Nautilus* struck after a scant fifteen-minute battle, having sustained considerable damage and casualties. Boyce and his first lieutenant were severely wounded.[13]

Immediately after the engagement, the master intendant informed the Americans that peace existed and he could prove it. Despite this assertion, Warrington began removing some of the prisoners to the *Peacock* on the evening of 30 June. The next morning, however, he permitted the master intendant to go ashore to locate the corroborating evidence. Warrington must have had second thoughts, because he

began returning the prisoners to their brig even before the master intendant had reappeared with the proof of peace. Disappointment echoed in
Midshipman Rodgers's journal entry when he reflected that "thus are
our bright prospects blighted." Twenty-three hours after Warrington
acknowledged that the war was over, the *Peacock* sailed for America.[14]

Departing the Sunda Strait on 2 July 1815, Warrington took a
leisurely four months to sail home, which should have allowed him
plenty of time to compose a detailed account of his voyage. Apparently
he did not avail himself of that extra time, because when he arrived in
New York on 30 October, he waited three days before addressing Secretary of the Navy Benjamin W. Crowninshield. This first, very short letter mentioned in one sentence that while cruising in the Sunda Strait
"we made four captures, two of which were burnt, a third was given up
to carry 150 prisoners into Batavia and the fourth released, as from her
we learnt that a peace had been made." This letter focused on the prize
goods captured and did not mention the casualties the *Nautilus* suffered. Nine days later Warrington wrote a more detailed letter to
Crowninshield because he feared that other accounts of the rencontre
with the East India Company brig would surface.[15]

While the *Peacock* sailed westward toward home, the controversy
surrounding her captures in June 1815 surfaced immediately, because
the captains of the captured merchant vessels wrote to their respective
owners, and the Bench of Magistrates in Batavia took depositions
from the crew of the *Nautilus*. These documents decrying the illegality
of the postwar captures and Warrington's alleged unwarrantable conduct toward the *Nautilus* began winding their way up the chain of
command of the East India Company from Batavia to Bombay to
London. On 22 July, W. Eatwell, the commander of the Honorable
Company's (East India Company) Cruiser *Benares* and the senior officer at Batavia, reported the incident to Henry Meriton, the superintendent of the Honorable Company's Marine in Bombay, because the
Nautilus's captain and first lieutenant were still too incapacitated to
make an official report. Lieutenant Boyce had been hit by grapeshot and
a thirty-two-pound shot had shattered his leg, resulting in its amputa-
tion. In September, Meriton forwarded the documentation on to Sir
Evan Nepean, Bart., governor in council of the East India Company

at Bombay, who lamented that Lieutenant Boyce's actions to defend the British flag had such serious consequences for himself personally. Meriton characterized Warrington's actions as "wanton and unjustifiable," especially when "opposed to a Vessel of such inferior force." [16]

After receiving initial reports of the incident, Robert, Viscount Castlereagh, British foreign secretary, drafted instructions to assist his newly appointed minister to the United States, Charles Bagot, in preparing a remonstrance to President James Madison and Secretary of State James Monroe. Bagot received two versions of this instruction. The initial draft instruction dated December 1815 contained two abrasive paragraphs not included in the second. In the first, Castlereagh vented his rage over Warrington's "shamefull conduct" and his "Malice & cruelty." The foreign secretary demanded complete indemnification for the destroyed ships and cargoes and suitable punishment for Warrington. Castlereagh, ever the diplomat, excised the strong words from the second official letter that he sent to Bagot. [17]

Bagot's negotiations relating to the *Peacock* reflected Castlereagh's diplomatic efforts to conciliate the Americans. This issue was minor compared to others that confronted the two former enemies—commercial concerns such as the fisheries, trade in the West Indies, and alien port duties; boundary disputes; and captured slaves and the slave trade. But Bagot persisted calmly and methodically to force a resolution while he was minister from 1816 to 1819. [18]

After a seven-week voyage across the Atlantic, Bagot arrived at Annapolis on 17 March 1816, where a newspaper article on the *Nautilus/ Peacock* affair in the *Maryland Republican* confronted him immediately. The news story attempted to correct the misrepresentations reprinted in American papers from the *Calcutta Times,* by printing Warrington's 11 November 1815 letter to Secretary Crowninshield. The Annapolis newspaper had copied this article from an earlier one in the *National Intelligencer.* The affair had merited national currency by February 1816, because Warrington mentioned to Crowninshield his concern about reading inaccurate reports of the incident in the Boston papers. He asked the secretary to publish his 11 November letter to clear his name, and he stated his willingness to have a court of inquiry investigate the matter. [19]

Warrington experienced postwar career insecurity because his fellow officers had received many of the choicer commands while he was still cruising in the East Indies. Upon his return, he repeatedly requested the command of a frigate, only to be told that "his claims shall receive due attention." Finally on 27 February the secretary ordered him to take the frigate *Macedonian* on a special diplomatic mission to Latin America.[20]

Meanwhile, a month after Warrington expressed concern with the newspaper reports about him, Minister Bagot, recently ensconced in Washington, visited Monroe on 26 March 1816, and the secretary professed to be entirely ignorant of the *Nautilus* affair. Apparently Monroe was not so avid a reader of American newspapers as was Bagot. In a formal letter of complaint against Warrington addressed to the secretary of state two days later, Bagot characterized the incident involving the *Nautilus* as one of "wanton violence" that was a "direct infraction of the conditions of that Peace which is now so happily restored between the two Countries." He cited the second article of the Treaty of Ghent as the basis for the British claims for indemnification for the three merchant vessels captured in June 1815 after the ninety-day limit for captures taken south of the equator. As regards the attack on the *Nautilus,* Bagot said it was Warrington's duty to delay precipitous action if he suspected a ruse, in order to obtain confirmation of peace, because "the decided superiority of his force" gave him the advantage against the brig at any time. Furthermore, Bagot remarked that if Warrington believed that Lieutenant Boyce was telling the truth, he had no right to insist on the "humiliation of striking his Flag." Bagot concluded his complaint by reiterating his government's confidence that the American government would act justly toward these claims.[21]

Monroe expressed the government's "great regret" that "incidents of a nature so distressing should have occurred." He assured Bagot that further communication on the subject would follow as soon as the secretary of the Navy had concluded an informal inquiry into "all the circumstances connected with these unfortunate events." Certainly this conciliatory stance boded well for future negotiations. Bagot related these exchanges to Viscount Castlereagh, noting that he would defer presenting the depositions until after Crowninshield had reported his findings to Monroe. From the outset of this inquiry it was evident to Bagot that Monroe offered no vindication of Warrington's conduct.[22]

While Bagot and Monroe exchanged notes and visits regarding the *Peacock's* actions, Warrington was preparing to take Christopher Hughes Jr. on a special mission to South America. Just before departing Boston Harbor on this diplomatic cruise, Warrington wrote Crowninshield on 29 April reiterating his request for a court of inquiry into his conduct in the Indian Ocean. He specifically wanted to prove that he lacked sufficient knowledge of the peace to warrant suspending hostilities any sooner. The secretary had never responded to his first request made on 27 February. Perhaps Crowninshield did not reply because he did not wish voluntarily to institute an inquiry that might tarnish the Navy's reputation and also because in the February letter Warrington had merely expressed his willingness for an inquiry and had not forcefully requested one.[23]

In responding to Monroe's request for an informal inquiry, Crowninshield merely provided him with Warrington's two official reports written in November 1815 and his letter of 27 February 1816. In early May, President Madison decided to assemble a formal court of inquiry as soon as Warrington returned from his diplomatic assignment. Monroe informed Bagot of this development and invited him to forward any evidence he wished for the court to review. Bagot sent Monroe copies of letters from the chairman of the East India Company to Lord Castlereagh, letters from Captain Eatwell of the Honorable Company's Cruiser *Benares* to the governor in council at Bombay, and depositions of the *Nautilus's* crew taken in Batavia.[24]

Once the president ordered the Navy to convene a court, Crowninshield took the initiative and assumed the adversarial role of rebutting the evidence of the British. His correspondence of 22 June 1816 with Attorney General Richard Rush illustrates the Navy's intention to defend Warrington during the inquiry by posing to the witnesses those questions that would exonerate him. Crowninshield asked Rush's assistance in framing the court's questions "in order to arrive at a fair and honourable result." In replying to this request, Rush hesitated at first to offer advice, because he claimed insufficient familiarity with the case and recommended that members of the court formulate their questions as the inquiry developed. Rush provided Crowninshield with several broad queries whose tone placed Warrington in a more favorable light. What did the captain know about the possible existence of peace? How much substance was there to any rumors? What was the *Nautilus's* appearance when the *Peacock* first encountered her? Was there reason to fear a ruse? What was Warrington's conduct before he opened fire? What was correct naval procedure when one vessel knows positively that there is peace and the other is ignorant or doubtful? What should weigh more heavily—humanity or a high state of vigilance and discipline? Besides tailoring special interrogatories to specific witnesses, Rush also recommended that the court emphasize the honor of the naval flag and Warrington's distinguished naval career.[25]

By the end of June 1816, one year after the events in the Sunda Strait, Crowninshield ordered Commodore William Bainbridge to convene a court of inquiry composed of himself and Captains Jacob Jones and Charles Morris; George Blake would serve as judge advocate. In a separate letter, also dated 29 June, Crowninshield forwarded the attorney general's opinions and questions to Bainbridge for the court's use. Bainbridge, however, could not convene the court until Warrington returned from his mission to rescue Americans imprisoned by the Spanish in South America. Warrington arrived at Annapolis on 7 July, but delays postponed the start of the court of inquiry in Boston until 3 September.[26]

The British documents submitted as evidence for the court's review argued the following: that the Americans ignored mounting rumors of peace from the captured crew of the *Venus* and the *Brio de Mar;* that precipitous action was not necessary, because the *Nautilus's* vastly inferior size posed no significant threat; that the deputy master intendant from Anjier who had boarded the *Peacock* fifteen minutes before the battle had spoken of the peace to the first lieutenant and purser; and that Warrington's order to Lieutenant Boyce to haul down his colors as a token, if peace really did exist, was an unreasonable demand. Captain Warrington did not testify at the court of inquiry. Instead, the court questioned the *Peacock's* top three lieutenants, the sailing master, and the purser, all of whom supported their captain in most of the details of the events. The court fashioned its questions to rebut the British contentions and to highlight Warrington's moderation. The Americans reported hearing only vague, unsubstantiated rumors of peace. They all recounted that the *Nautilus* flew no white flag or other signal of a truce when approaching them and her tampions were out, indicating she was prepared for battle. The *Peacock's* lieutenants all agreed that they had acted quickly and decisively in attacking the brig because they feared she would escape and seek the protection of the fort at Anjier Point. The *Peacock's* first lieutenant denied hearing about the peace from the deputy master intendant, whereas the purser acknowledged discussing it with him. The court took special care to prove Warrington's moderation by emphasizing that initially he ordered only a single bow gun fired instead of a broadside and that he permitted no plundering of the enemy vessel. Since Warrington's order to Boyce to haul down his colors precipitated the attack, it is noteworthy that the court never asked the American witnesses whether they considered that demand reasonable.[27]

The court of inquiry completed its work on 9 September 1816, but Monroe did not contact Bagot until 31 October about its findings. The secretary reported that the naval inquiry concluded that this "much to be lamented disaster" had occurred because the *Nautilus* had not hoisted a flag of truce or taken other measures that would have indicated peace existed. The court exonerated Warrington because he had "no knowledge of the Peace, until after the action was terminated." The American government accepted no responsibility for the incident, and the president merely "regretted" that "such an unfortunate event should have occurred." Delays in copying the documents at the Navy Department prevented Monroe from giving Bagot the court's report and the full text of the inquiry until 4 and 30 November respectively.[28]

Bagot's official response to Monroe regarding the naval court's conclusions reflected his diplomatic restraint. He noted that the two countries' versions of the attack differed considerably in their facts and that he had no idea if the prince regent would find the American court's ruling satisfactory. While he awaited future instructions on the matter, Bagot reiterated his countrymen's claims for indemnification for the three merchant vessels captured by the *Peacock*. The court of inquiry had not addressed this issue at all, and Bagot gently insisted that the American government comply with the stipulations of the second article of the treaty.[29]

In a dispassionate dispatch to Lord Castlereagh on 9 November, Bagot criticized the court's summary report for its lack of evidence and also mentioned that he had renewed the claims for the *Union*, the *Venus*, and the *Brio de Mar*. In another letter written the next day to a colleague, William Hamilton, at the Foreign Office, Bagot vented his true emotions. He was "very angry at their Report about Captn. Warrington.... There never was so impudent or so weak a defence." Bagot told Hamilton that his response to Monroe on the subject had merely laid the groundwork for a "further remonstrance" if the Foreign Office so ordered.[30]

The *Nautilus/Peacock* affair receded into the background after this November 1816 diplomatic exchange. There is no concrete evidence that the British pursued their claims against Warrington any further. Instead, the protestations of the owners of the three captured merchant vessels now came to the fore, but only because Bagot in his 6 November letter to Monroe had reiterated the claims that he had first set forth in his 28 March remonstrance. The American government had done nothing to resolve the complaint of illegal seizures in the ensuing seven months.[31]

As the central issue changed focus from an inquiry into the *Nautilus* affair to restitution for the three merchant vessels, Warrington and the Navy Department figured more prominently. James Scott & Co. of Calcutta, the owners of the *Venus*, through their American representative, the legal firm of S. Smith & Buchanan Company of Baltimore, took the lead in demanding indemnification. The latter's correspondence with the Navy and State Departments from February to October 1817 illustrates the bureaucratic nightmare of adjudicating what the British and their American agents considered to be a plain and equitable claim.

Crowninshield, acting at the behest of the State Department, wrote to Warrington on 26 December 1816 to inform him that Charles Bagot had made preliminary claims for indemnifying losses suffered by the owners of the *Union*, the *Venus*, and the *Brio de Mar*. The Navy secretary requested a list of the amount and disposition of all the captured property. Warrington responded three weeks later with a general, narrative description that lacked the specificity needed for adjudicating claims. The firm of S. Smith & Buchanan, writing directly to Crowninshield in early February 1817, claimed $17,453.75 plus interest of 6 percent from 21 June 1815, the date of the capture.[32]

Crowninshield denied that his department had jurisdiction over the case, asserting that the claimants must resort to an admiralty court to determine whether the second article of the Treaty of Ghent applied to them. On 22 February, Bagot submitted the *Venus's* affidavits to Secretary Monroe, but the latter also affirmed that the admiralty courts had jurisdiction.[33]

Since both the Navy and State Departments denied jurisdiction of the claim, S. Smith & Buchanan awaited the libel decision of the U.S. District Court for the Southern District of New York. In May, that court, recognizing the validity of the *Venus's* claim, sent her representatives the proceeds of the property subject to libel. Now S. Smith & Buchanan had proof that this was no longer an "alleged, but an acknowledged violation of the Treaty of Ghent." Their efforts to obtain restitution still faced further hurdles. Crowninshield maintained that now the State Department had jurisdiction and the latter told the Baltimore law firm that it could not act without a detailed statement of the value of the goods appropriated by Warrington for use of his ship. When S. Smith & Buchanan wrote Crowninshield about Warrington's inability to provide the requisite information, the Navy secretary wrote them back in May that his department was not trying to delay the disposition of the case. He blamed instead Warrington's inability to furnish him with a detailed list with prices. The department had first written to Warrington in December. It was now May.[34]

From May until October there was a continuous barrage of correspondence between Warrington and the Navy Department about obtaining the necessary documentation, and between S. Smith & Buchanan and the department about the constant delays. Crowninshield's chief clerk, Benjamin Homans, who acted for the secretary during his extended summer leave in 1817, badgered Warrington to act quickly because the matter had taken a diplomatic course. Homans demanded that Warrington send the *Peacock*'s logbook or a certified copy of it to Washington. Warrington was not sure where the logbook was and said he did not believe it was his job to provide prices for every item. He suggested that the department add 20 or 25 percent to American prices in order to determine the cost of supplies in the East Indies. Homans caustically reminded Warrington on 17 July that he had caused his own predicament by not adhering to Article 39 of the Naval Regulations, which required commanders of public vessels to send the department at the end of a cruise a general copy of the regular journal kept on board their ship. Warrington had failed to do this when he returned from his last cruise.[35]

S. Smith & Buchanan, obviously agitated, at one point threatened to turn the matter over to the British minister. Finally, in late August, Warrington arrived in Washington and provided the department with an acceptable list. The State Department had to approve the appropriation, however, and another six weeks passed before Homans could transfer the funds to the *Venus*'s representatives. Still, S. Smith & Buchanan was not satisfied, because the $8,182 award was still $7,697.29 short of their original claim. Homans referred the *Venus*'s agents to Congress for reclamation of this remaining amount.[36]

S. Smith & Buchanan finally resorted to Minister Bagot to press their claims further. Bagot had waited patiently while the American agents had sought relief from the U.S. District Court for the Southern District of New York and the Navy Department. In January 1818 he reentered the negotiations and approached the new secretary of state, John Quincy Adams, with the final claim. The following month, Adams forwarded the *Venus*'s affidavits to the chairman of the House Ways and Means Committee. Persistence paid off. The very last item of the congressional appropriation act for the support of the government in 1818 contained an allocation for not more than $7,678 for indemnifying the owners of the *Venus* in full, except for an interest payment.[37]

In 1818 the owners or representatives of the other two vessels, the *Union* and the *Brio de Mar,* submitted their claims with supporting affidavits to the Foreign Office, which forwarded the files on to Bagot, who presented them to the State Department, which in turn tendered them to Congress. The second session of the Fifteenth Congress on 3 March 1819 appropriated $15,000 to the insurers of the *Brio de Mar* and $61,451 to the owners and underwriters of the *Union*. Bagot's dispatch No. 66 to Castlereagh noted that Congress had allotted the entire amount claimed by the *Brio de Mar* but only $61,451 of the $84,925 that the owners of the *Union* had claimed. The British minister, however, conceded that the latter had included an amount for some future losses, which Congress was justified in not paying. Despite this partial rebuff, the representatives for the *Union* persisted, and in 1828 Congress appropriated another $23,474, which was full payment of their claim.[38]

By 1828 the American government had satisfied all the claims put forward by the owners and insurers of the three merchant vessels captured by the *Peacock* in violation of the second article of the Treaty of Ghent. These were, indeed, as one of the vessels' agents had noted, plain and equitable claims. More striking was the apparent silence about any indemnification for the alleged "wanton violence" against the *Nautilus*. After Bagot forwarded the report of the naval court of inquiry to Viscount Castlereagh, the records are silent. Perhaps the foreign minister decided quietly to end this thorny, but peripheral, diplomatic problem. Both the United States and Great Britain had more important issues to resolve and perhaps this was one of those examples of Castlereagh's conciliatory policy in the postwar era. The foreign secretary in a secret and confidential dispatch to Bagot in November 1817, a year after the court of inquiry and in the midst of the indemnification claims, wrote: "The avowed & true Policy of Great Britain, being, in the existing State of the World, to appease Controversy, & to secure, if possible, for all States a long interval of Repose."[39]

What happened to the *Peacock*, the *Nautilus*, Warrington, and Boyce? The *Peacock* suffered only minor damage during the encounter and continued to serve the Navy for another thirteen years in normal peacetime activities. She ferried diplomats to Europe, ferreted out pirates in the Caribbean, and protected American commerce in the Pacific. On a cruise in 1827, a whale struck the *Peacock*, resulting in her decommissioning and being broken up the next year. The *Nautilus* suffered severe damage to her hull and rigging from the 30 June 1815 attack, but was repaired and returned to service in the East India Company's fleet.[40]

For several years after the court of inquiry, Warrington resided in Norfolk, Virginia. Except for an assignment to survey ports and harbors on the East Coast, Warrington did not command a ship again until 1820, when Secretary of the Navy Smith Thompson offered him the frigate *Guerriere* in the Mediterranean. The *Peacock/Nautilus* incident did not harm Warrington's career, as prestigious positions highlighted his last thirty years in the Navy—commissioner of the Navy Board, commandant of the Norfolk Navy Yard, and acting secretary of the Navy. He died in 1851 while serving as the chief of the Bureau of Ordnance after almost fifty-two years in the Navy.[41]

While Lewis Warrington lived to be sixty-eight years old, Charles Boyce, captain of the *Nautilus*, survived into his nineties. Charles R. Low, a lieutenant in the British Indian Navy, wrote a history of that service that was published in 1877. While researching the *Nautilus/Peacock* affair, Mr. Low contacted the then ninety-two-year-old Boyce and reprinted the latter's 24 September 1815 official report to the East India Company. Boyce had retired from that service in 1817 as the result of the severe injuries incurred during the engagement, but, according to Mr. Low, Boyce had the last laugh. Boyce claimed that he was still receiving a pension that the U.S. Congress had voted for him some sixty years previously.[42]

Notes

1. William Jones to Stephen Decatur, 23 Nov. 1814, National Archives (hereafter DNA), Naval Records Collection of the Office of Naval Records and Library (hereafter RG45), Private Letters, (hereafter PL), 1814, p. 213; Decatur to Benjamin W. Crowninshield, 18 Jan. 1815, DNA, RG45, Captains' Letters to the Secretary of the Navy (hereafter CL), 1815, vol. 1, no. 50 (M125, roll no. 42); "Logbook of U.S. Ship *Peacock*, L. Warrington commander, kept by Midshipman Hill Carter, April 1, 1814–July 19, 1815," entries for 23–26 Jan. 1815, Colonial Williamsburg Foundation Library, Shirley Plantation Research Collection, Box 84, Folder 2; "Journal of William T. Rodgers Midshipman United States Navy on board United States Sloop of War *Peacock* 1813–1815," entries for 24–26 Jan. 1815, Library of Congress, William T. Rodgers Papers.

2. Rodgers Journal, 26 Jan., 14 Feb., 1, 13 Mar., 25, 27–28 Apr. 1815.

3. *The Public Statutes at Large of the United States of America from the Organization of the Government in 1789, to March 3, 1845*, vol. 8, *Treaties between the United States of America and Foreign Nations, from the Declaration of the Independence of the United States to 1845* (Boston: Little, Brown and Company, 1867), treaty: 218–23; article two: 219.

4. Rodgers Journal, 21, 24–26 Mar., 10, 13 Apr. 1815, James Biddle to Benjamin W. Crowninshield, 8 Apr. 1815, DNA, RG45, CL, 1815, vol. 3, no. 27 (M125, roll no. 44); Lewis Warrington to Crowninshield, 9 Apr. 1815, DNA, RG45, CL, 1815, vol. 3, no. 32 (M125, roll no. 44).

5. Rodgers Journal, 25, 27–28 Apr. 1815.

6. Ibid., 28 Apr. 1815.

7. Biddle to Decatur, 10 June 1815, DNA, RG45, CL, 1815, vol. 4, unnumbered, follows no. 19 (M125, roll no. 45); Rodgers Journal, 28–30 Apr. 1815.

8. Rodgers Journal, 16-17, 28 May, 7-9 June 1815. John Jacob Astor had offered Decatur space for some of his provisions on his merchant brig *Macedonian* that was sailing for the East Indies. The *President* and this brig left Sandy Hook together. The latter watched helplessly as the frigate succumbed to the British squadron. Decatur to Crowninshield, 30 Dec. 1814, DNA, RG45, CL, 1814, vol. 8, no. 148 (M125, roll no. 41) and John Hayes to Henry Hotham, 17 Jan. 1815, Public Record Office (hereafter UkLPR), Admiralty 1/508, fols. 387–90.

9. Rodgers Journal, 13–14 June 1815.

10. Carter Logbook, 13–23 June 1815.

11. Carter Logbook, 24–30 June 1815; Rodgers Journal, 24–28 June 1815.

12. "Logbook of U.S. Ship *Peacock* of 18 guns, L. Warrington, Esq. commander, kept by Midshipman William H. Baldwin, January 30–July 10, 1815," Maryland Historical Society, MS 2315, 30 June 1815; Carter Logbook, 30 June 1815; Rodgers Journal, 30 June 1815.

13. Rodgers Journal, 30 June 1815.

14. Rodgers Journal, 30 June 1815, 1–2 July 1815.

15. Warrington to Crowninshield, 2 Nov. 1815, DNA, RG45, CL, 1815, vol. 6, no. 2 (M125, roll no. 47); Warrington to Crowninshield, 11 Nov. 1815, DNA, RG45, CL, 1815, vol. 6, no. 17 (M125, roll no. 47).

16. Robert Boon to Messrs. Arnot & Fairlie, 3 July 1815, UkLPR, Great Britain. Foreign Office Records (hereafter FO) 5/111, fols. 320–21; W. Eatwell to Henry Meriton, 22 July 1815, enclosed in DNA, Records of the Office of the Judge Advocate General (Navy) (hereafter RG125), Court of Inquiry of the "Rencontre between U.S. Ship *Peacock*, and the British East

India Company's Brig *Nautilus*," vol. 7, no. 244, 35–37 (M273, roll no. 7); Henry Meriton to Sir Evan Nepean, 13 Sept. 1815, enclosed in ibid., 39–40.

17. Draft of a letter from the Foreign Office to Charles Bagot, Dec. 1815, UkLPR, FO 5/108, fols. 15–16; Robert Viscount Castlereagh to Bagot, 2 Jan. 1816, UkLPR, FO 5/113, fols. 3–4.

18. A recent thesis by James S. Krysick entitled "The Diplomatic Career of Sir Charles Bagot, The Early Years: London, Paris, Washington, St. Petersburg (1807–1824)" (Ph.D. diss., Marquette University, 1988) does not mention the *Peacock* controversy.

19. *Maryland Republican* (Annapolis), 16 Mar. 1816, is enclosure no. 3, UkLPR, FO 5/114, fol. 28 in Bagot to Lord Castlereagh, 7 Apr. 1816, UkLPR, FO 5/114, fols. 19–21; Warrington to Crowninshield, 27 Feb. 1816, DNA, RG45, CL, 1816, vol. 1, no. 97 (M125, roll no. 48).

20. Warrington to Crowninshield, 11 Nov. 1815, DNA, RG45, CL, 1815, vol. 6, no. 19 (M125, roll no. 47); Crowninshield to Warrington, 20 Nov. 1815, DNA, RG45, Secretary of the Navy Letters to Officers, Ships of War (hereafter SNL), vol. 12, p. 220 (M149, roll no. 12); Warrington to Crowninshield, 30 Nov. 1815, DNA, RG45, CL, 1815, vol. 6, no. 68 (M125, roll no. 47); Crowninshield to Warrington, 2 Dec. 1815, DNA, RG45, SNL, vol. 12, p. 228 (M149, roll no. 12); Warrington to Crowninshield, 4 Dec. 1815, DNA, RG45, CL, 1815, vol. 6, no. 73 (M125, roll no. 47); Crowninshield to Warrington, 12 Dec. 1815, DNA, RG45, SNL, vol. 12, p. 236 (M149, roll no. 12); Warrington to Crowninshield, 16 Jan. 1816, DNA, RG45, CL, 1816, vol. 1, no. 36 (M125, roll no. 48); Crowninshield to Warrington, 25 Jan. 1816, DNA, RG45, SNL, vol. 12, p. 261 (M149, roll no. 12); Crowninshield to William Bainbridge, 27 Feb. 1816, DNA, RG45, SNL, vol. 12, p. 281 (M149, roll no. 12).

21. Bagot to Monroe, 28 Mar. 1816, UkLPR, FO 5/114, fols. 22–25, enclosure no. 1 of Bagot to Castlereagh, 7 Apr. 1816, UkLPR, FO 5/114, fols. 19–21.

22. Monroe to Bagot, 3 Apr. 1816, DNA, General Records of the Department of State (hereafter RG59), Notes from the Department of State to Foreign Ministers and Consuls in the United States, 1793–1834, vol. 2, pp. 135–36 (M38, roll no. 2); copy also in UkLPR, FO 5/114, fols. 26–27, which is enclosure 2 of Bagot to Castlereagh, 7 Apr. 1816, UkLPR, FO 5/114, fols. 19–21.

23. Crowninshield to Warrington, 2 Apr. 1816, DNA, RG45, SNL, vol. 12, p. 302 (M149, roll no. 12); Warrington to Crowninshield, 29 Apr. 1816, DNA, RG45, CL, 1816, vol. 2, no. 91 (M125, roll no. 49); Warrington to Crowninshield, 27 Feb. 1816, DNA, RG45, CL, 1816, vol. 1, no. 97 (M125, roll no. 48).

24. Bagot to Castlereagh, 3 May 1816, UkLPR, FO 5/114, fols. 36–37 contained five enclosures: unnumbered, Monroe to Bagot, 3 May 1816, fols. 38–39; no. 1, Crowninshield to Monroe, 29 Apr. 1816, fols. 40–41; no. 2,

Warrington to Crowninshield, 2 Nov. 1815, fols. 42–43; no. 3, Warrington to Crowninshield, 11 Nov. 1815, fols. 44–45; no. 4, Warrington to Crowninshield, 13 Apr. 1816, fol. 46; Bagot to Monroe, 9 May 1816, is enclosure no. 7, fols. 138–39 in Bagot to Castlereagh, 4 June 1816, UkLPR, FO 5/114, fols. 128–31.

25. Crowninshield to Richard Rush, 22 June 1816, DNA, RG45, Miscellaneous Letters Sent by the Secretary of the Navy (hereafter MLS), vol. 12, p. 456 (M209, roll no. 4); Rush to Crowninshield, 24 June 1816, DNA, RG45, Letters Received by the Secretary of the Navy from the Attorney General of the United States Containing Legal Opinions and Advice 1807–1825, no. 25 (M1029).

26. Crowninshield to Bainbridge, 29 June 1816, DNA, RG45, SNL, vol. 12, pp. 348–49 (M149, roll no. 12); Crowninshield to Bainbridge, 29 June 1816, DNA, RG45, SNL, vol. 12, p. 349 (M149, roll no. 12).

27. DNA, RG125, Court of Inquiry, vol. 7, no. 244 (M273, roll no. 7)

28. Monroe to Bagot, 31 Oct. 1816, UkLPR, FO 5/115, fols. 155–56 is enclosure no. 1 in Bagot to Castlereagh, 9 Nov. 1816, UkLPR, FO 5/115, fols. 153–54; the 31 Oct. 1816 letter is also in RG59, Notes to Foreign Ministers, vol. 2, p. 187 (M38, roll no. 2); notation in State Department letter book, 4 Nov. 1816, ibid. Monroe to Bagot, 30 Nov. 1816, UkLPR, FO 5/115, fols. 195–96 and enclosure of entire court of enquiry, fols. 197–212, all of this enclosed in Bagot to Castlereagh, 3 Dec. 1816, FO 5/115, fols. 193–94; another copy of this 30 Nov. 1816 letter, with no court of inquiry report, is in RG59, Notes to Foreign Ministers, vol. 2, 190 (M38, roll no. 2).

29. Bagot to Monroe, 6 Nov. 1816, UkLPR, FO 5/115, fols. 165–66 is enclosed in Bagot to Castlereagh, 9 Nov. 1816, UkLPR, FO 5/115, fols. 153–54.

30. Bagot to Castlereagh, 9 Nov. 1816, UkLPR, FO 5/115, fols. 153–54; Bagot to William Hamilton, 10 Nov. 1816, UkLPR, FO 5/115, fols. 187–89.

31. Bagot to Castlereagh, 9 Nov. 1816, UkLPR, FO 5/115, fols. 153–54; Bagot to Monroe, 28 Mar. 1816, UkLPR, FO 5/114, fols. 22–25 is enclosure no. 1 of Bagot to Castlereagh, 7 Apr. 1816, UkLPR, FO 5/114, fols. 19–21.

32. Crowninshield to Warrington, 26 Dec. 1816, SNL, vol. 12, p. 444 (M149, roll no. 12); Warrington to Crowninshield, 17 Jan. 1817, CL, 1817, vol. 1, no. 26 (M125, roll no. 52); S. Smith & Buchanan to Crowninshield, 3 Feb. 1817, DNA, RG45, Miscellaneous Letters Received by the Secretary of the Navy, 1801–84 (hereafter MLR), 1817, vol. 1, no. 117 (M124, roll no. 78).

33. Crowninshield to S. Smith & Buchanan, 12 Feb. 1817, DNA, RG45, MLS, vol. 13, p. 37 (M209, roll no. 5); Bagot to Monroe, 22 Feb. 1817, RG59, Notes from the British Legation in the U.S. to the Department of State, 1791–1906, vol. 9, note of 22 Feb. 1817 (M50, roll no. 10); Monroe to Bagot, 26 Feb. 1817, RG59, Notes to Foreign Ministers, vol. 2, p. 205 (M38, roll no. 2).

34. S. Smith & Buchanan to Crowninshield, 21 May 1817, DNA, RG45, MLR, 1817, vol. 4, no. 39 (M124, roll no. 79); Crowninshield to S. Smith & Buchanan, 23 May 1817, DNA, RG45, MLS, vol. 13, p. 77 (M209, roll no. 5).

35. Warrington to Crowninshield, 19 June 1817, DNA, RG45, CL, 1817, vol. 3, no. 29 (M125, roll no. 54); Homans to Warrington, 30 June 1817, DNA, RG45, SNL, vol. 13, p. 39 (M149, roll no. 13); Warrington to Homans, 14 July 1817, DNA, RG45, CL, 1817, vol. 3, no. 78 (M125, roll no. 54); Homans to Warrington, 17 July 1817, DNA, RG45, SNL, vol. 13, p. 49 (M149, roll no. 13).

36. S. Smith & Buchanan to Crowninshield, 7 Aug. 1817, DNA, RG45, MLR, 1817, vol. 5, no. 55 (M124, roll no. 80); Statement of Warrington regarding the amount of species and stores taken from *Venus* and applied by him for naval purposes to the amount of $8,182, 29 Aug. 1817, DNA, RG45, MLR, 1817, vol. 5, no. 95 (M124, roll no. 80); S. Smith & Buchanan to Crowninshield, 26 Sept. 1817, DNA, RG45, MLR, 1817, vol. 6, no. 15 (M124, roll no. 80); Homans to S. Smith & Buchanan, 9 Oct. 1817, DNA, RG45, MLS, vol. 13, p. 119 (M209, roll no. 5); S. Smith & Buchanan to Crowninshield, 11 Oct. 1817, DNA, RG45, MLR, 1817, vol. 6, no. 48 (M124, roll no. 80); Homans to S. Smith & Buchanan, 13 Oct. 1817, DNA, RG45, MLS, vol. 13, p. 120 (M209, roll no. 5).

37. Bagot to John Quincy Adams, 6 Jan. 1818, RG59, Notes from British Legation, vol. 10, note of 6 Jan. 1818 (M50, roll no. 11); Bagot to Monroe, 22 Feb. 1817, RG59, Notes from British Legation, vol. 9, note of 22 Feb. 1817 (M50, roll no. 10). A notation on the docket says that the enclosed affidavit listing the value of the contents of the *Venus* was sent to the chairman of the Committee of Ways and Means on 27 Feb. 1818. Congress acted quickly to satisfy the claim by 9 Apr. 1818. *The Public Statutes at Large of the United States of America from the Organization of the Government in 1789, to March 3, 1845*, vol. 3 (Boston: Little, Brown, 1861), 423.

38. *The Public Statutes at Large of the United States of America from the Organization of the Government in 1789, to March 3, 1845*, vol. 6, *The Private Statutes at Large of the United States of America, from the Organization of the Government in 1789 to March 3, 1845* (Boston: Little, Brown, 1862), 394.

39. Bradford Perkins, *Castlereagh and Adams: England and the United States 1812–1823* (Berkeley: University of California Press, 1964), 197, 200–202; Perkins does not mention the *Peacock* affair; Castlereagh to Bagot, 10 Nov. 1817, UkLPR, FO 5/120 fol. 67.

40. U.S. Naval History Division, *Dictionary of American Naval Fighting Ships*, vol. 5 (1970; reprint, Washington, D.C.: Government Printing Office, 1979), 240–41; Deposition of Master Joseph Bartlett, 7 July 1815, and W. Eatwell to Henry Meriton, 22 July 1815, enclosed in DNA, RG125, Court of Inquiry, vol. 7, no. 244; Charles Boyce to John Lowe, 24 Sept. 1815, quoted

in Charles Rathbone Low, *History of the Indian Navy (1613–1863)*, vol. 1 (London: Richard Bentley and Son, 1877), 287.

41. Crowninshield to Warrington, 13 June 1818 and 4 March 1820, DNA, RG45, SNL, vol. 13, pp. 204 and 462 (M149, roll no. 13); Warrington to Smith Thompson, 10 Mar. 1820, CL, 1820, vol. 1, no. 98 (M125, roll no. 66); and Dumas Malone, ed., *Dictionary of American Biography*, vol. 19 (New York: Charles Scribner's Sons, 1943), 492–93.

42. Low, *History of the Indian Navy*, 284–88.

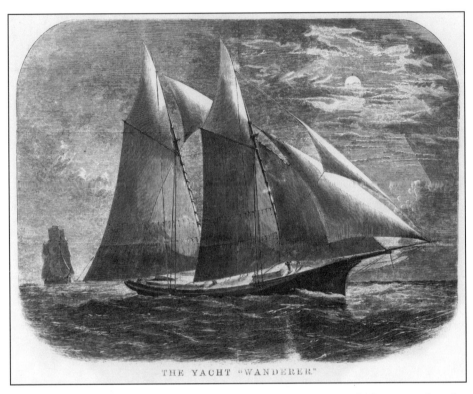

THE YACHT "WANDERER."

The sleek and speedy schooner *Wanderer,* captained by William C. Corrie, outfoxed government officials and outraced vessels of the U.S. Navy's African Squadron to smuggle more than 400 slaves into the Dubignon Plantation on Jekyll Island, Georgia, in November 1858. Proceedings against the slaver, Captain Corrie, and crew-members occurred in federal courts at Boston, Charleston, and Savannah.

7

War on the Slave Trade: Changing Fortunes in Antebellum U.S. Courts of the Mid-Atlantic South

Peter G. Fish

Constitutional Origins

Wars on crime have a long history in American political life. Periodically the national government has assumed the role of policeman to suppress a specific perceived social evil. The contemporary international war on drugs had its antecedents in the Prohibition era war on rum. That war, in turn, echoed an earlier one waged by the United States largely on the sea—the war on the slave trade. Adjudication of cases arising out of the federal government's enforcement of the anti–slave trade laws before the Civil War enmeshed judges and juries of the United States courts of the mid-Atlantic South in the key component of the historic African diaspora and in the leading moral and political issue of the antebellum period—slavery.

From the establishment of the United States government in 1789, the institution of slavery challenged the nation's democratic Constitution. That Constitution incorporated tenets of republican ideology ascendant in eighteenth-century America, but the "higher law" elements of republicanism withered when confronted with the practice of slavery.[1] The Constitution starkly manifested the divorce in its explicit recognition of the legality of slavery, the limited personhood of slaves and even the at least temporary lawfulness of slave importations into the United States.[2]

Behind the text lay the original understanding of the framers. The Constitution and the essential compromises that made its ratification possible were, declared Georgia's Constitutional Convention veteran Abraham Baldwin, "to ensure the peace and equal rights and properties of the various states."[3] And slavery, William L. Smith of South Carolina declared, was "the palladium of the property of our country."[4] That institution and the related African slave trade figured importantly in generating oratorical stridency in the First Congress. Its predecessor had banned the trade during the Revolutionary War and by 1787 all states except Georgia had prohibited or limited it.[5]

Prevailing state restrictions discouraged the Constitutional Convention from imposing immediate prohibitions while encouraging an extended period of national powerlessness over the importing trade.[6] Silence at the state ratification conventions, other than in that of the slave-exporting state of Virginia, generally greeted the unamendable importation provision.[7] The implicit linkage between abolition of the slave trade and abolition of slavery surfaced in the First Congress, igniting a lengthy and "warm debate" on what southerners regarded as the Constitution's absolute ban on congressional power over either slavery or the slave trade.[8] The constitutional text guaranteed until 1808 the "importation of such persons as any of the States now existing shall think proper to admit . . . but a Tax or duty may be imposed on such Importation, not exceeding ten dollars for each Person."[9] That language, clear on first impression, evinced a porous quality, notwithstanding a House resolution guaranteeing "that Congress shall have no authority to interfere in the immigration of slaves, or in the treatment of them within any of the States."[10]

Constitution framer and Virginia congressman James Madison fueled an interpretative approach. He conceived that Congress "might be able to give some testimony of the sense of America with respect to

The West African Connection, showing slave collection points to and from which vessels in the unlawful Atlantic slave trade were seized and carried into U.S. courts situated in ports of the mid-Atlantic South.

the African trade until the time arrived when [Congress] might abolish the importation of slaves. . . ."[11] Other than the constitutionally authorized per capita tax, which Congress never implemented, Madison believed that "there were a variety of ways by which [Congress] could countenance the abolition [of the slave trade] through regulation. . . ."[12] Although he did not spell out the sources of congressional power over the subject, others did. They named the commerce clause (Art. I, sec. 8, cl. 3) and the power "to define and punish Piracies and Felonies committed on the high seas" (Art. I, sec. 8, cl. 10).[13] Subsequently mentioned was that portion of the same clause empowering Congress "to define and punish . . . offenders against the Law of Nations," a law that one congressman asserted, "unquestionably gave Congress a full power over the subject, independently of that derived from [its] right to regulate commerce."[14] Whatever the foundation and scope of congressional power over the African trade before 1808, the temporary negative on the exercise of that power clearly suggested the affirmative, that Congress enjoyed post-1808 plenary authority over the subject.[15]

"War" and Courts

Beginning in 1794, by ever more comprehensive statutes, Congress made unlawful distinct categories of conduct relating to the slave trade. Eventually, statutes subjected American citizens and their vessels to penalties for engaging in the slave trade if (1) while within (infra presida) the United States or in international waters, vessels had been built, fitted out, and equipped for the trade, (2) after fitting and equipping but before loading and while on the high seas or hovering off the African coast, they awaited the assembling and purchasing of human cargoes, or (3) they actually loaded, carried, or unloaded such cargoes. However distinct the categories affected, the enforcement record depended on a variety of factors: available policing resources, judges and juries in criminal prosecutions, and judges in nonjury civil proceedings in admiralty against the instruments and contents of the unlawful commerce. As it turned out, the long-lived war brought relatively few offenders to trial.[16]

Offenders who were apprehended and charged with violating national laws aimed at the slave trade appeared before federal judges.[17] The judges and their courts, in what is now the United States Fourth Circuit, served the slave states of Maryland, Virginia, North Carolina, and South Carolina.[18] The Judiciary Act of 1789 divided these states among two of the three circuits created by that act, the middle and the southern.[19] From 1802 to 1842, they fell within the fourth, fifth and sixth circuits;[20] thereafter to the Civil War, they lay within the fourth and sixth circuits.[21]

Within the boundaries of the multistate circuits were districts composed of single states or portions thereof. A resident judge appointed for each district within the several circuits held court at various fixed localities within his district, often in ports of entry along the mid-Atlantic

South's maritime frontier. Circuit courts periodically sat in each district to hear appeals from district courts and to try important civil and criminal cases.[22] The circuit courts were staffed by a district judge and a justice of the United States Supreme Court, each of whom "rode" his allotted circuit to hold in each of its districts the scheduled sessions of the circuit court.[23] Thus, circuit courts presided over by the chief justice or associate justices with whom the resident district judge sat were structurally linked to the highest court in the land.

The overlapping judicial personnel served to mitigate the development of disharmonious interpretations of national law spawned by potentially localistic proclivities of the district judges. Even so, judicial uncertainty initially perplexed federal judges and juries in criminal prosecutions as they grappled with novel laws and sometimes ambiguous statutory language. Clarification of law during the 1820s still left judges and jurors confronted with the task of applying the law to elusive facts arising out of criminal undertakings. As the secession crisis of 1860–61 neared, sectionalism in a politically and geographically isolated South threatened the integrity of national law on a subject fraught with hard choices for United States judges.

Congress Speaks

Memorable Supreme Court cases on the slave trade involved questions of international law and especially the existence of a law of nations founded on inalienable natural rights and justice.[24] Statutory law enacted by Congress, not "higher law," provided most of the legal grist for federal trial courts from Baltimore to Charleston. Congressional animosity toward the slave trade, which surfaced in the First Congress, bore fruit in the Third. The Act of 22 March 1794 followed Madison's earlier suggestion that Congress could interdict the American slave export and carrying trade. Made unlawful was "carrying on the slave trade from the United States to any foreign place or country."[25] The law barred American citizens and foreigners alike from building, fitting, equipping, loading, or otherwise preparing "any ship or vessel, within any port or place of the . . . United States . . . [or] causing to sail therefrom for the purpose" of trading in slaves between and among foreign countries and prohibited American citizens from receiving on board or transporting persons into a foreign country "for the purpose of selling them as slaves."[26]

Violators faced fines and forfeiture of their vessels, the latter a juryless proceeding in admiralty. No enforcement resources were provided until 1800 when legislation that year authorized public and private vessels commissioned by the United States to seize slavers as maritime prizes and extended the law's prohibitions to citizens holding a financial interest in, or employment in, foreign or American-flagged vessels in the foreign trade.[27] Importation of slaves into the United States otherwise continued to enjoy explicit constitutional protection until 1808.

Judicial Uncertainty

Enforcement of the initial prohibitions got off to a halting start. Few slave trade cases made their way to federal court dockets, largely because apprehension of violators was almost fortuitous. For those few cases tried before 1800 in the South Carolina admiralty court presided over by slaveholding plantation owner Thomas Bee, whom President George Washington had appointed to the post in 1790, ignorance of facts or law was the best defense.[28] Bee turned a friendly ear to shipowners' pleas, except in a clear-cut case wherein he adjudged the vessel "unfit for sea."[29] Forfeiture proceedings failed against the brig *Harriet,* owned by a Charleston merchant who successfully argued his status as a bona fide purchaser without notice of the vessel's previous illegal use in the foreign slave trade.[30]

When in *Leonard v. Caskin* an American vessel was apprehended carrying ten slaves from Martinique to Havana, Bee placed a heavy burden of proof on the capturing vessel. He opined that the mere presence of slaves and the circumstances of the ship and its ports of call "might give cause for suspicion, but no more," of an unlawful intent to sell those aboard. "The bare transportation of Negroes from one place to another without proof of an intention to sell, will not incur this penalty," he declared.[31]

In Maryland, however, District Judge James Winchester, an Adams appointee,[32] allowed admission of a flawed indictment, to no great effect in the case of mariner Vickery charged under the 1800 act. Vickery had served aboard an American schooner transporting nine slaves from Nevis, an island in the Leeward Islands, to Cumana on the South American mainland. Notwithstanding an indictment charging Vickery with serving in a vessel that departed from Martinique in the Windward Islands rather than from Nevis, Winchester held that the words of the statute, "from one foreign place to another," sufficed. The jury agreed, returning "a verdict of guilty without retiring." But Winchester, like Bee, temporized on grounds "that the prisoner was ignorant that he was committing a violation of any law," and sentenced Vickery to pay a $10.00 fine and serve twenty-four hours in prison.[33]

The statutory text suffered judicial revision at Bee's hands in a case arising immediately after the constitutionally prescribed twenty-year slave importation window closed on 1 January 1808. The Act of 1807 superceded slave-importing South Carolina's "open door" policy adopted in 1803 and authorized the president to employ the United States Navy to search for and arrest slave smugglers in coastal waters and on the high seas.[34] Civil and criminal penalties imposed were heavy in order to deter prospective participants and to render the act self-enforcing.[35] The measure had been passed nearly a year in advance of its effective date in order to give ample notice to shipping interests. Nevertheless, Charleston shipowners and merchants petitioned Congress for relief.[36] Rebuffed there, the Charleston traders' plea found a more sympathetic reception in the local federal court.

Seizure by the revenue cutter *Gallatin* of the schooner *Kitty* in Stono Inlet near Charleston on 16 January 1808 precipitated an extraordinary incident of judicial lawmaking. The *Kitty*'s capture and subsequent legal proceedings in Bee's court ended an incredible saga of ill luck. Having sailed from Charleston in November 1806 and reaching the African coast in January 1807, the *Kitty*'s crew suffered hunger, illness, drunkenness, death, and desertion. Unavoidable inordinate delays ensued. With only thirty-two Africans aboard, the *Kitty* finally made for Charleston in mid-November 1807. Howling head winds and raging early winter seas turned a usual six-week voyage into a harrowing eight-week nightmare, causing the battered schooner to arrive more than two weeks after her human cargo had become illegal under the 1807 act.

The owners' tale of woe moved Bee to exempt the *Kitty* from the letter of the law. Since slave importation had been lawful when the voyage commenced, the judge believed that perhaps the captain, like Vickery in Winchester's court, had remained ignorant of the 1807 act until his return. "But if the act had been known to him," the judge declared, "unavoidable accident and invincible necessity prevented his sailing sooner." In Bee's view, the case before him was one "of hardship, occasioned by no fault of the party." According to Bee, Congress had fortuitously empowered the court to exercise "a discretionary power in extreme cases, of which this is surely one."[37] In fact, the act contained no such provision.

Law's Ambiguity

Bee's chilly reception of the 1807 act suggested judicial vacillation in the face of the law's new commands. As soon as it became apparent, the statutory text proved ambiguous. The published legislative history provided little clarification. Debate on the act in bill form had centered on the measure's perceived domestic impact related to the disposition in American ports of slaves taken from laden vessels and to the exempted interstate coastal slave trade.[38] Rarely, however, was a laden slaver apprehended "red-handed," the clear case apparently contemplated by the act's framers. An exception involved the Dutch schooner *Louisa*.[39] That involving the cargoless brig *Caroline*,[40] in contrast, attested to the protracted litigation necessary to clarify the meaning of the 1807 act where only circumstantial evidence of slave trading existed.

Sheer good fortune marked the government's case in St. George Tucker's court at Norfolk for the newly created Eastern District of Virginia against the *Louisa*'s incidental participation in the international slave trade[41]. Libels filed by United States Attorney Robert Stannard stipulated infractions of the 1807 act by Christoffel Rasmyne, the schooner's opportunistic master, who had reached Norfolk from Jamaica via St. Barthelemy in the West Indies. In the

Virginia port, four youths, apparently free members of the vessel's crew, disappeared, sold in Portsmouth by Rasmyne, who predictably absconded while the schooner's owner characteristically disclaimed any knowledge of the alleged illegalities.[42] The *Louisa*, however, remained in the hands of Tucker's court. And so did the $1,200 bill of sale for the four ex-crewmen transformed into slaves.[43] The incontrovertible evidence doomed the schooner to condemnation and forfeiture to the government under the 1807 act in the clearest of clear-cut cases.[44]

The long-running saga of the *Caroline* attested to the myriad obstacles impeding enforcement of the anti–slave trade laws when violators were not caught "red-handed." Prosecutions early foundered on failings in legislative craftsmanship and on the specificity of pleadings made by federal prosecutors. The 1794 act rendered it unlawful for any person to "build, fit, equip, load, or otherwise prepare any ship or vessel...for the purpose of carrying on any trade or traffic in slaves." Subsequent language, however, applied the punishment of forfeiture only to "any ship or vessel...so fitted out...or...caused to sail."[45] Only this latter clause found its way into the 1807 act.[46]

United States Attorney Thomas Parker filed a libel in the Circuit Court for the District of South Carolina alleging that, pursuant to the 1794 act, the *Caroline* "was built, fitted, equipped, loaded, or otherwise prepared" for the slave trade or, alternatively, that the vessel was "caused to sail" for that purpose.[47] Presiding over the court was Sixth Circuit justice William Johnson, no friend of illicit slave trading notwithstanding his South Carolina birth and residency as well as slave ownership.[48] Johnson considered the case on its merits, and owing to "sufficient evidence having been adduced of intentions to carry on the slave trade, either abroad or at home, and a consequent violation either of the act of 1794, or of the act of 1807," he decreed condemnation and forfeiture.[49]

On appeal, the Supreme Court in 1813 reversed the decree and remanded the case involving both the brig and the ship *Emily* to Johnson's circuit court. In the high court, Chief Justice John Marshall heeded the claimant's argument that a libel in admiralty must match the precision of common law pleadings and that the language of Parker's libel had been "altogether vague, uncertain and informal."[50] In his *Brig Caroline* opinion, the Chief Justice manifested his usual caution

in matters involving slavery, which institution he never vocally supported, and the slave trade, which he considered "a horrid traffic de-
tested by all good men."[51] Warning that "the peculiar odium attached
to the traffic ought not to affect the legal questions which belong to
the case," Marshall stressed the high value of objectivity in the law.[52]
Arguably, his demanding approach reflected a desire to recognize the
developing supremacy of congressional power to define crimes as well
as to heed the judiciary's institutional imperatives in the law enforcement context. Without information confined to the activity proscribed
by statute that gave rise to the stipulated penalty, neither the claimant
nor the court could guess whether the government actually possessed
evidence of "fitting"—the single act that could support a forfeiture
under the 1807 act. As he put it, "If several acts be prohibited under
several penalties, and on one of them, the penalty of forfeiture be inflicted, the information must charge, in explicit terms, that the particular crime to which the law has annexed forfeiture as a penalty, has been
committed, or the court cannot adjudge the thing to be forfeited."[53]

Parsing the statutory language in his inimitable fashion, Marshall
explained, "To build a vessel is to construct her, to fit her out, is to prepare her for sea after she has been constructed."[54] Because only the latter act merited imposition of the penalty of forfeiture, charging a vessel
with actions other than fitting rendered the libel vague and incapable of
sustaining the prescribed penalty.[55] Thus, the chief justice required the
government to confine its allegations in libels of slavers to those acts
set forth in the statute that were directly linked to the stipulated punishment. Tersely holding the libel "too imperfectly drawn, to own a
sentence of condemnation thereon," the high court directed the circuit
court to entertain an amended libel.[56] As amended, the libel alleged
that both vessels had been "fitted out" for the slave trade.[57]

Sixth Circuit justice William Johnson, early in 1821, affirmed the
district court's condemnation decree in the case now styled as the *Ship
Emily and Brig Caroline v. United States*.[58] "These vessels arrived in this
port in the condition of ordinary merchantmen," he recounted, although
one of them had apparently been previously "employed as a Guinea
Man." Yet, when seized, they were fitted out as slavers. Witness after
witness answered affirmatively to Johnson's query: "whether either of

[the vessels] were so actually fitted when seized or at any time before when in your hands, and whether they were fitted for that Trade when they were taken out of your hands." One marine artisan testified that both "were as much fitted for the African Slave Trade as any vessel he had ever seen."

True, neither had been completely fitted out when it cleared the port. But, Johnson noted that the fitting continued thereafter. In the Gulf Stream, the *Emily* loaded "a Camboon . . . such as is only used in a slaving voyage."[59] Both the ship and the brig featured "new gratings and bulk heads . . . such as are only fit for slaving voyages and not for merchant service, . . . new necessary tubs and eating tubs, . . . the necessary tub . . . [being] peculiar to slaving vessels, [in that] [n]o other description of vessels carry them [because] the Crews are trusted to visit the quarter galleries." The evidence adduced led Johnson to reject the claimant's argument that the statute's term, "fitting out," required that the vessel when seized be 100 percent equipped for the slave trade and not in some partial state of preparation. "These vessels," the circuit justice observed, "were in such an advanced state of equipment as qualified them to proceed immediately on such a voyage." The government did not have to "wait until they have driven the last nail in the last cleat before it can seize for the offence of fitting out."[60] The Supreme Court brethren emphatically agreed with Johnson in affirming his circuit court decision favorable to prosecution of the slave trade war.[61]

Three years later, in January 1827, Associate Justice Joseph Story reaffirmed in *United States v. Gooding* the doctrine of fitment laid down in the *Emily and Caroline*.[62] First heard in the Circuit Court for the District of Maryland, the *Gooding* case reached the Supreme Court on a certificate of division between District Judge Elias Glenn and Fourth Circuit Justice Gabriel Duvall.[63] Its facts suggested the growing sophistication of those engaged in trafficking in humans. En route from Baltimore to St. Thomas in the West Indies, the Baltimore-built *General Winder*, carrying fitments peculiarly adapted to the slave trade, rendezvoused with a companion vessel transporting additional "peculiar fitments," which, when transferred, completed the *General Winder*'s fitting for what turned out to be a profitable voyage carrying 290 inhabitants of West Africa to slave markets.[64] The subsequent indictment and his newsworthy criminal trial at Baltimore put owner John Gooding in the dock.

Gooding, President John Quincy Adams icily described, was "a respectable man . . . a warm patriot in the late war [of 1812] with Great Britain . . . [with] a large and helpless family, and, when going to wreck and ruin, speculated in the slave trade to save himself. . . ."[65] Defending him against Attorney General William Wirt and District Attorney Nathaniel Williams were those whom Wirt identified as five of the "most eminent counsel at the bar."[66] Their defense echoed that unsuccessfully proffered by predecessors in the *Emily and Caroline*. Citing that case as controlling precedent, Story held "that any preparations for a slave voyage, which clearly manifest or accompany the illegal intent, even though incomplete or imperfect, and before the departure of the vessel from port, do yet constitute a fitting out within the purview of the statute."[67] Certified to the circuit court, Gooding's case went to the jury. The jurors duly acquitted the local notable, demonstrating the government's difficulty in securing convictions of those accused of slave trading.[68]

Reorganized Enforcement

The slave trade issue won renewed congressional attention as sectional differences over the admission of new states became exacerbated before their temporary settlement under the Missouri Compromise of 1820.[69] Beginning in 1818, Congress moved to strengthen the nation's laws against the trade. The Act of 20 April 1818 both shifted the burden of proof to the defendant to show that any person of color brought in was not a slave and enhanced penalties for violations.[70] The "Act in Addition," passed the next year, empowered the president to dispatch American naval vessels to African waters to interdict and seize American slavers and carry them into ports from which they had sailed.[71]

The 1819 act also sought to rectify a serious shortcoming in prior laws on the subject. The fate of slaves taken from intercepted vessels had heretofore been left to the tender mercies of local sheriffs, who disposed of them according to applicable state laws.[72] After 1819, such slaves carried into southern ports, instead of being sold by state officials, were to be placed in the custody of the United States marshal for "safekeeping, support, and removal beyond the limits of the United States." To this end, Congress authorized the appointment of receiving agents stationed on the West African coast.[73]

As President Monroe went about organizing the Navy's African Squadron as authorized by the 1819 act, Congress further strengthened the hand of the federal government.[74] A select House committee chaired by Virginia congressman Charles Mercer called for an all-out war against what its report termed "this odious traffic."[75] From this committee came an expanded definition of piracy, which made pirates of American citizens who engaged in, acted in, aided in, or abetted a variety of enumerated transactions associated with the slave trade. Conviction by a jury in a federal circuit court exposed offenders to the death penalty.[76] It was a punishment long sought by antislavery advocates, one deemed sufficient to pierce "straight to the heart of the African Connection."[77]

Notwithstanding enhanced statutory prohibitions against traffickers in the nefarious trade, enforcement efforts in the 1820s and 1830s were desultory and tangible results were few.[78] Americans continued to smuggle hapless Africans into Cuba, Brazil, and the United States even in the face of various risks.[79] These included the usual perils of the sea to a perishable cargo and an international maritime police force led by Great Britain. That nation outlawed slavery in its colonies beginning in 1834 and then joined with Spain in authorizing Royal Navy vessels to seize suspected slavers as prizes and to bring them before mixed commissions at Sierra Leone and Havana for condemnation and forfeiture.[80] American flag vessels were not formally subject to seizure by British cruisers. Considerations of national sovereignty and memories of boardings and impressment during the Napoleonic wars lingered and vexed development of a unified policy for suppressing the slave trade.[81]

Slave traders took advantage of the enforcement lacunae. They clothed their vessels with indicia of American nationality during the outward half of the voyage to avoid unlikely apprehension by thinly deployed American naval vessels, while flying the "Stars and Stripes" to ward off interdiction by elements of the more potent British force.[82] The return trip was a different matter. With Americans aboard slavers defined as pirates under the 1820 act, American citizenship exposed master and crew alike to a fate unique to their nationality—death. A second set of papers bearing a foreign nationality, a foreign flag, and transformation of foreign "passengers" on the outward voyage into a vessel's captain and mates became a necessity.[83]

Seizures of American-flagged vessels by British cruisers whose captains doubted their true nationality nevertheless occurred. Such interdictions challenged American sovereignty. Vociferous protests emanated from Washington until Secretary of State Daniel Webster in the Tyler administration resolved the dispute together with that enveloping the Canadian boundary. The Webster-Ashburton Treaty of 1842 bound the United States and Great Britain to station along the 3,000-mile African coast a "sufficient and adequate" naval force of "not less than eighty guns," comprising between four and five vessels, for the "suppression" of the slave trade.[84] Even with the requisite force available, the U.S. Navy's African Squadron projected an insufficient presence to accomplish the assigned policing duties. Heat and tropical diseases decimated crews, while the tiny armada's base in the Cape Verde Islands put it a month's sail from the Congo Basin to which region the illegal trade had migrated southward in the late 1840s from collection points north of the equator. For American slavers, the squadron's occasional presence presented a relatively low risk or even afforded an effective shield against the more formidable Royal Navy's force, an immunity only partially mitigated by joint Anglo-American cruising arrangements. In the face of this augmented maritime police force, American participation in the trade waxed and waned during the 1840s and 1850s.[85]

Parsing the Evidence

As in the past, application of the strengthened anti–slave trade laws challenged prosecutors and judges alike. Red-handed apprehension of vessels laden with slaves occurred, but not often. American cruisers patrolling the African coast during the two decades ending in 1859 managed to seize only two fully loaded slavers.[86] Subsequent transfer of the Navy's base from the Cape Verde Islands to Loanda (St. Paul de Loanda), south of the Congo River, dramatically changed the enforcement results. In

1860 alone, squadron vessels interdicted seven slavers carrying a total of 4,300 humans.[87]

Among the prizes apprehended that year was the 230-ton brig *Storm King* built in Talbot County Maryland in 1854 and owned by a Marylander. The *Storm King* had cleared the Port of New York in May 1860 notwithstanding issuance of a libel on the eve of its departure. Off the mouth of the Congo River, the Navy's first-class steam sloop *San Jacinto* cut short all prospects for a successful slaving voyage.[88] Lieutenant Aaron K. Hughes led the boarding party onto the *Storm King*'s deck, where he lifted the deck hatches to discover that the openings were "filled with the heads of naked Africans [held] in the hold . . . without distinction of sexs [*sic*]."[89] A census revealed the presence of 619 captives—130 women, 68 girls, 160 men, and 261 boys—all sold by a Spanish factor and then transported in launches to the *Storm King*, which was "laying too" preparatory to its short-lived flight to the high seas.

In addition to the utterly incriminating cargo, the brig featured other indicia of a slaver, including missing name plate and colors, a logbook "with some of the leaves torn out," firearms, two slave decks wholly uncharacteristic of ordinary merchantmen, vast quantities of foodstuffs and water, a Hispanic crew, and Captain John Lockhart of New York claiming the status of a passenger. A *San Jacinto* prize crew released the kidnapped Africans at the American Colonization Society's Liberian refuge in Monrovia and carried the *Storm King* and its crew into the country's premier naval base at Gosport and into the hands of the United States marshal for the Eastern District of Virginia for eventual condemnation in that district's court, presided over from 1844 to 1861 by James Dandridge Halyburton.[90]

Unlike the *Storm King*, apprehended suspected slavers were more likely than not to lack a human cargo and to be incompletely equipped for the trade. Masking the real purpose of voyages to and from West Africa were a variety of deceptive practices honed in privateering associated with the War of 1812 and the Latin American wars of independence.[91] Navy Secretary Abel P. Upshur warned of them in instructions given in 1843 to the African Squadron's first commander, Commodore Matthew C. Perry.[92] Upshur rued that "the cunning of the slave trader . . . is constantly devising new disguises and schemes of deception by which he may elude detection and escape the consequences of his crimes. No one supposed," the secretary observed, "that vessels destined for the slave trade will *exhibit* any of the usual arrangements for that business." He noted what federal judges well knew—"the slavers do not carry within themselves any positive proof of their guilt, except before they reach the coast, and after they leave it with slaves on board."[93] In the guise of honest merchantmen, but endowed with a plethora of deceptive devices, they moved swiftly and covertly to contract with local slave factors, unload incriminating trading goods, hover offshore, return to the collection station (barracoon), load, and depart swiftly and surreptitiously.[94] Thus in cases of unladen slavers, federal prosecutors, judges, and juries faced circumstantial evidence, each element of which could be viewed in a light favorable or unfavorable to the government.

Although caught "red-handed," the *Storm King* had provided other clues to its unlawful enterprise. These typically included physical characteristics of the vessel, its fittings and equipment, cargo, papers, and the personnel. The unladen brig *Triton of New Orleans,* apprehended by the Navy steamer *Mystic* north of Kabinda, near the mouth of the Congo River, and like the *Storm King* carried into Gosport, revealed incriminating circumstantial evidence: name painted over, manifest "lost" overboard, American colors absent, eighty casks of water, a slave deck in place, bags of coins, and the crew's dunnage packed for a flight to shore.[95]

With its hold filled with wooden planks sufficient to build a slave deck, the bark *Julia Dean,* seized in 1858 by the Navy sloop *Vincennes* off Cape Coast Castle in modern Ghana, lacked an accurate crew manifest and an identifiable consignor for the voyage. Other papers received close scrutiny, especially the charter party agreement, which stipulated the destination and duration of the voyage, and the still intact logbooks. The voyage seemingly cost too much.[96]

That circumstance in *United States v. Panther* raised the suspicions of Judge Robert Budd Gilchrist in the District of South Carolina.[97] Gilchrist as United States attorney had stood fast for enforcement of federal tariff laws in the Nullification crisis of 1831, a factor that figured importantly in his appointment to the bench by President

Andrew Jackson in 1839.[98] Specifically, Gilchrist wondered why the maritime contract made in Rio de Janeiro described a trip from that port to specific West African ports, "and thence to . . . ports of discharge *in Brazil,*" while the American consul at Rio had approved a voyage "to the coast of Africa and *back to the United States.*" The judge perceived the latter as "fair and legitimate," while a voyage from the coast of Africa to Brazil, where the slave trade remained legal, is "not [i]nfrequently of a different character."[99] An excessive number of sailing days suggestive of a hovering strategy on the African coast pending the locating and loading of a slave cargo marked the *Julia Dean's* logbook.[100]

The *Panther's* similar record led Gilchrist to ask why a vessel, chartered at $1,750 a month, carrying an African-bound cargo valued at only $2,750 and reporting trading activity confined to two ivory teeth and fourteen gallons of palm oil, was anchored first in the Congo River, then moved to Kabinda, idled there for months, then sailed south to Ambiz, and returned to the Congo River before retracing her route to Kabinda, where the African Squadron's sloop of war *Yorktown* seized the suspected slaver.[101] The inordinate number of days led Gilchrist to take judicial notice of the fact that the *Panther's* loitering occurred in "a section of country notorious as a slave mart."[102] The papers also denoted ports of origin; these raised suspicions, particularly if the port was New York City. Officials there habitually cleared questionably equipped vessels linked to an international crime syndicate and destined for dubious ports of call.[103] Among those departing from New York were the bark *William G. Lewis,* seized by the Navy sloop *Dale* at Punta da Lenha, a trading post thirty miles up the Congo River, and the schooners *Advance* and *Rachael P. Brown,* both taken by the Navy sloop *Germantown* at the Portuguese outpost of Porto Praia in the Cape Verde Islands, all carried into Halyburton's court.[104]

American shipmasters and crews might or might not be aboard at the moment of capture, as were Captain Lockhart and the *Panther's* master, whose unsavory reputation put Gilchrist on guard. Unique to the United States, the death penalty prescribed by the 1820 act encouraged at least the American captain on reaching the African coast to sell, or appear to sell, his vessel or otherwise transfer his command to

Hispanics.[105] If apprehended, Americans typically claimed the status of passengers and manifested complete ignorance of a single African confined aboard their laden vessels, or more credibly for sailors, of their ultimate destination when they signed the shipping articles.[106] Thus a crewmember aboard the brig *Excellent*, seized off the African coast in 1850 by the Navy sloop *John Adams* and carried into Norfolk, thought his voyage from Rio de Janeiro at ordinary wages as distinguished from high slave trade wages would take him to California in Gold Rush days.[107]

Chief Justice Taney's Crusade

Ambiguous statutory language, the usual array of deceptive practices characteristic of the slave trade, and defendants represented by leading members of the American bar confronted Chief Justice Roger B. Taney. Riding the Fourth Circuit, he launched a veritable judicial crusade against building of vessels expressly for the slave trade. The crusade accorded with his belief that the South's firmest protection for its peculiar institution rested on the pro-slavery Constitution of 1787 and on the supremacy of national law in pursuance of that end.[108] His fidelity to national law surfaced at the November 1839 term of the Circuit Court for the District of Maryland. The judicial signals then and thereafter emitted by the chief justice and the associate justice riding the Fourth and Sixth Circuits stretching from Maryland to the Georgia line favored the development of harmonious national slave trade law such that the judges of the mid-Atlantic South from 1837 to 1861 condemned fourteen of the nineteen vessels libeled by the government as suspect slavers.[109] Andrew H. Foote of the African squadron considered the forfeiture record as evidence of the efficacy of judicial enforcement of the anti–slave trade laws. Criminal prosecutions before local jurors were another matter.[110]

Taney opened the autumn 1839 Maryland circuit court at Baltimore in the wake of a remarkable set of events. The previous June, Her Majesty's brig *Buzzard* sailed into New York harbor accompanied by two "American" prizes, both suspected slavers. Three more such vessels, all schooners, including the *Catherine* of Baltimore, embarrassingly followed.[111] Astounding too were the events that unfolded late in August 1839 off Long Island, where the 120-ton Baltimore-built schooner *Amistad* of Havana had been seized by a revenue cutter following a slave mutiny, led by Cinque, and a thwarted attempt to reach Africa.[112] Carried into New London, Connecticut, the jailed human cargo became a cause célèbre that mobilized New England abolitionists and ignited two years of litigation wherein were juxtaposed in historic proportions issues of human freedom and property rights, international and domestic law, and natural and positive law.[113]

As suggested by the origins of the *Catherine* and the *Amistad,* Baltimore's entrepreneurial class played a significant role in facilitating the unlawful "middle passage" trade in "black ivory." From its shipyards, even in the midst of economic depression, came fast, if flimsily constructed, clipper-style schooners for the slave trade. Rigged with at least one mast with fore and aft sails, the shallow-draft vessels averaging 200 tons represented a technological advance conducive to shortened sailing times, enhanced survival rates for their perishable cargoes, and augmented profits.[114] The Chesapeake industry benefited immensely from a preexisting network spawned by the Latin American wars of independence against Spain and Portugal lasting into the 1820s. Baltimore's pan-American "privateering" enterprise, always in conflict with proclaimed American neutrality, relied on a web of relationships peopled by faithless American diplomatic representatives; shady American, Spanish, and Portuguese brokers; dummy owners; real and fictitious buyers; "flag captains"; and ethnically diverse crews, all awash in a sea of fraudulent documents.[115]

The Baltimore connection, its tentacles extending over thousands of nautical miles through Havana and Bahia in Brazil to and from the African coast, implicated members of Baltimore's elite.[116] Among them was Bremen-born John F. Strom, who participated in the slave trade as a factor, in which capacity he facilitated the construction of two "clipper-built" schooners, including the *Ann.* Strom, representing the Brazilian firm of DaCosta & Co. through its Havana-based agent DeSilva, for whom two Hispanic captains acted as construction supervisors, contracted with a Fell's Point shipyard to build the two vessels for which purpose DeSilva paid him $14,000 of the total bill of $18,000 before the port's customs collector acted. No structural features suggested a slaver. Only the *Ann*'s cargo suggested a criminal purpose: spars and 1,300 feet of one-inch pine boards for a slave deck to rest on two 150-gallon water casks, and stone ballast.[117] Also facing serious criminal charges in Taney's court that term were other leading citizens of Baltimore, Robert W. Allen and John Henderson, co-owners of the British prize *Catherine*, and Francis T. Montell, owner of the Baltimore-built schooner *Elvira*.[118] Their acute legal problems signaled an intensified effort on the part of United States Attorney Williams to crush a local cornerstone of the African slave trade—the building, fitting out, and equipping of the vessels employed in it. Associate Justice Joseph Story's classmate at Harvard,[119] Williams targeted factor Strom. Enforcing the 1818 act, he triumphed in the federal district court. That court condemned the *Ann* and ordered its sale, the proceeds of which amounted to $4,256.33.[120]

In his appeal to Chief Justice Taney's circuit court, Strom was represented by one of the nation's great courtroom litigators, Reverdy Johnson, who asserted that the prosecution must prove that his client actually intended to build, equip, and employ vessels for the slave trade. Without proof of scienter or guilty knowledge imputed to Strom, the government had no case.[121] Taney disagreed. "Here we have an owner, here is a factor, and here is a master," he noted. "If any one of the three intended the vessel to be employed in the slave trade, she is liable to forfeiture. . . . It is not necessary to bring home the knowledge or purpose to either of the other two."[122] Concealment of a guilty knowledge behind layers of real or paper agents, however, rendered truth an ever-elusive element. Proof of any one of the defendants' unlawful intent depended on finding of facts sufficient to overcome "any reasonable doubt."

The facts struck Williams as virtually conclusive. The lumber, water casks, and ballast aboard the *Ann* all suggested a criminal intent to convert the merchantman into a slaver at some indeterminate time and place. Johnson successfully explained away the evidence as suggesting vessels built and loaded for use in either legal or in illegal maritime commerce.[123] Other evidence, however, proved decidedly inculpatory. Conversation between DeSilva's Hispanic captains and a local pilot-turned-government witness revealed an always-suspect interest in recruiting an American flag captain for the *Ann* to deter its seizure by Britain's African Squadron. An indelicate inquiry by Strom at the customshouse was deemed by Taney as evidence "of conscious guilt." Flight of DeSilva's captain-agents confirmed the chief justice in his certainty of their guilty knowledge, for they were "the best witnesses that the owner could have had if the vessels were intended for lawful commerce.... From these circumstances," he concluded "that the owner, masters and factor were all *particips crimins.*"[124]

Williams's case against owners Allen and Henderson also seemed airtight. The *Catherine* had arrived in New York's harbor reeking of tell-tale attributes of a slaver.[125] The Baltimore grand jury indicted Allen under the 1818 act for fitting out "in the port of Baltimore...a certain vessel called 'The Catherine' with intent to employ the said vessel in procuring Negroes from the foreign country, to wit, from the continent of Africa to be transported to another place...to be sold as slaves."[126]

Resting his case on the *Emily and Caroline* and *United States v. Gooding,*[127] the prosecutor maintained that establishing guilt did not require "that her fitments should be complete for such a trade when leaving the United States, or that she should have on board any fitments peculiarly required for such trade." Furthermore, if Allen personally or through an agent knowingly permitted any "supposed Purchaser or Purchasers...at the Havana (if the Jury find there was a sale) to use the *Catherine's* original American register, for a slaving voyage, then he sent away the said Schooner with intent to employ her in the slave trade." Incriminating, too, was the absence of a bill of sale suggesting that Allen and Henderson held title to the vessel "up to the time of capture on the Coast of Africa."[128]

The defense characteristically denied everything. The schooner's master, James Swedge, could not recall the presence of a single fitting suitable for the slave trade when he departed from Baltimore for Cuba.[129] As for co-owners Allen and Henderson, they claimed utter innocence. Both intended merely to build and equip a vessel for sale at Havana and naturally "had no interest or no part in her subsequent proceedings."[130] As for the lack of a bill of sale, its substitute was a power of attorney delivered by Swedge to an American front man in

Havana, accompanied by discharge of the American crew in the presence of the American vice consul and surrender of the register to that official of dubious integrity. "The sale at Havana was an actual honest bona fide sale," the captain protested, its consummation to occur on the African coast by delivery of the vessel to its Hispanic crew-purchasers.[131] This duplicitous transformation of the *Catherine*'s nationality undid the government's case. The jury deadlocked in December 1839.[132] Retrial at the circuit court's April 1840 session concluded with the jury's cryptic report: "that the United States have failed to produce sufficient evidence to convict him as charged in the Indictment.... We therefore find the said Allen Not Guilty."[133]

The companion case against *Elvira*'s owner, Francis T. Montell, tried at the same 1840 circuit court term, went no better for the government. Defended by a litigation team also spearheaded by Johnson, Montell claimed to have merely exercised his right as an American citizen to sell the schooner at Havana to Spanish "purchasers," who unexpectedly turned out to be participants in the international slave trade. Again evidence of the "sale" to be consummated by delivery of the vessel at Galenas (Gallinas), a Gambian outpost, was sparse. Other facts emitted a distinctly incriminating tinge, including shuffling of crew-passenger nationalities, changing flags, and inexplicably dropping overboard the American register required by the 1792 registry return act to be delivered to a government official upon sale of an American vessel.[134] Such incriminating circumstances hardly fazed defense counsel Johnson. He argued the sale was bona fide and his client ignorant of the loss of the register. The petit jury agreed. After deliberating "a few minutes they returned a verdict of not guilty."[135]

Roundly defeated in his primary cases, the persevering Williams resorted to secondary attacks on Montell, Allen, and Henderson. None involved juries. All involved statutory interpretation for the judge. Success in the district court capped his suit against Montell for forfeiture of a $1,200 bond posted to secure return of the *Elvira*'s register. Classification of the recovered bond as a penalty or forfeiture determined whether involved custom collectors, naval officers, and surveyors received as a reward a moiety of the proceeds.[136] Appealed to the circuit court, the question impressed Taney as a novel one "of some difficulty," because, as he observed, "penalties and forfeitures imposed by statute are not usually provided for by bond and security given in advance." Further reflection, however, convinced him that the bond "is not a liquidated amount of damages due upon a contract, but a fixed and certain punishment for an offense." That the "security is taken before the offense is committed, in order to secure the payment of the fine if the law should be violated" did not diminish its status as a penalty.[137]

Williams pursued an identical harassing strategy against Allen and Henderson. Fourth Circuit Justice Taney readily sustained his motion to exclude the admission of the libel decision in the case of the *Catherine* handed down in the Southern District of New York.[138] Dismissal there of the government's libel by Judge Samuel R. Betts, characteristically casting benign glances upon slave traders, did not impress Taney as conclusive evidence of the schooner's nationality.[139] Far more convincing of "her American character" would have been a sentence of condemnation under the law proscribing American slave trading, he acidly observed. Nor did he read Betts's opinion as even relevant to the bond forfeiture question because civil judgments could not be applied to either criminal proceedings or suits for penalties.[140] His recently delivered opinion in the *Montell* case meant "that a suit upon a bond of this kind, though in form, a civil suit and sounding in contract, is yet, in substance and reality, a suit for a penalty inflicted for an offence against the law."[141]

Allen, Henderson, and Montell beat back the serious charges levied against them. They merely forfeited their registry bonds. But they lost intangible assets as well. Taney saw to it that they lost their reputations and that their fates would serve as a cautionary tale for the Baltimore community. Before him had paraded as witnesses the city's leading merchants, who heaped encomiums on Strom's "high character as a merchant and a man or probity," on Allen's "good character and high standing," and on Montell as "a high-minded honorable man [of] irreproachable character," utterly incapable of intentionally fitting out a slaver.[142] The evidence before the chief justice suggested venture capitalists whose characters differed markedly from those so generously ascribed to them. In affirming the district court's forfeiture decree against Strom, the circuit justice roundly denounced the Baltimore factor for conduct constituting nothing less than "a gross fraud on the American character" as well as a prevailing community-wide "feeling of connivance at a violation of the laws . . . so great. . . . [as to bring] disgrace upon the American flag and the character of the city."[143] That the criminal prosecution had failed at the hands of local jurors displeased Taney. He promptly availed himself of a pending Supreme Court case, *United States v. Morris*, to vindicate prosecutor Williams's reliance on the *Emily and Caroline* and *Gooding* precedents to establish criminal intent.[144]

Fidelity to Law

Perplexing questions of statutory interpretation confronted other judges in the mid-Atlantic South as they grappled with often skillfully argued slave trade cases.[145] However intricate the law, they followed Taney's lead and made good-faith efforts to fathom the meaning of statutes in accordance with the unmistakable intention of Congress to suppress the slave trade—at least they did until the late 1850s when intervening and overwhelming exogenous influences permeated the judicial process. Robert Budd Gilchrist of the District of South Carolina pondered implications of the anti–slave trade statutes and prior judicial interpretations of them when he considered the case of *United States v. Panther,* discussed above.[146] Proceedings involving the 407-ton, American-owned double decked bark seized while hovering off Kabinda late in 1845 raised significant questions about the meaning of language found in the several slave trade acts.[147] Whether in the words of the 1800 act the bark carried Africans or had ever carried them during its voyage such as to be "employed or made use of in the transportation or carry-ing of slaves from one foreign country to another" impressed him as immaterial.[148] Relying on Circuit Justice Joseph Story's decision in the *Brig Alexander* which had figured in the government's argument in the then-recent *Morris* case, Gilchrist warmly quoted the recently deceased New Englander, who concluded that Congress intended that "the employment in the business and for the purposes of the slave trade, and not merely the actual transportation of slaves, should be prohibited and punished."[149] The language of the 1819 act further supported what he regarded as a congressional purpose "to subject equally to forfeiture the vessel, which may have taken on board any Negro, etc., and the vessel, which may only be intended for that purpose."[150]

Gilchrist also turned a deaf ear to predictable contentions that every fitting and item of equipment found aboard the *Panther* had a plausible innocent purpose and that, even if any or all lacked such a purpose, the loading had occurred beyond the boundaries of the United States.[151] Gilchrist, as Taney had, relied on the *Emily and Caroline* and *United States v. Gooding* decisions.[152] Thus, he held that both statutes focused on "the intent with which the preparations are made; and the provisions or equipments which are suitable for lawful voyages, and therefore innocent in themselves, will nevertheless subject the vessel to forfeiture, if they are intended for the slave trade." That the 1800 act made no mention of equipment suggested merely that it was the vessel's "employment, and the ownership therein [by] citizens of the United States, or other persons residing within the same, which brings her within the purview of the statute."[153]

Language in the 1818 act might be read narrowly to require personal involvement by the owner, captain, or supercargo in fitting out or having control over a slaver. Section 3 of the act penalized "every person or persons so building, fitting out, equipping, loading, or otherwise preparing or sending away, or causing any of the acts aforesaid to be done, with intent to employ such ship or vessel" in the slave trade.[154] Ironically, Story in his 1827 *Gooding* opinion seemingly read the section 3 language to mean that the owner or master committed no crime if he "had fitted out the vessel, to be employed by some other person in the slave trade." Only if he "fitted her out with the intention of employing her himself in that trade" did he fall within the statutory proscription.[155] To make such a distinction respecting situations rife with deception would undermine the nation's proclaimed war on the slave trade.

Gilchrist parsed the *Gooding* opinion to explain Story's phraseology as pertinent to the special facts of that case.[156] Fortifying Gilchrist in his interpretation was an 1824 Supreme Court decision left undisturbed three years later by Story wherein Justice Bushrod Washington asserted that a plain reading of the same text made clear Congress' intention "to prevent citizens of, or residents within the United States, from affording any facilities to this trade, although they should have no interest or property in the slaves themselves, and although they *should not be immediately instrumental to the transportation of them from their native country.*"[157] A decree of forfeiture against the *Panther* followed as did its subsequent affirmance by the Sixth Circuit Court.[158]

The South Carolina jurist did not stand alone in faithfully seeking and fairly construing congressional intentions embodied in the text of successive anti–slave trade laws. Halyburton in the Eastern District of Virginia faced, in April 1860, a statutory conundrum similar to that which had confronted the by now-deceased Gilchrist nearly fifteen years earlier. The case of *United States v. Alice Rogers* differed materially from that of the *Panther.*[159] The former's facts were clear, so clear that the government had "proved beyond controversy that the master of the vessel took from Jamaica two free Negroes and *landed* them and *offered them for sale,* claiming them as his own property in the town of Hampton" in Virginia, where a reward-seeking water-borne posse seized the vessel.[160]

The applicable law, however, impressed President Tyler's appointee and kin of both Martha Washington and Jeffersonian apostle William Branch Giles as decidedly unclear, if not in conflict.[161] The 1807 and 1818 acts each punished different offenses and imposed different punishments. The latter apparently repealed the first six sections of the former, leaving intact only section seven.[162] That section made unlawful "any ship or vessel ... found ... or hovering on the coast ... having on board any Negro, mulatto, or a person of colour, for the purpose of selling them as slaves, or with intent to land the same."[163] Its violation exposed wrongdoers to forfeiture of the involved "ship or vessel, together with her tackle, apparel, and furniture, and the goods or effects found on board" as well as to a $10,000 maximum fine and a minimum imprisonment of two years ranging to a maximum of four.[164]

The government argued that actual landing only consummated a chain of actions criminalized by the 1807 act. Therefore, section 7 applied to James Brayley, master of the Canadian schooner, because, before the landing at Hampton, "the vessel was in a river or bay, or hovering on the coast of the United States with the Negroes on board."[165] Halyburton resisted this reasoning on both textual and practical grounds.

The judge thought that the 1818 act controlled the case because section 6 clearly prohibited holding, selling, or otherwise disposing of any "person of colour... brought in, as a slave." Its punishment specified a fine ranging from $1,000 to $10,000 and a jail term of from three to seven years.[166] Under it, the judge imposed on Brayley the harsher statutory minimum punishment authorized by the 1818 act for his minor part in the vast Atlantic slave trade.[167]

Forfeiture also proved to be a vexing problem. Section 4 of the 1818 act made it a crime, with forfeiture of vessel, equipment, and cargo stipulated, to take on board in any foreign country "any person of colour for the purpose of selling such as a slave."[168] But evidence relating to the apparently voluntary boarding of the youths, possibly as crew members, suggested the sale strategy as a late developing idea on Brayley's part.[169] Therefore, only the more general language of section 1 seemed to apply. Its language made unlawful the bringing in from any foreign country of any person of color with intent to sell as a slave. Forfeiture of the offending vessel, but not of its equipment or cargo, befell violators.[170]

Sorting through the language of the two provisions, Halyburton deemed it "wholly inadmissible" for there to exist side by side two conflicting laws for the punishment of the *same* offense and decreed condemnation under section 1, exclusive of the schooner's paraphernalia and cargo.[171] He thereby gave public notice of the perils of even minor participation in the international slave trade and of the financial rewards awaiting those who contributed to the apprehension of slave traders.

Changed Directions

While Halyburton in Virginia labored as late as mid-1860 to apply anti–slave trade laws faithfully, his counterpart in the South Carolina district took a different tack. Gilchrist's death in 1856 signaled a fundamental change in the reception accorded those laws after President Franklin Pierce appointed passionate states' righter Andrew Gordon Magrath to fill the vacancy.[172] Magrath ascended the bench in a political context that had substantially changed in the decade since Gilchrist handed down his *Panther* decision. The heated Kansas question, mob-actuated resistance to enforcement of the Fugitive Slave Act, the Buchanan administration's resolve to enforce the slave trade ban as a demonstration of its sectional evenhandedness, publication of North Carolinian Hinton Rowan Helper's antislavery tract on *The Impending Crisis of the South: How to Meet It,* and John Brown's Harper's Ferry raid and his subsequent execution-martyrdom roiled the political atmosphere riven by sectional conflict.[173] Meanwhile, South Carolina became the center of agitation for reopening the slave trade, a step perceived as bolstering southern political power by virtue of the Constitution's "three-fifth's" proviso, ameliorating labor shortages linked to escalating cotton prices, and attesting to the moral rightness of the institution of slavery.[174] Gilchrist's successor carried that cause into the federal courtroom and set his face implacably against the slave trade laws by infusing with politics his interpretation of them and of the evidence adduced by the government's enforcement effort.

Magrath's approach became apparent after a naval prize crew from the sloop *Marion* brought the ketch *Brothers* into Charleston in November 1858. The Charleston-owned *Brothers* was a typical unladen slaver case. A three-hour chase off Mayumba, north of the Congo River, ended with a shot across the ketch's bow from the African Squadron's vessel and subsequent discovery of virtually all the attributes of a slaver: Spanish crew paid high wages, rum, $8,416 in cash, unmanifested lumber, two tons of rice, 100 barrels of bread, preserved fish, dried beef, water casks, iron cooking boiler, 500 wooden spoons, five cases of drugs, and five kegs of vinegar.[175] A clearer case of fitting out, equipping, and causing to sail in pursuance of the unlawful trade could hardly be imagined, but not to editor Robert Barnwell Rhett. His incendiary Charleston *Mercury* decried "the brilliant and peculiarly American crusade of playing police, and interfering against Americans engaged in trade between foreign countries."[176] Magrath echoed the *Mercury.* He could not "discover what there is in this cargo which of itself leads to a conclusion of a criminal purpose or excludes the fact of such articles having been intended for a lawful purpose."[177] The pieces of the evidentiary mosaic offered by the government simply did not create an ultimately incriminating pattern. Rather each piece, viewed in light of its most lawful uses, remained discreet and disconnected from every other, forming no guilty configuration discernible to the naked eye. Acquittals and dismissals of libels followed in the train of Magrath's crabbed treatment of the facts.[178]

Law as well as facts received singular treatment at the hands of Magrath, whose handiwork in the case of the *Brothers* had been preceded by that in the sensational politicized *Echo* case and followed by that in the even more sensational case of the *Wanderer*.[179] Capture of the Baltimore-built brig *Echo*, ex-*Putnam, New Orleans,* by the Navy brig *Dolphin* near Key Verde, off the eastern tip of Cuba, seemingly presented the clearest of cases. Apprehension of the 188-ton slaver with its name painted over occurred as it signaled to land 320 Africans, survivors, after the forty-four day voyage, of 455 originally boarded at Kabinda.[180] Those still living ranged in age from five to twenty-five years; they emerged emaciated, haggard, and "afflicted with diseases of the eye and the skin, and dysentery" from shipboard conditions described by naval officers as "filthy to the last degree."[181]

The subsequent incarceration of 306 survivors, first in Castle Pinckney and then in Fort Sumter, agitated Charlestonians and fueled their anxieties over domestic security.[182] No sooner had Magrath disposed of the *Echo* case than he became embroiled in criminal proceedings against William C. Corrie, master of the celebrated slaver *Wanderer*.[183] Corrie and the *Wanderer* achieved lasting fame by completing the only known successful large-scale slaving expedition to the United States between 1820 and the Civil War. The 235-ton yacht, built in 1857 for a member of the New York Yacht Club, had a length and beam exceeding that of the *Echo*, while its sailing speed of twenty knots rivaled that of the great clipper ships. Amid glittering events staged by Charleston society in a city seething over sectional politics on the eve of secession, Corrie surreptitiously loaded the *Wanderer* with provisions unusual for a mere pleasure yacht and eventually cleared for St. Helena, 1,200 miles west of Africa. Sighted off the Congo River by vessels of the British and American African Squadrons, the *Wanderer* speedily vanished. Aboard were some 490 Africans, of which an estimated 409 survivors were disgorged in late November at Georgia's isolated Dubignon-owned Jekyll Island.[184]

Constitutional Attack: The *Echo*

The *Echo* trials stood as the high-water mark of constitutionally based slave trade litigation in districts from Maryland to South Carolina during the quarter century before the Civil War. In the dock in federal courts at Charleston and Columbia were sixteen crewmen of the *Echo* charged with the capital crime of piracy under the 1820 act.[185] Their fates seemed sealed; Navy Lieutenant John N. Maffit had caught them "red-handed" aboard the laden slaver.[186] Among the skilled attorneys defending the English- and Spanish-speaking mariners was the South's foremost advocate for reopening the slave trade, Leonidas W. Spratt, who assailed the constitutionality of the 1820 act.[187] The prosecutorial efforts of United States attorney James Conner, aided by South Carolina attorney general Isaac W. Hayne, initially foundered when in November 1858 the Columbia grand jury balked at handing down an indictment. By the following April, word that the case afforded a prime opportunity to test the constitutionality of the prohibitory acts encouraged the Charleston grand jury to indict the imprisoned mariners.[188]

The 1820 act symbolized for South Carolinians what one *Echo* defender called "our vassalage and subordination to that spirit of fanaticism, which now governs the North—and throughout the North, the country."[189] Was it not anomalous that the recently decided *Dred Scott* decision barred congressional inference with slavery in the territories, notwithstanding broad constitutional power over them while "advocates were found who contended for a power in Congress to interfere with, control, regulate and destroy slavery on the high seas." How could it be that congressional omnipotence "extended as far as a . . . Federal ship could sail?"

A question of law lay before the court, but "political considerations," even the "social existence of the South," permeated the courtroom arguments.[190] Politics favored strict construction of the constitutional text. Nowhere within the four corners of the Constitution could attorneys for the *Echo*'s crew find once-apparent express or implied powers for suppressing the slave trade. The Constitution enumerated a congressional power to define and punish piracies, but they contended that *defining* piracy did not mean the same thing as *declaring* it.[191] The former required establishing as a crime that which already existed, to wit robbery on land which act became piracy on the sea. Resort to original-ism suggested that in 1789 neither municipal law nor the law of nations defined slave trading as piracy.[192] Defender Richard DeTreville even challenged the affirmative implications of Article I, section 9, which Chief Justice Marshall had articulated in his *Gibbons* opinion.[193] The expiration in 1808 of the protective provision did not release power to prohibit the slave trade based on the commerce clause, which did not avail anyway because it permitted only "regulation," not prohibition, of commerce "*with,* not *between,* foreign nations."[194] Similarly, there existed no resultant national power over "ships and the persons sailing in them" that accorded the United States extraterritorial jurisdiction.[195]

Special Counsel Hayne, voicing assurances that he "had been brought up in the straightest sect of the Pharisees," maintained that a proper interpretation of the Constitution required consideration of "the whole Constitution, and . . . the structure of our system of Govern-ment."[196] The powers enumerated in Article I provided a starting point. Among them was the commerce and the "necessary and proper" clause.[197] He asked, "Where . . . would be the sanction to the regula-tions of commerce, without the right to prescribe a rule of conduct to our ships and those sailing in them . . . and to our citizens engaged in commerce on the high seas, under a penalty for disobedience of law." Defining and punishing crimes committed on the high seas aboard American vessels, whether or not those vessels carried on commerce "with" or "between" the United States and foreign nations, fell within the powers granted Congress. As for the defendant's construction of the piracy clause, Hayne's search of word meanings, of original intent at the Founding and of subsequent legislative practice all failed to sup-port a power-draining construction of the word *define.* The slave-trade provision manifestly demonstrated, he insisted, "that, after 1808, it was intended that Congress should have the right of prohibition."[198]

Sixth Circuit Justice James M. Wayne of Georgia, presiding over the *Echo* trials, largely ignored the courtroom debate over the scope of constitutional powers vested in Congress except to quash DeTreville's bold assertion that it lay within the jury's power "to judge as well of the law as of the fact; ... to [construe] the Constitution ... and decide whether Congress has, or has not assumed to itself powers which are not in it."[199] Constitutional interpretation, Wayne sternly responded, "is confided to the judiciary." To accept De Treville's suggested democratization of constitutional law meant erosion of decisional authority and spawning of disharmonious national law. Worse still, jury nullification of congressional legislation portended dire political consequences. Popular judicial activism could jeopardize hard-won constitutional gains for the South secured by the Supreme Court under Chief Justice Taney's leadership, a point Wayne had made in his separate 1849 *Passenger Cases* opinion.[200] Not until he charged the grand jury assembled at Savannah in the Southern District of Georgia in November 1859 to consider the fate of some of the *Wanderer*'s crew did Wayne fully address the constitutional issues raised the previous April in the *Echo* trials. He then denounced any restrictive construction of congressional power to define piracy as it had been defined "from remote antiquity." The commerce clause, in his view, clothed Congress with "plenary and conclusive" power to regulate the slave trade while the piracy provision authorized it to permit oceanic policing "without limitation." Laws suppressing the trade were therefore unquestionably "necessary and proper." Supportive judicial precedents abounded, nor had any "question ... been decided in the Circuit or in the Supreme Court, which in any manner impugns their validity or constitutional enactments."[201] Magrath, however, took a very different view.

Mangling Statutory Text: The *Wanderer*

The district judge's nullificationist tendencies found an outlet in the case of the *Wanderer*. The main proceedings occurred in the Georgia district, where the government lost.[202] However, one key participant, Captain William C. Corrie, was missing. He soon materialized in his hometown of Charleston, where he found refuge in Magrath's court. Notwithstanding government efforts to remove Corrie from Charleston to Savannah, Magrath saw to it that they failed.[203] When a grand jury charge by Wayne resulted in "no true bill" and exposed Corrie to arrest and removal to Georgia to face a piracy charge under the 1820 act, the circuit justice and district judge initially divided on the question of the jury's reconsideration of its decision. Wayne, however, backed down. As Magrath hoped or perhaps expected, "the Grand Jury then came into court with a presentment, charging Wm. C. Corrie with a violation of the [1820 act], and asking the Court to make the necessary orders for his prosecution."[204] Brought within the protective umbrella of the South Carolina court, the *Wanderer's* master basked in freedom while on bail, granted by Magrath, pending resolution of the capital charge against him.[205]

The proceedings against Corrie never rested on the law's substance. The district judge availed himself of the opportunity thus presented to fuse law and emotive politics and construe the act of 1820 to conform to local public opinion. Without the restraining influence of the absent Justice Wayne at the April 1860 term of the circuit court at Charleston, Magrath freely ventilated his views on policy. The issue before him involved only a procedural question—whether to accept U.S. Attorney Conner's motion to discontinue (*nolle prosequi*) the case against Corrie in order that the defendant might be prosecuted in the Southern District of Georgia.[206] Having noisily retained jurisdiction, Magrath proceeded to gut the act. "It has been said, that by this Act of Congress, the slave trade has been declared piracy," the district judge intoned. As had counsel for the *Echo* crewmen, he could uncover no such purpose in either the text or in its legislative history. Nothing in the text nor in its legislative or judicial antecedents permitted an inference "that the slave trade is piracy because seizing and decoying on a foreign shore a Negro or mulatto, with intent to make him a slave, is so declared." All Congress sought by enacting the 1820 law, in Magrath's view, was to suppress conventional acts of piracy associated with the then-extant pan-American privateering.

The conclusion was inescapable: Congress had yet to make "the slave trade a piracy."[207] Admittedly the Constitution endowed Congress with sufficient power to define the crime of piracy to encompass international slave trading. However, the current moment was not 1789 nor even 1820. Congressional power to regulate or prohibit the slave trade had been "granted at a time and under circumstances which are so wholly different from the time in which we live and the circumstances which surround us," he observed. New conditions imperatively demanded a changed Constitution to overcome the consequences of an original improvident grant of unrestricted national power over the trade. That was an arduous undertaking, "one for the States by whom the grant of power was made."[208] No matter what Congress did, with or without a constitutional amendment, Magrath waxed confident that the requisite intent to support the charge of piracy involved proof of an "intent to make such Negro or mulatto a slave," an argument previously made by Spratt in the *Echo* trials. To "make a slave," required proof that the subject's antecedent condition had not been one of servitude; otherwise no intent existed "to make a slave or rob him of his right to freedom."[209] To this argument, Unionist Wayne would accord no credence. "Whether they were slaves or not in Africa... has nothing to do with the law," he asserted. "They may have been free there; not very probable. They may have been slaves. It is a matter of no consequence what their antecedent condition may have been."[210]

Fusing Law and Politics

The South Carolinian's performances in the celebrated *Echo* and *Corrie* proceedings proved to be omens. On trial in Magrath's court was the very supremacy of national law. What was that law, *Echo* defense counsel DeTreville asked jurors? Was it not merely "the law of that majority whose country lies to the East and North of Mason and Dixon's line— a majority eager to promote their [*sic*] own prosperity, and not less eager to destroy yours [and of]... a Government as foreign to you as is the Government of France on all matters of internal polity, but more especially on the subject of slavery."[211] In trials suffused with emotionalism and before a judge steeped in states' rights ideology, prosecutor Conner labored at an impossible task—to separate law and politics. He fruitlessly urged that, "Public opinion is to be respected in its proper sphere, but its voice must be silent in a court house, and fearful terrible indeed, will be the day whenever the hall of justice shall be converted into a political arena."[212] Wayne, too, urged the *Echo* jurymen to enforce the slave trade law, not to nullify it. "It was said that this law was an insult to the freemen of a slave community," that it jeopardized the institution of slavery. To the contrary, he asserted that national law, including the oft-denigrated fugitive slave law, acknowledged the constitutionality of holding slaves as property.[213]

When Connor and Wayne strove to curb emotion with reason, politics with law, and nullification with appeals to national supremacy founded on a pro-slavery Constitution, time was running out. "Where," DeTreville queried, will South Carolina find relief "from the reckless legislation of the Black Republican majority, into whose hands the Federal Government will before long fall?"[214] The jurors in the *Echo* trials resoundingly answered, bringing in verdicts of acquittal within ninety minutes, notwithstanding that the laden slaver had been apprehended "red-handed." That the government successfully condemned the vessel and received a paltry $1,679.10 for it at a court-ordered sale provided small consolation.[215] Federal justice dispensed by a faithless judge and feckless jurors had seemingly been harnessed to sectional politics. The outcome predictably ignited the wrath of anti-slavery advocates and their political vehicle, the rising Republican party, dashed the hope of Buchanan's attorney general, Jeremiah Sullivan Black, for judicial adherence to the "principles of obedience, loyalty and good order, in which the whole nation is interested," and unraveled the slave trade laws in the District of South Carolina, an event that augured ill for national supremacy in a union of putatively united states.[216]

Conclusion

Writing at the end of the nineteenth century, eminent black intellectual and civil rights leader W. E .B. DuBois lamented the failure to suppress the international slave trade. "On the whole," he thought it "plain that, although in the period from 1807 to 1820 Congress laid down broad lines of legislation sufficient, save in some details, to suppress the African slave trade to America, yet the execution of these laws was criminally lax."[217] Some eighty years later, historian Warren S. Howard echoed DuBois in decrying the failure of the war on the unlawful trade. His masterful study of the subject was nothing less than "a story of a crime that was *not* punished."[218] Whether responsibility for results falling short of victory in the nation's earliest international war on crime lies with the police effort, the prosecution, or the judiciary will always be a matter of debate.[219] Reliable and complete empirical evidence on the maritime crime is as elusive as the enterprise itself. Nevertheless, the enforcement of laws aimed at suppressing the Atlantic trade in humans is a matter of official record, albeit some of it unpublished. The scant number of captured suspect vessels over a period of more than sixty-five years during the age of sail in transition to that of steam suggests the simple difficulty of apprehending with limited maritime police resources a variety of disguised slavers captained by clever and experienced rogues. The enforcement shortcomings thus manifested an apprehension problem of significant dimensions, not a judicial failing ascribable to United States courts.

The outcomes of admiralty and criminal proceedings held in federal courts involving slavers, vessel owners, officers, and crew members hardly supports a view of the federal judges in the mid-Atlantic South as nullifiers of law. To be sure, initial judicial contact with the prohibitory statutes vesting the national government with vast plenary authority over one subject of commercial life gave pause to some judges and juries. Shortcomings in legislative craftsmanship and imprecision in the language of the government's charges bedeviled federal courts during the chief justiceship of John Marshall. Even in the face of challenges posed by statutory language combined with vexing evidentiary problems associated with the deceptive practices endemic to the trade, and confronted by arguments advanced on behalf of defendants by some of the nation's leading courtroom litigators of the day, federal judges in states of the modern Fourth Circuit honored their oaths of office almost until secession swept them away. They were men who deeply believed in southern political principles. Yet day in and day out, they, if not the juries whom they charged, separated law from politics and interpreted the statutes enacted by Congress to combat the nefarious maritime trade in a manner that resulted in the laws' enforcement. Among them was *Dred Scott* author Roger B. Taney, whose mobilization of Baltimore public opinion against the building of vessels for the slave trade may, in Howard's view, have been the only real victory achieved in a war that began in 1794.[220]

Georgia native and Supreme Court justice James M. Wayne and Judge Halyburton in Virginia's Eastern District who, like Magrath, would soon resign his office to become judge of the Confederate District Court, remained faithful to their judicial oaths even as the national fabric frayed in 1860.[221] Only in seething South Carolina late in the antebellum period did national law succumb to sectional politics. There, Andrew Gordon Magrath labored to delegitimize that law at the dawning of a new and fateful day in national life. In defiance of constitutional commands and of positive law, and in defense of the institution of slavery, Magrath sacrificed on the altar of state sovereignty the nation's commitment to an international war against oceanic traffic in humans. His exceptional performance suggests the availability of a politicized judicial path that other federal judges of the mid-Atlantic South might have taken, but one which they eschewed.

Acknowledgments

This revision of a paper presented at the Twenty-first Annual Meeting of the North American Society for Oceanic History, Newport, Rhode Island, on 19 April 1997, derives from my work on the development of the United States courts of the Fourth Circuit sponsored by the U.S. Court of Appeals for the Fourth Circuit, Richmond, Virginia. I am deeply indebted to Mrs. Doris C. Cross for production of this paper.

Notes

1. G. Edward White, *The Marshall Court and Cultural Change, 1815–1835*, vols. 3 and 4 of *Oliver Wendell Holmes Devise History of the Supreme Court*, ed. Paul A. Freund and Stanley N. Katz (New York: Macmillan, 1988), 703 [2 vols. in one with continuous pagination].

2. U.S. Constitution, art. 4, sec. 2, cl. 3 (fugitive slaves); art. 1, sec. 2, cl. 3 (three fifths ratio); art. 1, sec. 9, cl. 1 (importation to 1808); see also William M. Wiecek, *The Sources of Antislavery Constitutionalism in America, 1760–1848*, (Ithaca, N.Y.: Cornell University Press, 1977), 62–63.

3. Charlene Bangs Bickford, Kenneth R. Bowling, and William Charles DiGiacomantonio, eds., *Documentary History of the First Federal Congress of the United States of America*, vol. 12, *Debates in the House of Representatives: Second Session, January–March 1790* (Baltimore, Md.: Johns Hopkins University Press, 1994), 303.

4. Ibid., 310.

5. James Oakes, "'The Compromising Expedient': Justifying a Proslavery Constitution," *Cardozo Law Review* 17 (May 1996): 2023–24, 2027–31. See also Donald L. Robinson, *Slavery in the Structure of American Politics, 1765–1820* (1971; reprint, New York: Norton, 1979), 297, 299.

6. William E. B. DuBois, *The Suppression of the African Slave Trade to the United States of America, 1638–1870*, (1896; reprint, New York: Social Science Press, 1954), 60.

7. Oakes, "Compromising Expedient," 2023, quoting "George Mason and James Madison debate the Slave-Trade Clause (17 June 1788)." See also U.S. Constitution, art. 5, prohibiting amendments prior to 1808 of art. 1, sec. 9, cl. 1 (importation of slaves) and art. 1, sec. 9, cl. 4 (direct taxation apportioned according to state populations); Gary M. Anderson, Charles K. Rowley, and Robert D. Tollison, "Rent Seeking and the Restriction of Human Exchange," *Journal of Legal Studies* 17 (1988): 85–92.

8. Charlene Bangs Bickford and Helen E. Veit, eds., *Documentary History of the First Federal Congress of the United States of America*, vol. 6, *Legislative Histories: Mitigation of Fines Bill [H.R.38] through Resolution on Unclaimed Western Lands*, (Baltimore, Md.: Johns Hopkins University Press, 1986), 1900, referring to Slave Trade Bill (May 18, 1789, 1st Cong., 1st sess. H.R. 30); see also Bickford, et al., *Documentary History of the First Federal Congress*, vol. 12, 282, 816; Robinson, *Slavery in the Structure of American Politics*, 302–10.

9. U.S. Constitution, art. 1, sec. 9, cl. 1.

10. Bickford, et al., *Documentary History of the First Federal Congress*, vol. 12, 341, referring to "Report of the Committee of the Whole House" (March 23, 1790).

11. Charlene Bangs Bickford, Kenneth R. Bowling, and Helen E. Veit, eds., *Documentary History of the First Federal Congress of the United States of America*, vol. 10, *Debates in the House of Representatives, First Session: April–May 1789* (Baltimore, Md.: Johns Hopkins University Press, 1992), 636. On the range of potential interpretations of U.S. Constitution, art. 1, sec. 9, cl. 1, see Walter Berns, "The Constitution and the Migration of Slaves," *Yale Law Journal* 78 (1968): 198.

12. Robinson, *Slavery in the Structure of American Politics*, 323; Bickford, et al., *Documentary History of the First Federal Congress*, vol. 12, 304–5, 312, 792.

13. Bickford, et al., *Documentary History of the First Federal Congress*, vol. 12, 821–22.

14. *Annals of Congress*, 9th Cong., 2d sess., 1806–7, pt. 16: 271.

15. Ibid., 226. See *Gibbons v. Ogden*, 22 U.S. (9 Wheaton), 1, 191, 206–7 (1824).

16. Philip D. Curtin, *The Atlantic Slave Trade: A Census* (Madison: University of Wisconsin Press, 1969), 250 (estimating diversion by international enforcement efforts of only 8 percent of total imports of Africans to the Americas from 1811 to 1870).

17. See Dwight F. Henderson, *Congress, Courts, and Criminals: The Development of Federal Criminal Law, 1801–1829* (Westport, Conn.: Greenwood Press, 1985), 3–18.

18. "Number and Composition of Circuits," *U.S. Code*, Title 28, sec. 41, (1994).

19. Act of Sept. 24, 1789, ch. 20, secs. 2, 4, *The Public Statutes at Large of the United States of America*, 8 vols. (Boston, Ma., 1845–67) (hereafter, *Stats. at Large*), 1 (1845): 73–74.

20. Act of Apr. 29, 1802, ch. 31, sec. 4, *Stats. at Large* 2 (1845): 156.

21. Act of Aug. 16, 1842, ch. 180, sec. 1, *Stats. at Large* 5 (1846): 507.

22. See Russell A. Wheeler and Cynthia Harrison, *Creating the Federal Judicial System*, 2d ed. (Washington, D.C.: Federal Judicial Center, 1994), 4.

23. Ibid., 7–8; "Federal Judges Arranged Chronologically under Their Respective Circuits and Districts," 1 F. Cas. xiii, xiv–xv (1898).

24. *The Antelope*, 23 U.S. (10 Wheaton), 66 (1825); *The Amistad*, 40 U.S. (15 Peters), 518 (1841).

25. Act of Mar. 22, 1794, ch. 11, *Stats. at Large* 1 (1845): 347 (emphasis added).

26. Ibid., 348–49.

27. Act of May 10, 1800, ch. 51, secs. 1, 2, 4, *Stats. at Large* 2 (1845): 70–71.

28. Admiralty Final Record Books and Minutes for the District of South Carolina, 1790–1857, Records of the District Courts of the United States, RG 21, National Archives and Records Service, Washington, D.C., in microfilm (M1182) rolls 1, 2.; U.S. Department of Commerce and Labor, Bureau of the Census, *Heads of Families at the First Census of the United States Taken in the Year 1790: South Carolina* (Washington, D.C.: GPO, 1908), 8. Bee served from June 14, 1790 to February 18, 1812, "Federal Judges," xxvii.

29. Unreported case, *Edward Boss of the Schooner Experiment v. Sloop Betsy* (D.S.C. Sept. 29, 1800), Admiralty Final Records (M1182), roll 2.

30. Unreported case, *United States v. Brig Harriet* (D.S.C. June 10–12, 1799); ibid., roll 1.

31. *Leonard v. Caskin*, 15 F. Cas. 337 (D.S.C. 1799) (No. 8,257).

32. Winchester served from October 31, 1799 to April 5, 1806, in "Federal Judges," xxi.

33. *United States v. Vickery,* 28 F. Cas. 374 (C.C.D.Md. 1803) (No. 16,619).

34. Act of Mar. 2, 1807, ch. 22, sec. 1, *Stats. at Large* 2 (1845): 426; Robinson, *Slavery in the Structure of American Politics,* 318–19.

35. Act of Mar. 2, 1807, ch. 22, secs. 1–5, 7, *Stats. at Large* 2 (1845): 426.

36. *Annals of Congress,* 10th Cong., 1st sess., 1807, pt. 17: 1243.

37. *United States v. The Kitty,* 26 F. Cas. 791, 792 (D.S.C. 1808) (No. 15, 537). Ironically, Bee imposed costs on claimants because the apprehending naval officer "did no more than obey a positive law."

38. *Annals of Congress,* 9th Cong., 2d sess., 1806–7, pt. 16: 167–87, 200–4, 225–26. See also Robinson, *Slavery in the Structure of American Politics,* 324–36.

39. Unreported case, *United States v. Schooner Louisa* (E.D.Va. Nov. 15, 1819), Minute Books, 1819–1850, in Admiralty Case Files of the U.S. District Court for the Eastern District of Virginia 1801–1861, Records of the District Courts of the United States, RG 21, National Archives and Records Service, Washington, D.C., in microfilm (M1300) roll 1.

40. See *The Brig Caroline,* 5 F. Cas. 90 (C.C.D.Va. 1819) (No. 2,418). This opinion was incorrectly attributed by John C. Brockenbrough, compiler of Marshall's circuit court opinions, to the C.C.D.Va. and dated 1819 rather than to the Supreme Court of the United States and dated March 16, 1813. The error has been corrected in Charles H. Hobson, ed., *The Papers of John Marshall,* vol. 8, *Correspondence, Papers, and Selected Judicial Opinions: March 1814–December 1819* (Chapel Hill: University of North Carolina Press, 1995), 404.

41. Tucker served from January 19, 1813 to April 8, 1825, in "Federal Judges," xxvii; Act of Feb. 4, 1819, ch. 12, *Stats. at Large* 3 (1846): 478 (dividing Virginia into an Eastern and Western District).

42. Unreported case, *United States v. Schooner Louisa,* in Admiralty Case Files, in microfilm roll 7, Interrogatories before District Judge St. George Tucker; Deposition of the Claimant Joseph John King [owner] to the Schooner *Louisa* (Aug. 14, 1817), in ibid.

43. Bill of Sale, 1 July 1817, ibid.

44. Acts of Mar. 2, 1807, ch. 22, secs. 4, 5, *Stats. at Large* 2 (1845): 426, 427.

45. Act of Mar. 22, 1794, ch. 11, sec. 1, *Stats. at Large* 1 (1845): 347, 347–48.

46. Act of Mar. 2, 1807, ch. 22, sec. 2, *Stats. at Large* 2 (1845): 426.

47. *The Brig Caroline v. United States,* 11 U.S. (7 Cranch), 496–97 (1813).

48. John T. Noonan Jr., *The Antelope: The Ordeal of The Recaptured Africans in the Administrations of James Monroe and John Quincy Adams* (Berkeley: University of California Press, 1977), 62; White, Marshall Court, 689.

49. *The Brig Caroline,* 11 U.S. (7 Cranch), 498–99.

50. Ibid., 499–500.

51. *The Brig Caroline,* 5 F. Cas. 90; White, *Marshall Court,* 689–90; John Marshall to R. R. Gurley, December 14, 1831, ibid., 690.

52. *The Brig Caroline,* 5 F. Cas. p. 91; Donald M. Roper, "In Quest of Judicial Objectivity: The Marshall Court and the Legitimization of Slavery," *Stanford Law Review* 21 (1969): 532, 536–39.

53. *The Brig Caroline,* 5 F. Cas., 90, 92.

54. Ibid. See also Jordan M. Smith, "The Federal Courts and the Black Man in America 1800–1883, A Study of Judicial Policy Making" (Ph.D. diss., University of North Carolina at Chapel Hill, 1977), 91-94.

55. See *The Emily and The Caroline v. United States,* 22 U.S. (9 Wheaton), 381, 386–90 (1824).

56. *The Brig Caroline,* 11 U.S. (7 Cranch), 500.

57. *The Emily and The Caroline,* 385–88.

58. Unpublished opinion, *Ship Emily v. the United States and Brig Caroline v. The United States,* (C.C.D.S.C., Mar. 6, 1821, entered Dec. 8, 1821), Minutes, Circuit and District Courts, District of South Carolina, 1789-1849 and Index to Judgments, Circuit and District Courts, 1792-1874, Records of the District Courts of the United States, RG 21, National Archives and Records Service, Washington, D.C., in microfilm (M1181) roll 2.

59. Ibid. (presumably referring to a "camboose" or galley aboard a slaver).

60. Ibid.

61. *The Emily and The Caroline,* 381, 389 (per Smith Thompson, J.).

62. *United States v. Gooding,* 25 U.S. (12 Wheaton), 459 (1827).

63. Ibid., 467. Glenn served from August 31, 1824 to March 28, 1836, in "Federal Judges," xxii.

64. *Gooding,* 465–66.

65. Charles Francis Adams, ed., *Memoirs of John Quincy Adams, Comprising Portions of his Diary from 1795 to 1848,* vol. 7 (Philadelphia: J. B. Lippincott & Co., 1875): 305.

66. Henderson, *Congress, Courts, and Criminals,* 198.

67. *Gooding,* 473.

68. See Henderson, *Congress, Courts, and Criminals,* 199.

69. See Robinson, *Slavery in the Structure of American Politics,* 407–23.

70. Ch. 91, secs. 3 and 4, 6, 7 and 8, *Stats. at Large* 3 (1846): 450–52.

71. Act of Mar. 3, 1819, ch. 101, sec. 1, *Stats. at Large* 3 (1846): 532.

72. Homer S. Cummings and Carl McFarland, *Federal Justice: Chapters in the History of Justice and the Federal Executive* (New York: Macmillan, 1937), 165. See *The Josefa Segunda*, 23 U.S. (10 Wheaton), 312 (1825).

73. Act of Mar. 3, 1819, ch. 101, secs. 1, 2, *Stats. at Large* 3 (1846): 532–33.

74. U.S. Congress, House, *Message of the President of the United States of America [Interpretation of the Slave Trade Act of 1819]*, 16th Cong., 1st sess., Exec. Doc. No. 11 (1819). See Henderson, *Congress, Courts, and Criminals*, 186; DuBois, *Suppression of the African Slave Trade*, 251.

75. *Annals of Congress*, 16th Cong., 1st sess., 1820, pt. 36: 2210.

76. Ibid., 2210–11; Act of May 15, 1820, ch. 113, secs. 3, 4, *Stats. at Large* 5 (1846): 600–1.

77. *Annals of Congress*, 9th Cong., 2d sess., 1806–7, pt. 16: 483–84 (reporting defeat of a capital punishment sanction to be included in what became the Act of March 2, 1807, ch. 22, *Stats. at Large* 2 [1845]: 426); see also *Annals of Congress*, 15th Cong., 2d sess., 1819, pt. 33: 280 (reporting the death in the Senate of a similar amendment); Smith, "the Federal Courts and the Black Man," 65.

78. DuBois, *Suppression of the African Slave Trade*, 158.

79. Warren S. Howard, *American Slavers and the Federal Law: 1837–1862* (Berkeley: University of California Press, 1963), vii.

80. John R. Spears, *The American Slave-Trade: An Account of Its Origin, Growth and Suppression* (1900; reprint, Williamstown, Mass.: Corner House Publishers, 1970), 176; Howard, *American Slavers*, 30–31.

81. W. E. B. DuBois, "The Enforcement of the Slave-Trade Laws," in *Articles on American Slavery*, vol. 2, *Slave Trade and Migration: Domestic and Foreign*, ed. Paul Finkelman (New York: Garland Publishers, 1989), 109, 171.

82. Act of Mar. 3, 1819, ch. 101, sec. 1, *Stats. at Large* 2 (1845): 532; see Spears, *American Slave Trade*, 149–50; DuBois, *Suppression of the African Slave Trade*, 158.

83. Act of May 15, 1820, ch. 113, secs. 4, 5, *Stats. at Large* 3 (1846): 600, 601; see the *Baltimore Sun*, April 30, 1840, 1.

84. "A Treaty to Settle and Define the Boundaries between the Territories of the United States and the Possessions of Her Britannic Majesty in North America," 9 August 1842, art. 8, *Stats. at Large* 8 (1846): 572, 576; see Howard, *American Slavers*, 40.

85. Howard, *American Slavers*, 6, 40–43, 68.

86. Ibid., 42.

87. Ibid., 59.

88. Ibid., 127–29, 137–38, 261; see also U.S. Congress, House, *African Slave Trade: Message of the President of the United States,* 36th Cong., 2d sess., Exec. Doc. No. 7 (1860), 459.

89. Unreported case, *United States v. the Brig Storm King* (E.D.Va. Nov. 17, 1860), Admiralty Case Files, in microfilm (M1300) roll 18, Deposition of Aaron K. Hughes, Aug. —, 1860.

90. Ibid.; Howard, *American Slavers,* App. A, p. 221. Halyburton served from June 15, 1844, to April 17, 1861, in "Federal Judges," xxvii.

91. Henderson, *Congress, Courts, and Criminals,* 111–59; Jerome R. Garitee, *The Republic's Private Navy: The American Privateering Business as Practiced by Baltimore during the War of 1812* (Middletown, Conn.: Wesleyan University Press, 1977), 228.

92. Howard, *American Slavers,* 42.

93. Abel P. Upshur to Matthew C. Perry, March 30, 1843, in U.S. Congress, House, *Instructions to the African Squadron: Message from the President of the United States,* 35th Cong., 2d sess., Exec. Doc. No. 104 (1859), 5.

94. Ibid.; see Andrew H. Foote, *Africa and the American Flag* (New York: D. Appleton Co., 1854), 217.

95. Unreported case, *United States v. the Brig Triton of New Orleans* (E.D.Va. Oct. 10, 1860), Admiralty Case Files, in microfilm (M1300) roll 18.

96. Unreported case, *United States v. the Barque Julia Dean* (E.D.Va. Jul. 11, 1859), ibid., in microfilm roll 17.

97. Unreported case, *United States v. The Panther,* U.S. Records of the Supreme Court of the United States, Appellate Case File 3150, RG 267, National Archives, Washington, D.C.

98. Gilchrist served from October 30, 1839 to May 1, 1856, "Federal Judges," xxvi; see John Belton O'Neall, *Biographical Sketches of the Bench and Bar of South Carolina,* vol. 1 (Charleston, S.C.: S. G. Courtenay and Co., 1859), 206-7.

99. Unreported case, *The Panther.*

100. Unreported case, *Barque Julia Dean.*

101. Unreported case, *The Panther,* printed record, 64–65.

102. Ibid., 65 (citing Conrad Malte-Brun, *Universal Geography,* vol. 1 [Philadelphia: A. Finley, 1827], 192, 586).

103. Howard, *American Slavers,* 50–51.

104. Unreported case, *United States v. the Barque William G. Lewis* (E.D.Va. Aug. 10, 1858), Admiralty Case Files, in microfilm (M1300) roll 16; unreported case, *United States v. The Schooner Advance* (E.D.Va. Nov. 5 [?], 1853), ibid., in microfilm roll 13; unreported case, *United States v. the Schooner Rachel P. Brown* (E.D.Va. June 17, 1853), ibid., in microfilm roll 14.

105. See Rachel P. Brown; Robinson, *Slavery in the Structure of American Politics*, 342.

106. See J. Woodruff, *Report of the Trials in the Echo Cases in Federal Court, Charleston, S.C., April, 1859; together with Arguments of Counsel and Charge of the Court* (1859; reprinted in *The African Slave Trade and American Courts: The Pamphlet Literature*, vol. 2, *Slavery, Race and the American Legal System, 1700–1872*, 5th ser. [New York: Garland Publishers, 1988], Paul Finkelman, ed., 118–19, 121), reporting Leonatas Spratt's argument.

107. Unreported case, *United States v. the Brig Excellent* (E.D.Va. Nov. 9, 1850), Admiralty Case Files, in microfilm (M1300) roll 13, Deposition of William Temple.

108. See *Prigg v. Pennsylvania*, 41 U.S. (16 Peters), 539, 626–33 (Taney, C. J., concurring) (1842); *Passenger Cases*, 48 U.S. (7 Howard), 282, 463–94 (Taney, C. J., dissenting) (1849); *Dred Scott v. Sandford*, 60 U.S. (19 Howard), 393 (per Taney, C. J.) (1857).

109. Howard, *American Slavers*, App. A, 213–21.

110. Foote, *Africa and the American Flag*, 356.

111. Howard, *American Slavers*, 37.

112. Howard Jones, *Mutiny on the Amistad: The Saga of a Slave Revolt and Its Impact on American Abolition, Law, and Diplomacy* (New York: Oxford University Press, 1987), 3-30.

113. Ibid., 47 ff; See *Gedney v. L'Amistad*, 10 F. Cas. 141 (D. Conn. 1840) (No. 5, 294a), *aff'd in part, rev'd in part sub nom. The Amistad*, 40 U.S. (15 Peters), 518 (1841); Robert M. Cover, *Justice Accused: Antislavery and the Judicial Process* (New Haven, Conn.: Yale University Press, 1975), 109-12; Harold M. Hyman and William M. Wiecek, *Equal Justice under Law: Constitutional Development, 1835–1875*, (New York: Harper & Row, 1982), 103.

114. Howard, *American Slavers*, 30, 32; see also Garitee, *Republic's Private Navy*, 228–30; Roger Anstey, "The Volume of the North American Slave-Carrying Trade from Africa: 1761–1810," in *Articles on American Slavery*, vol. 2, 18; David Eltis, "The Impact of Abolition on the Atlantic Slave Trade," in *The Abolition of the Atlantic Slave Trade: Origins and Effects in Europe, Africa, and the Americas*, eds. David Eltis and James Walvin (Madison: University of Wisconsin Press, 1981), 155, 161.

115. Howard, *American Slavers*, 31–36.

116. Ibid., 38.

117. The *Baltimore Sun*, May 20, 1840, p. 1.

118. Howard, *American Slavers*, 38–39; the *Baltimore Sun*, May 20, 1840, p. 1.

119. Gerald T. Dunne, *Justice Joseph Story and the Rise of the Supreme Court* (New York: Simon and Schuster, 1970), 22.

120. *African Slave Trade: Message of the President,* 627.

121. The *Baltimore Sun,* May 20, 1840, p. 1.

122. Ibid.; *Strom v. United States,* 23 F. Cas. 240, 241–42 (C.C.D.Md. 1840) (No. 13,539).

123. The *Baltimore Sun,* May 20, 1840, p. 1.

124. Ibid.

125. Howard, *American Slavers,* 163.

126. Unreported case, *United States v. Robert W. Allen* (C.C.D.Md. Dec. 7, 1839), Indictment . . . True Bill of the Grand Jury of the United States for the Fourth Circuit in and for the District of Maryland (signed Nathaniel Williams, U.S. Atty.) (D.Md. Nov. 23, 1839), Criminal Case Files of the U.S. Circuit Court for the District of Maryland, Records of the District Courts of the United States, RG 21, National Archives and Records Service, Washington, D.C., in microfilm (M1010) roll 3.

127. 22 U.S. (9 Wheaton), 381 (1824); 25 U.S. (12 Wheaton), 460 (1827).

128. *Robert W. Allen,* Criminal Case Files, Prayers on the Part of the Prosecution, n.d., microfilm (M1010) roll 3. See also ibid., *United States v. John Henderson* (C.C.D.Md. April —, 1839; *nolle prosequi*); ibid., *United States v. Francis Montell* (C.C.D.Md. April 29, 1840).

129. Ibid., *Robert W. Allen,* Deposition of James Swedge, November 20, 1839.

130. Ibid., Proffered charges, n.d.

131. Ibid., Deposition of James Swedge; see also Howard, *American Slavers,* 163.

132. *United States v. Robert W. Allen* (C.C.D.Md. December 7, 1839) (hung jury before Taney, C. J. and Upton S. Heath (D. Judge), in *Minutes of the U.S. Circuit Court for the District of Maryland, 1790–1911,* Records of the District Courts of the United States, RG 21, National Archives and Records Service, Washington, D.C., in microfilm (M931) roll 2; see also Howard, *American Slavers,* 224. Heath served from April 4, 1836, to February 21, 1842, in "Federal Judges," xxii.

133. *United States v. Robert W. Allen* (C.C.D.Md. Apr. 25, 1840) (verdict of "not guilty" before Taney, C. J. Heath (D. Judge), in Minutes, microfilm (M931) roll 2; see also Howard, *American Slavers,* 224.

134. The *Baltimore Sun,* April 30, 1840, p. 1; Act of Dec. 31, 1792, ch. 45, sec. 7, *Stats. at Large* 1 (1845): 290.

135. The *Baltimore Sun,* Apr. 30, 1840, p. 1.

136. Act of Dec. 31, 1792, ch. 1, sec. 29, *Stats. at Large* 1 (1845): 287, 298-99; Act of Aug. 4, 1790, ch. 35, sec. 12, *Stats. at Large* 1 (1845): 145, 157.

137. *United States v. Montell,* 26 F. Cas. 1293, 1294–95 (C.C.D.Md. 1841) (No. 15,798).

138. *Allen v. United States,* 1 F. Cas. 518, 519 (C.C.D.Md. 1840) (No. 240) referring to *The Catherine,* 25 F. Cas. 337 (C.C.S.D.N.Y. 1840) (No. 14,755).

139. Howard, *American Slavers,* 161–62.

140. Allen, 1 F. Cas., 519.

141. *United States v. Montell,* 26 F. Cas., 1293.

142. The *Baltimore Sun,* May 20, 1840, p. 1; Howard, *American Slavers,* 39.

143. The *Baltimore Sun,* April 30, 1840, p. 1.

144. 39 U.S. (14 Peters), 464, 476 (1840).

145. See unreported case, *United States v. Jason S. Pendleton (Brig Montevideo)* (C.C.D.Md. April 30, 1845), (indictment quashed); *United States v. Jason S. Pendleton (Brig Montevideo)* (C.C.D.Md., May 1, 1845) (ordered to appear at June, 1845 term of D.Md.) in *Minutes of the U.S. Circuit Court,* microfilm (M931) roll 2. See Howard, *American Slavers,* 225, 243 (wherein the U.S. Attorney reduced charges from a capital crime under the Act of May 15, 1820, ch. 11, secs. 4, 5, *Stats. at Large* 3 (1846): 600, 601, to a misdemeanor under the Act of May 10, 1800, ch. 51, sec. 2, *Stats. at Large* 2 (1845): 70, and won convictions under the latter); unreported case, *The Panther;* Howard, *American Slavers,* 225 (wherein the master of the American bark *Panther* won an acquittal in the District of South Carolina).

146. Unreported case, *The Panther.*

147. Howard, *American Slavers,* 214; Acts of Mar. 22, 1794, ch. 11, sec. 1, *Stats. at Large* 1 (1845): 347, 348-49; May 10, 1800, ch. 51, sec. 1, ibid., 2 (1845): 70, 71; Apr. 29, 1818, ch. 91, sec. 2, ibid., 3 (1846): 450, 451; Mar. 3, 1819, ch. 101, sec. 1, ibid., 3: 532, 533.

148. Act of May 10, 1800, ch. 51, sec. 2, *Stats. at Large* 2 (1845): 70.

149. The Alexander, 1 F. Cas. 362, 363, (C.C.D.Mass. 1823) (No. 165), quoted in unreported case, *The Panther,* printed record, 61–62, and cited by the United States in *United States v. Morris,* 39 U.S. (14 Peters), 464, 469 (1840). Associate Justice Joseph Story died on September 10, 1845.

150. Unreported case, *The Panther,* printed record, 62; Act of Mar. 3, 1819, ch. 101, sec. 1, *Stats. at Large* 3 (1846): 532, 533 (subjecting to arrest and prosecution for violation of the prohibition imposed by the Act of Mar. 2, 1807, ch. 22, *Stats. at Large* 2 [1846]: 426, on the importation of slaves by "all ships or vessels of the United States . . . which may have taken on board, or which may be intended for the purpose of taking on board, or transporting, or may have transported, any negro.")

151. See Act of Mar. 22, 1794, ch. 11, sec. 1, *Stats. at Large* 1 (1845): 347-49; Act of Apr. 20, 1818, ch. 91, sec. 2, ibid., 3 (1846): 450-51.

152. 22 U.S. (9 Wheaton), 381 (1824); 25 U.S. (12 Wheaton), 460 (1827).

153. Unreported case, *The Panther,* printed record, 61.

154. Act of Apr. 20, 1818, ch. 91 sec. 3, *Stats. at Large* 3 (1846): 450, 451.

155. Unreported case, *The Panther,* printed record, 62, citing *Gooding,* 478.

156. Gooding was erroneously charged with an intent that the vessel *should be employed* in the slave trade. See Act of Mar. 22, 1794, ch. 11, sec. 2, *Stats. at Large* 1 (1845): 347, 349 ("shall be employed in such trade or business") and imposing a maximum fine of $2,000 instead of charging him with an intent to *employ her* (emphasis added); see Act of Apr. 20, 1818, ch. 91, sec. 3, *Stats. at Large* 2 (1845): 450–51 ("with intent to employ such ship or vessel in such trade or business") and imposing a maximum fine of $5,000 and seven years of imprisonment.

157. *The Merino, The Constitution, The Louisa,* 22 U.S. (9 Wheaton), 391, 404 (1824), quoted in unreported case, *The Panther,* printed record, 63 (emphasis added).

158. Howard, *American Slavers,* 99, 215.

159. See unreported case, *United States v. Schooner Alice Rogers* (E.D.Va. May 4, 1860), Admiralty Case Files, in microfilm (M1300) roll 18.

160. Ibid., Unpublished opinion (emphasis in the original); see Act of Apr. 20, 1818, ch. 91, secs. 4, 6, *Stats. at Large* 3 (1846): 450, 451-52, especially sec. 6 providing "one moiety to the use of the United States, and the other to the use of the *person or persons* who shall sue for such forfeiture, and prosecute the same to effect" (emphasis added).

161. See Armistead M. Dobie, "Early Federal District Judges in Virginia Before the Civil War," *Federal Rules Decisions* 12 (1952): 451, 473 (1952).

162. Act of Apr. 20, 1818, ch. 91, sec. 10, *Stats. at Large* 3 (1846): 450, 453.

163. Act of Mar. 2, 1807, ch. 22, sec. 7, *Stats. at Large* 2 (1845): 426, 428.

164. Ibid.

165. Unpublished opinion, *Alice Rogers.*

166. Act of Apr. 20, 1818, sec. 6, *Stats. at Large* 3 (1846): 452.

167. Unpublished opinion, *United States v. James Brayley and James Melville* (E.D.Va. May 3, 1860), Admiralty Case File, in microfilm (M1300) roll 18. The jury acquitted First Mate Melville.

168. Act of Apr. 20, 1818, sec. 4, *Stats. at Large* 3 (1846): 451.

169. Unpublished opinion, *Alice Rogers,* testimony of Edward J. Butler; of Thomas Latimer.

170. Act of Apr. 20, 1818, sec. 1, *Stats. at Large* 3 (1846): 450-51.

171. Unpublished opinion, *Alice Rogers* (emphasis in original).

172. Magrath served from May 12, 1856 to November 7, 1860, in "Federal Judges," xxvi; see John Barnwell, *Love of Order: South Carolina's First Secession Crisis* (Chapel Hill: University of North Carolina Press, 1982), 172; Leroy F. Youmans, *Sketch of the Life of Governor Andrew Gordon Magrath: Prepared for the Charleston Year Book 1895* (Charleston, S.C.: Walker, Evans and Cogswell Co., 1896), 3.

173. James M. McPherson, *Battle Cry of Freedom: The Civil War Era*, vol. 6 of *Oxford History of the United States*, C. Vann Woodward, ed., (New York: Oxford University Press, 1988), 145–69 (Kansas), 201–13 (Harpers Ferry); Michael Kent Curtis, "The Crisis over The Impending Crisis: Free Speech, Slavery, and The Fourteenth Amendment," in *Slavery and the Law*, ed. Paul Finkelman (Madison, Wis.: Madison House, 1996), 161–205; Frederick S. Calhoun, *The Lawmen: United States Marshals and their Deputies, 1789–1989* (Washington, D.C.: Smithsonian Institution Press, 1990), 81, quoting Jeremiah S. Black to James Connor, October 6, 1858.

174. See DuBois, *Suppression of the African Slave Trade*, 170–78; Ronald T. Takaki, *A Pro-Slavery Crusade: The Agitation to Re-open the African Slave Trade* (New York: Free Press, 1971), 1–8, 23–85; Takaki, "The Movement to Re-open the African Slave Trade in South Carolina," in DuBois, *Articles on American Slavery*, 364–69.

175. Howard, *American Slavers*, 96–97.

176. Ibid., quoting *Mercury* (Charleston, S.C.) n.d., n.p.

177. Ibid., 96–97.

178. Ibid., 97–99.

179. Woodruff, *Report of the Trials; United States v. Corrie*, 25 F. Cas. 658 (C.C.D.S.C. 1860) (No. 14,869); see Tom Henderson Wells, *The Slave Ship Wanderer* (Athens: University of Georgia Press, 1967).

180. Woodruff, *Report of the Trials*, 62–63; U.S. Congress, House, *Message from the President of the United States to the Two Houses of Congress at the Commencement of the Second Session of the Thirty-fifth Congress*, 35th Cong., 2d sess., Doc. No. 2 (1858), 69.

181. Woodruff, *Report of the Trials*, 64.

182. Ibid., 62; *Message from the President*, 31–32.

183. *United States v. Corrie*, 25 F. Cas., 658.

184. Wells, *Slave Ship Wanderer*, 1, 4–5, 8, 13–14, 24–25, 30–31; see also Robert Ralph Davis Jr., "Notes and Documents, Buchanian Espionage: A Report on Illegal Slave Trading in the South in 1859," *Journal of Southern History* 37 (1974): 271–78; *The Wanderer*, 29 F. Cas. 150 (D. Mass. 1860) (No. 17,139), citing Act of Apr. 20, 1818, ch. 91, *Stats. at Large* 2 [1845]: 450.

185. Woodruff, *Report of the Trials*, 55, 61-62. See Act of May 15, 1820, ch. 113, secs. 4 and 5, *Stats. at Large* 3 (1846): 600, 601, making it unlawful

for American crew members to serve on vessels owned in whole or in part by American citizens, to land on foreign shores, and there kidnap "any negro or mulatto," to bring to and forcibly confine him or her to a vessel with an intent "to make such negro or mulatto a slave" or actually to sell, transfer or to attempt to do so on land, and classifying such captors as pirates and subjecting them to death "on conviction... before the circuit court of the United States for the district wherein... brought or found."

186. *Message from the President,* 31. Maffit later achieved fame as commander of the Confederate raider *Florida.* Howard, *American Slavers,* 76–77.

187. Woodruff, *Report of the Trials,* 64; Takaki, "Movement to Re-open," 364–65; Takaki, *Pro-Slavery Crusade,* 215–16.

188. Takaki, *Pro-Slavery Crusade,* 215–16; see Alexander A. Lawrence, *James Moore Wayne: Southern Unionist* (Chapel Hill: University of North Carolina Press, 1943), 166, quoting Andrew G. Magrath to James M. Wayne, September 11, 1858.

189. Woodruff, *Report of the Trials,* 130, reporting DeTreville's argument.

190. Ibid., 83–84, 92, reporting Bellinger's argument.

191. U.S. Constitution, art. 1, sec. 8, cl. 10 (providing that "the Congress shall have power... to define and punish Piracies and Felonies committed on the high Seas"); Woodruff, *Report of the Trials,* 143, reporting DeTreville's argument.

192. Woodruff, *Report of the Trials,* 74, reporting Gregg's argument.

193. Ibid., 143, reporting DeTreville's argument; see also *Gibbons v. Ogden,* 206–7.

194. U.S. Constitution, art. 1, sec. 8, cl. 3; Woodruff, *Report of the Trials,* 144, reporting DeTreville's argument.

195. Woodruff, *Report of the Trials,* 73, reporting Gregg's argument.

196. *Argument before the United States Circuit Court by Isaac W. Hayne, Esq., on the Motion to Discharge the Crew of the Echo delivered in Columbia, S.C. December, 1858* (1859; reprinted in *African Slave Trade*), 38–39.

197. U.S. Constitution, art. 1, sec. 8, cls. 3, 18.

198. *Argument before the United States Circuit Court,* in *African Slave Trade,* 40, 42–53.

199. Woodruff, *Report of the Trials,* 142, reporting DeTreville's argument.

200. Ibid., "The Judge's Charge," 161–63; 48 U.S. (7 Howard), 283, 411–15, (1849), (Wayne, J., concurring). See also Takaki, *Pro-Slavery Crusade,* 103–33 (considering nonconstitutional arguments against legalizing the slave trade).

201. Charge to the Grand Jury, 30 F. Cas. 1026, 1030, 1032 (C.C.D.Ga. 1859) (No. 18,269a).

202. Howard, *American Slavers*, 146; Takaki, *Pro-Slavery Crusade*, 209–10.

203. Howard, *American Slavers*, 149.

204. *United States v. Corrie*, 25 F. Cas. 658, 659 (C.C.D.S.C. 1860) (No. 14,869); the Act of May 15, 1820, vested jurisdiction in the U.S. circuit court of the state in which an offender was "brought" or "found" (ch. 113, sec. 3, *Stats. at Large* 3 [1846]: 600). Corrie had been "found" in the District of South Carolina for originally committing an offense outside the boundaries of any state (*United States v. Corrie*, 659). The constitutional requirement that trial be held in "the State and District wherein [crimes] have been committed" (U.S. Constitution, amendment 6) did not apply. Instead, the Constitution fixed trials of offenses "not committed within any State, . . . at such place or places as Congress may by law have directed." (U.S. Constitution, art. 3, sec. 2, cl. 3). And that place could only be South Carolina! "Rightful jurisdiction of the case once vested in the Circuit Court of the United States for the State of South Carolina," Magrath proclaimed, "it became exclusive of jurisdiction elsewhere; and the accused could not be transported to a different District for trial." (*United States v. Corrie*, 661).

205. *United States v. Corrie*, 659.

206. Ibid., 669.

207. Ibid., 662–64; see Act of May 15, 1820, ch. 113, secs. 4, 5, *Stats. at Large* 3 (1846): 600, 601.

208. *United States v. Corrie*, 664–65.

209. Ibid., 669; Woodruff, *Report of the Trials*, 123, reporting Spratt's argument.

210. Woodruff, *Report of the Trials*, 165, reporting "The Judge's Charge."

211. Ibid., 134, 136, reporting DeTreville's argument.

212. Ibid., 158, providing an abstract of the argument of James Connor, Esq., U.S. attorney.

213. Ibid., 166, reporting "The Judge's Charge."

214. Ibid., 136, reporting DeTreville's argument.

215. Ibid., 167, reporting the verdict; *African Slave Trade*, 628.

216. See Howard, *American Slavers*, 147; Cummings and McFarland, *Federal Justice*, 183, quoting Jeremiah S. Black to James Connor, March 17, 1860.

217. DuBois, *Suppression of the African Slave Trade*, 129.

218. Howard, *American Slavers*, vii (emphasis in original).

219. See Robinson, *Slavery in the Structure of American Politics*, 338–39.

220. Howard, *American Slavers*, 39.

221. William M. Robinson Jr., *Justice in Grey: A History of the Judicial System of the Confederate States of America* (Cambridge, Mass.: Harvard University Press, 1941), 18, reporting that Halyburton resigned on April 17, 1861; 129, reporting that Halyburton opened the Confederate States District Court for the Eastern District of Virginia on June 12, 1861; 3, reporting that Magrath resigned on November 7, 1860; 14, reporting that Magrath was appointed judge of the Confederate States District Court for the District of South Carolina on March 16, 1861; 126, reporting that Magrath opened the court on May 22, 1861.

Part Two

James Fenimore Cooper
and the Birth of
American Maritime
Experience

The Battle of Lake Erie, 10 September 1813

8

Enabling and Disabling the Lake Erie Discussion: James Fenimore Cooper and Alexander Slidell Mackenzie Respond to the Perry-Elliott Controversy

Hugh Egan

At half past two, the wind springing up, Captain Elliott was enabled to bring his vessel, the *Niagara,* gallantly into close action. I immediately went on board of her, when he anticipated my wishes, by volunteering to bring the schooners, which had been kept astern by the lightness of the wind, into closer action.[1]

This extract is taken from Oliver Hazard Perry's "after action" report to the secretary of the Navy, 13 September 1813. It concerns a crucial juncture in the Battle of Lake Erie three days earlier, during which Perry's squadron had captured the British squadron under the command of Robert Heriot Barclay. That one word, "enabled," perhaps hinting at a distinction between the ability to act and action itself, has disabled historical discourse on this matter, and goes to the heart of a controversy involving the performance of Captain Jesse D. Elliott during battle, the interpretation of that performance by Captain Perry, and the analysis of Captain Perry's interpretation by second-generation commentators James Fenimore Cooper and Alexander Slidell Mackenzie.

Beginning with Perry's report—which has been alternately termed sincere or strategic—the Battle of Lake Erie has generated such a voluminous and rarified textual response that a naval controversy begins increasingly to resemble a literary controversy. The affair has raised questions, for instance, about the elusive relationship between deed and document, about what constitutes appropriate evidence for an "objective" account of history, about author intention, textual ambiguity, and rhetorical strategy. The overlap of the military with the literary is all but inevitable, perhaps, given the participation in this affair of Cooper and Mackenzie. They both had careers that spanned naval and authorial ambition and that crossed each other at a number of historical flash points. At the very center of the issues, Perry's text serves as a sign of how opaque and resistant are those very accounts of the affair that was purported to be the most straightforward.

The circumstances of the battle are now the stuff of legend. With his own flagship, *Lawrence*, battered and crippled, Perry transferred his pennant by boat to the *Niagara*. He took over command of that vessel from Jesse D. Elliott, revived the American effort, divided the British squadron, and in fairly short order overwhelmed the two main British vessels, the *Detroit* and the *Queen Charlotte*. Shortly after the battle, Perry wrote his famous message to Major General William Henry Harrison, "We have met the enemy—and they are ours." [2]

The victory at Lake Erie straddles any number of paradoxes—such as the fact that Perry, after inspiring his crew never to give up the ship, did exactly that—but a whole series of historical ironies swirl around Perry's second in command, Jesse Elliott, for whom victory constituted a kind of professional defeat. [3] In the course of the three-hour battle, Elliott, commanding a vessel identical with Perry's, stayed largely out of the action for two-and-half hours, while the *Lawrence* was enduring heavy attack. He engaged in some distant fire with the British squadron, but never came to the direct aid of the *Lawrence*. Elliott claimed that the lightness of the wind kept him away and that, in addition, he did not want to break the line of battle established by Perry. After the conflict, however, both British and American seaman questioned Elliott's courage for avoiding the heavy fighting for as long as he did. The American resentment was spurred by the fact that the *Lawrence* had twenty-two men and officers killed, while the *Niagara* had only two.

It is in this context that we read Perry's after-action report, in which he officially praises Elliott, by saying that at a certain point Elliott was "enabled" to engage his vessel in close action with the enemy. The unanswered question is: did he do so? Perry states further, "Of Captain Elliott, already so well known to the government, it would be almost superfluous to speak. In this action he evinced his characteristic bravery and judgment; and, since the close of the action, has given me the most able and essential assistance."[4]

The naval bureaucracy followed suit with its own official praise of Elliott's conduct, even in the face of persistent rumors that condemned it. Newspaper accounts from England, reporting on the court of inquiry assembled to assess the performance of British commander Barclay, described Elliott as "making away" during the height of battle. In response to these allegations, Elliott demanded that an American court of inquiry clear his name, and this was done in April 1815.[5]

Here the matter rested until 1818, when Perry himself instituted court-martial charges against Elliott—both for his conduct during the battle and for his post-battle "intrigues" against Perry. Perry claims that his initial words of praise for Elliott were written in the interest of maintaining naval harmony after a great victory and screening Elliott from censure.[6] However, it was Perry's feeling that Elliott's conduct since the battle—in expressing public and covert resentment over Perry's exalted status—could no longer be met with silence or praise. Perry's charges were never officially examined or prosecuted. He was dead within a year, and perhaps the accusations seemed irrelevant as a result. At any rate, the circumstances of their withdrawal remain unresolved.[7]

The affair lay largely dormant for nearly twenty more years, although in the meantime Elliott managed to offend the Whig press on a number of political matters (he was a notorious Jacksonian) and each time would stir up the accusations of his cowardice during the Battle of Lake Erie.[8] James Fenimore Cooper then published his *History of the Navy* in two volumes in 1839. His account of the Lake Erie affair attempts painstakingly to avoid controversy and follows the official line of praise for all concerned. He simply noted the transfer of power on the *Niagara* from one commander to another, and summarized in this fashion:

> The personal deportment of Captain Perry, throughout the day, was worthy of all praise. He did not quit his own vessel when she became useless, to retire from the battle, but to gain it; an end that was fully obtained, and an effort which resulted in triumph.... For his conduct in this battle, Captain Perry received a gold medal from Congress. Captain Elliott also received a gold medal.[9]

Cooper included in his history Perry's praise for Elliott but does not mention that Perry withdrew that praise and filed court-martial charges five years later.

In attempting to avoid controversy, Cooper created it. He, too, was accused of "making away" from close action on this issue. In quick order there appeared three different condemnations of his account—authored by William Duer, Tristam Burges, and Alexander Mackenzie.[10] In each instance, Cooper proved immensely resistant to criticism. He went as far as to prosecute the publisher of Duer's review for libel, earning a judgment of $300. The Burges review, in turn, is perhaps best known for focusing on that word *enabled* and seeing it as an equivocation on Perry's part. Perry's camp was called upon to answer the question: why did the commander first praise Elliott and then, five years later, turn on him? Burges says that the praise wasn't really praise at all: "Here he saved Elliott, by a *benevolent ambiguity.* He says '*at half past two, the wind springing up,* Captain Elliott was ENABLED to bring his vessel, the *Niagara,* gallantly into close action.' He was ENABLED, he could say; he could *not* say he DID bring the *Niagara* into close action."[11]

A literary critic looking for signs of rhetorical hesitation or ambiguity in a text will almost certainly find them, and it appears that here Burges has willfully taken on that task. By magnifying a single word, he creates a stereoscopic view of Perry-as-warrior and Perry-as-author. His argument appears precious and overwrought, born of loyalty and defensiveness rather than a "search for truth," but once introduced it is difficult to dispense with. In fact, if read as a strategic exercise, Perry's report gives one plenty to work with. In addition to his use of "enabled," he praises Elliott first by claiming it is superfluous to speak of him, then by saying Elliott "evinced his characteristic bravery and judgment" (characteristically limited?), and finally by thanking him for able and essential assistance "since the close of the action" (hinting, perhaps, that he didn't render such assistance during the action).

Opened to this kind of analysis, Perry's official account, whose purpose was to give "the most important particulars of the action," is no longer the sincere, reflective narrative of an American hero, one whose motive was simply to match words to actions, but something more self-conscious and cagey, the beginning of a different kind of battle altogether. His report is but the first sign that, as the actual events of 1813 recede, deeds and texts begin to dissolve into one another, with texts becoming deeds, and the straightforwardness of a military victory remaking itself as a meditation on the nature of authorship and the control of historical discourse. In the Lake Erie affair, the thunder of canister would give way to the thunder of criticism and interpretation, with each succeeding layer of commentary received by the opponent as a blow that demanded equal response. As the battle moved into the realm of interpretation, the effects of these volleys could not be measured in terms of victory, defeat, or statistical tables of the wounded and dead. The rhetorical firepower, in fact, often undermines the very cause it seeks to serve.

Of all the reviews published, none struck home more deeply with Cooper, and none framed the issues of history and authorship more acutely, than those of Alexander Slidell Mackenzie. Mackenzie was related by marriage to the Perry clan and was, like Cooper himself, something of a sailor-author. Cooper had served three years in the Navy (1808–11), stationed on Lake Ontario; Mackenzie was a career Navy man who rose to the rank of captain. Both had published travel books on England in the 1830s, and both had published lead articles in the short-lived *Naval Magazine* in 1836 and 1837. They were, in a sense, literary competitors. In a letter to his wife in 1836, Cooper compared the sales of his own *Sketches of Switzerland* (1836) with Mackenzie's *Spain Revisited* (1836): "The Sketches have not sold very well, but stand very fair. About twice as many have sold as of Slidell's book, but they are puffing away at him, might and main."[12] A year later, the British *Quarterly Review* compared Cooper's irascible *England* (1837) unfavorably to Mackenzie's *The American in England* (1835):

No one complains of Captain Slidell's book—because it is written in good faith, and with good manners. His views, when erroneous, are not distorted either by vanity or malice; and hitting, as he does, much harder, and on sorer places than Mr. Cooper, his strictures may be read by an Englishman sometimes with profit—often with regret—but never with anything like the mingled disgust and contempt which are excited by the rancorous triviality of Mr. Cooper.[13]

Fanatically loyal to Perry, Mackenzie first commented on *Naval History* in the *North American Review* of October 1839. He himself engages in some equivocal praise at the beginning:

Mr. Cooper has made a valuable addition to the history of the country, in the work before us. He appears to have used a commendable diligence in searching out whatever facts our early history affords, illustrative of the origin and growth of the national navy, and has dressed them out in a form as attractive, perhaps, as the unconnected nature of the events, and the meagreness of the annals from which he derived his materials, permitted.[14]

Soon, however, Mackenzie is into the Battle of Lake Erie, accusing Cooper of tarnishing Perry's reputation by refusing to criticize Elliott, and by presenting "gross misrepresentations" of the battle itself. Twelve pages of the thirty-five-page review are devoted to correcting Cooper's rendition of Lake Erie.

Mackenzie's review put in motion a widening spiral of charge and countercharge between the two authors, with name calling escalating and pages increasing in every exchange. In his *Life of Perry* (1840), a biography written largely to refute Cooper's history, Mackenzie embraces Burges' view that the word *enabled* is an equivocation, explaining: "He leaves to Captain Elliott the benefit of the inference that, more than two hours after the *Lawrence* had been in close action, he actually did what he was enabled to do; which, by concurrent testimony of the officers of the squadron, except a few of those on the *Niagara*, he never did."[15]

In his postbattle report, according to Mackenzie, Perry "was torturing his ingenuity to keep honestly out of view the palpable misconduct of Captain Elliott."[16]

Because some of the material issues relating to Lake Erie were a matter for litigation in his suit against the publisher of William Duer's article, Cooper could not respond fully until 1843, when he published a hundred-page pamphlet, *The Battle of Lake Erie, Or Answers to Messrs. Duer, Burges, and Mackenzie*. Indeed, part of this story involved Cooper's continual promise throughout 1841 and 1842 to "do up" the whole Lake Erie matter in a form that could not be refuted.[17] And when he did finally respond, he opened as an avenging angel, sounding a note of biblical portentousness:

> The writer has not sought this discussion. It has been forced on him by his assailants, who must now face the consequences. For years the writer has submitted in comparative silence to gross injustice, in connection with this matter, not from any want of confidence in the justice of his case or any ability to defend himself, but, because he 'bided his time,' knowing, when that day should arrive, he had truth to fall back upon. . . . The day of reckoning has come at length, and the judgment of men will infallibly follow.[18]

Central to Cooper's attack is his impatience with the notion that Perry would "meditate any evasion" in his official report. He ridicules the idea of any "benevolent ambiguity" on Perry's part, writing that "In this section of the country, we have a good many 'benevolent ambiguities' practiced by a certain caste of lawyers. . . . Among gentlemen, every where, the benevolence would meet with but little respect, while the 'ambiguity' would excite disgust."[19]

As Cooper works through the layered nature of his refutation, however, he too begins to sound like a textual critic, examining specific word choice and weighing author intention. Focusing on Perry's phrase, "I immediately went on board of her" (in the sentence that follows the "enabled" passage) Cooper says

> Here we see Capt. Perry expressly referring to this change of position, this *coming* into close action . . . as giving him (Perry) an opportunity of making the change of vessel of which he speaks. The use of the word "immediately," too, shows this. It refers to time, of course; and to what time can Mr. Burges apply it, if it be not *immediately* after Capt. Elliot got "into close action." Does he think Perry

would have said "immediately after Capt. Elliott was ENABLED to get into close action, I went on board the *Niagara?*" This would have been a very complicated falsifying of the truth. Perry's language had no such object; it is simple, direct, and not to be misunderstood.[20]

The complexity of Cooper's analysis has the paradoxical effect of undermining the straightforwardness of his final statement. Cooper noted that Perry used the word *enabled* at another point in his official report, where it was "unequivocally used in direct connection with performance, and without any 'benevolent ambiguity.'" But again, the more Cooper assigned deliberate strategy to Perry's choice of specific words, the further he entered the realm of rhetorical instability and conceived of the battle as a text rather than an event. A tortured ingenuity might even be read into Cooper's historical summary: "For his conduct in battle, Captain Perry received a gold medal from Congress. Captain Elliott also received a gold medal." An implicit question— why did Elliott receive a medal?—is left unanswered. To the extent that his account engages in its own evasions, and that the very making of textual narrative invites this slipperiness, Cooper himself was guilty of the duplicity he found so impossible in Perry.

Still, Cooper pronounced, here and elsewhere in his writings from this period, a blunt philosophical positivism whereby facts should precede and determine opinions in a republic, and the corruption in the Perry case (and in America at large) is that these poles have been reversed. Opinions about Elliott's misconduct were, according to Cooper, "clearly in an unfit state to be received at all into the pages of history."[21]

Left unexamined, of course, is how the "pages of history" help to create the very events they receive. Cooper was clearly uncomfortable with the fragmentary, fluid, and irresolute path of historical truth as it makes its way into written accounts. In his pamphlet, some rather delicate textual exegeses on the positions of the vessels, the relative strengths of the British and American forces, the number of seamen dead or wounded—all of which respond to points of Mackenzie's—are weirdly combined with an ad hominem passion that all but overwhelms his scholarship. At times, Cooper's own fixed opinions determined his facts. The precision of the analysis often appears to have no historical purpose at all. Rather, framed by his own sense of outrage and irritation, Cooper's meticulous dissection of events illustrated his dilemma rather eloquently. He wished to demonstrate that the events of Lake Erie simply happened, and thereby fall outside any need for interpretation, but became increasingly implicated in the textual strategies he sought to discredit, including the ratcheting-up of condemnatory rhetoric. At one point he wrote: "I hope those persons who are ready to canonize Capt. Mackenzie as a saint, without waiting the customary century, will bear this whole matter in mind."[22]

The exchanges between Cooper and Mackenzie endured over four years, with their polemics spanning a variety of textual genres, including history, biography, essay, and review. Of course, these men were employed in other arenas during this time, Cooper as a novelist and Mackenzie as a naval captain. During the four-year span of controversy over Lake Erie, Cooper published eight novels, including *The Pathfinder* (1840), *The Deerslayer* (1841), and a number of sea novels. Mackenzie was involved in his own controversy when he hanged three men at sea aboard the *Somers* in December 1842. The men were suspected of mutiny, although no overt act of mutiny ever occurred, no trial was held to determine the truth of the accusation, and no chance given the accused to refute the charges against them. Mackenzie was tried for murder and other charges in a naval court; he was acquitted on all counts.

In fact, the *Somers* affair occurred just as Cooper was writing his Lake Erie pamphlet, and he could not resist adding references to the "mutiny" to his rhetorical arsenal. Speaking of how Elliott's reputation had been damaged by Mackenzie, Cooper wrote: "Let it be imagined, for a moment, that he had assumed the responsibility of executing three men without a trial, and then fancy the result! His life, justly or unjustly, would have been the forfeit."[23] There are more oblique references as well, such as when Cooper describes Mackenzie's character:

I think Captain Mackenzie's mind to be very singularly constituted, and that he did not mean all he has so clearly said. So many instances of this peculiarity of moral conformation have forced themselves on my notice, as to leave no doubt of its existence. Capt. Mackenzie can see only one side of a question. He is a man of prejudice and denunciation, and he accuses, less under evidence, than under convictions. Were he inspired, this last might do well enough; but, as he is only a man, and quite often wrong as right, fearful consequences have followed from his mistakes.[24]

At this point, Cooper appears to have moved from the historical events of Lake Erie to the more personal and less winnable battle of character assassination. In so doing, he left himself vulnerable to the very charge he leveled at Mackenzie: that he was a man of prejudice and denunciation.

Cooper would write an eighty-page "elaborate review" of the Mackenzie's court-martial trial, condemning once again the Emersonian tendency of the captain to "regard things as he has at first conceived them to be, and act under his conviction, rather than under the authority of evidence."[25] The *Somers* case, even more than the Lake Erie affair, inhered so fully in the complexities of language—in codes, handwriting, dictation, translation; in Mackenzie's own stylistic affectations in his written account of the incident; in contemporary sea fiction (including Cooper's own), which was said to have corrupted one of the conspirators; in literary grudges and literary fame—that the whole incident seems to issue from, as well as proceed into, written documents.[26] Cooper's review of Mackenzie's court-martial trial is, in its own right, an interesting and conflicted attempt to separate deeds from texts, facts from interpretation. In the *Somers* affair, this was simply impossible.

On the subject of Lake Erie, at least, Cooper began with the clarity of a victory at sea. The capture of six British vessels was not open to dispute, the facts were recorded and acclaimed, and they had, in this sense, the authority of evidence. Cooper assumed that the results of his textual assault would be similarly obvious. In a letter to Elliott, Cooper promised that Mackenzie "will be demolished." He later claimed that his Lake Erie pamphlet had "struck deep wherever it has been read," and that "Poor McKenzie is losing ground daily."[27] In the same drive for closure, some reviewers celebrated Cooper's Lake Erie pamphlet as the last word on the subject. One wrote in *The United States Magazine and Democratic Review* that "The controversy may now be considered at an end. Mr. Cooper has performed an operation analogous to that of the *Niagara* in the battle itself. He has not come into 'close action' till rather late in the day, perhaps, but after he has once fairly entered the enemy's line, scarce more than a single broadside of his heavy metal has been necessary to settle the question."[28]

Even this amusing conceit has its own paradox and loose end, demonstrating again that the battle cannot move from history to text in anything resembling a direct path. Cooper, the champion of Jesse Elliott, is metaphorically put in the position of Oliver Hazard Perry as he destroys the opposition. Cooper's pamphlet was not the last word, of course. In 1844 the embattled Mackenzie came out with a new edition of the *Life of Perry*, which contained a fifty-seven-page appendix responding to Cooper.[29] Here, he took Cooper's seamanship to task, saying it was all right for writing novels, but not for naval history. Cooper immediately promised another response, but none has been located. No doubt still "enabled," Cooper may have simply decided not to. Beginning with Perry's use of this term, a first sign that the battle had moved from the sea to the page, the authority of evidence in the Lake Erie affair yields increasingly to the predisposition of its interpreter.

Appendix: Cooper/Mackenzie Exchanges on the Subject of Lake Erie

May 1839: Cooper's *Naval History* published.

October 1839: Mackenzie's review in the *North American Review.*

1840: Mackenzie's *Life of Perry* published, the purpose of which is to restore the admiration of Perry, which Cooper had sought to diminish. Long chapters on Lake Erie directly rebut Cooper. Thirty-page appendix contains record of charges Perry brought against Elliott in 1818.

29 March 1841: Cooper's preliminary reply to Mackenzie's review of *Life of Perry* published in the *Evening Post.* Cooper says he cannot reply fully because the Duer suit is still being prosecuted and some of the facts bear materially on the Mackenzie review.

7 April 1841: Mackenzie's reply to Cooper published in the *Evening Post.*

May/June 1843: Cooper publishes his own brief biography of Perry in *Graham's Magazine.* Fifty-five of the eighty-six pages concern Lake Erie and its aftermath; they respond directly to Mackenzie's criticisms.

July 1843: Cooper responds fully to the Lake Erie affair with a pamphlet, *The Battle of Lake Erie, or Answers to Messrs. Burges, Duer, and Mackenzie.*

1844: Mackenzie brings out a new edition of his *Life of Perry,* which contains a fifty-seven-page appendix devoted to answering Cooper's points from the *Graham's Magazine* biography and *The Battle of Lake Erie* pamphlet.

Notes

1. William S. Dudley, ed., *The Naval War of 1812: A Documentary History*, vol. 2 (Washington, D.C.: Naval Historical Center, 1992), 557–58.

2. Gerard T. Altoff, "The Battle of Lake Erie: A Narrative," in *War on the Great Lakes*, eds. William Jeffrey Welsh and David Curtis Skaggs (Kent, Ohio: Kent State University Press, 1991), 5–16. For an account that includes maps illustrating the relative positions of the vessels during each half-hour of the battle, see Robert and Thomas Malcomson, *HMS* Detroit: *The Battle for Lake Erie* (Annapolis, Md.: Naval Institute Press, 1990), 94–111.

3. Before battle, Perry raised a flag with James Lawrence's famous words, "Don't give up the ship!" emblazoned on it. Edward L. Beach, *The United States Navy: 200 Years* (New York: Henry Holt and Company, 1986), 122.

4. Dudley, *Naval War of 1812*, 558.

5. David Curtis Skaggs, "Aiming at the Truth: James Fenimore Cooper and the Battle of Lake Erie," *Journal of Military History* 59 (April 1995): 250.

6. Perry's charges and supporting materials are published in the appendix of Russell Jarvis, *A Biographical Notice of Com. Jesse D. Elliott* (Philadelphia: Printed for the author, 1835), 447 ff.

7. Skaggs, "Aiming at the Truth," 248–49.

8. For an account of the strange career of Jesse D. Elliott, see Lawrence J. Friedman and David Curtis Skaggs, "Jesse Duncan Elliott and the Battle of Lake Erie: The Issue of Mental Instability," *Journal of the Early Republic* 10 (Winter 1990), 493–516.

9. James Fenimore Cooper, *History of the Navy of the United States of America* (Philadelphia: Lea and Blanchard, 1839), 402–4.

10. Duer's review was published serially in the *New-York Commercial Advertiser* on 8, 11, 14, and 19 June 1839; Tristam Burges, *The Battle of Lake Erie* (Philadelphia: Wm. Marshall & Co., 1839); [Alexander Slidell Mackenzie], *North American Review* 49 (October 1839): 432–67.

11. Burges, *The Battle of Lake Erie*, 52.

12. James Franklin Beard, ed., *The Letters and Journals of James Fenimore Cooper*, vol. 3 (Cambridge: Harvard University Press, 1960–68), 228.

13. *Quarterly Review* 59 (October 1837), 329.

14. Mackenzie, *North American Review*, 432.

15. Mackenzie, *The Life of Commodore Oliver Hazard Perry*, vol. 1 (New York: Harper & Brothers, 1840), 275.

16. Mackenzie, *The Life of Perry*, 277.

17. Cooper's letter of 29 March 1841 to the *Evening Post*, in which he gives a preliminary response to Mackenzie's *Life of Perry*. Beard, *Letters and Journals of Cooper*, 4:134.

18. Cooper, *The Battle of Lake Erie, or Answers to Messrs. Burges, Duer, and Mackenzie* (Cooperstown, N.Y.: Phinney, 1843), iii–iv.

19. Ibid., 23.

20. Ibid., 24.

21. Ibid., 35.

22. Ibid., 83.

23. Ibid., 49.

24. Ibid., 58.

25. *Proceedings of the Naval Court-Martial in the Case of Alexander Slidell Mackenzie* (Delmar, N.Y.: Scholars Facsimiles & Reprints, 1992), 279.

26. For my own account of the *Somers* affair, see the "Introduction" to *Proceedings*.

27. Beard, *Letters and Journals of Cooper*, 4:389, 400–401, 409.

28. Reprinted in ibid., 4:402.

29. Mackenzie, *The Life of Commodore Oliver Hazard Perry* (New York: Harper & Brothers, 1844), 271–328.

9

Nelson Resartus: Legitimate Order in Cooper's Fleet Novel

Robert D. Madison

The beginning of the year 1842 was a busy one for James Fenimore Cooper. He had published *The Deerslayer* in the autumn of the preceding year, the last of the Leatherstocking Tales and a work that would be acknowledged by future readers as a giant in American Literature. At the same time that he had been at work on *The Deerslayer*, he had also been revising and abridging his two-volume *History of the Navy of the United States of America* (1839, revised in 1840) for use as a text by midshipmen and apprentices. Cooper was, in his own eyes, as much a naval historian as he was a novelist—perhaps even more, as the evidence of the 1840s suggests.

Cooper had given up novel writing in the thirties, turning instead to strict social criticism of Europe and America and, increasingly, to naval affairs.[1] He had, in fact, prepared to write naval history for all his literary life. When he turned to naval materials for *The Two Admirals: A Tale* late in 1841, he was not simply experimenting with form.[2] He was using material in which he had immersed himself for over a

decade, and which in 1842 would produce (in terms of naval nonfiction) the biographies of three American naval officers (Somers, Bainbridge, and Dale) and a treatise on the British naval historian William
James. This last provided him with the themes of fleets and admirals;
the young United States had little experience with the former, and the
latter would not appear in America for over twenty years.

The Two Admirals began at first as a book about fleets; indeed, ships
were to be its only characters. That intention was almost entirely abandoned.[3] Instead, Cooper turned to naval character and his central portrait of the relationship between two differently tempered admirals.[4]
Oddly enough, Cooper, who had long been a proponent of the formation of the rank of admiral in the United States, did not develop this
polemical theme in the novel. Instead, he probed deeply into what has
been referred to in Navy education circles today as "the loyalty thing."

The Two Admirals chronicles the apoplexy and death of an English
baronet in 1745 and explores the legitimacy of his heirs' claims to wealth
and title, alongside an exploration of the legitimacy of the Stuart claim
to the throne of England. The first chapter's long discussion of the law of
the half blood—patently based on the discussion of Salic Law that opens
Henry V—prepares us for the issue. The outcome of the first half of
the book—a justification of the workings of the peerage and legitimate
claims through law—moves us far beyond the question of legitimacy.
We move into the second half of the book—the "sea novel" half—and
are presented with Admiral Richard Bluewater's dilemma: a choice between a legitimacy he believes (and that Cooper forces us to accede, however reluctantly) is true, and loyalty to Sir Gervaise Oakes, his commander and deepest friend.

The basis of this relationship, and many of the minor aspects of
plot, is drawn (as Richard H. Ballinger pointed out long ago) from
Robert Southey's *Life of Nelson* and the correspondence of Nelson's
close friend Collingwood.[5] Cooper's debt to his own *History of the
Navy*, also suggested by Ballinger, is certainly insignificant, however,
compared to what Cooper immersed himself in while responding to
the *Edinburgh Review*'s acclamation for Captain Chamier's edition of
William James's The *Naval History of Great Britain* (1837).[6]

This impressive sideshow of 1842 is the key to understanding
Cooper's sources in this book. Cooper's *Democratic Review* essay about

William James focuses (as did his knowledge) on the conflict between England and the United States, but *The Two Admirals* draws on the full range of British naval history, is set well before open hostilities between England and the colonies, and bears no biographical relationship to either Collingwood or Nelson, despite the plundering of works specifically by and about them.

In fact, Sir Gervaise Oakes, the commanding admiral, is patently based not on the close relationship between Nelson and Hardy or Collingwood, but on John Jervis, Earl St. Vincent. Jervis had been Nelson's mentor and sponsor; nevertheless, Nelson broke with him, as described by Robert Southey in *The Life of Nelson:*

> Then came the victory at Copenhagen: which Nelson truly called, the most difficult achievement, the hardest fought battle, the most glorious result, that ever graced the annals of our country. He, of course, expected the medal: and, in writing to Earl St. Vincent, said: "He longed to have it, and would not give it up to be made an English duke." The medal, however, was not given:—"For what reason," said Nelson, "Lord St. Vincent best knows."—Words plainly implying a suspicion, that it was withheld by some feeling of jealousy; and that suspicion estranged him, during the remaining part of his life, from one who had at one time been, essentially, as well as sincerely, his friend.[7]

In a book that dwells on the possibility of disloyalty, one also suspects the ever-present influence of the Perry-Elliott controversy as well. The key action of the book—Bluewater's hesitation and then succor of his friend—matches the Lake Erie relationship much more closely. Nelson, however, never hesitated. The three strands in the naval portion of the book can thus be recognized: the Nelson strand, bringing with it obvious names of subordinates and the major fleet maneuvers; the Jervis strand, focussing on the Admiral of Cooper's choice who best represented the impeccable tradition of British command at sea; and the Elliott strand, of fraternity gone wrong.[8]

The theme does, in fact, come from the intersection of the Nelson and Jervis strands, but they are twisted. The chief end of service in the naval world of *The Two Admirals* is gaining a peerage: becoming part of the established, the legitimate, unassailable order of things. "When your work is done," exclaims Sir Gervaise to subordinate Captain

Parker, "make the best of your way to the nearest English port, and clap a Scotchman on your shoulder to keep the king's sword from chafing it. They thought me fit for a knighthood at three and twenty, and the deuce is in it, Parker, if you are not worthy of it, at three and sixty." "You will be made Viscount Bowldero, for these last affairs," a wounded Bluewater advises his friend, Sir Gervaise; "Nor do I see, why you should again refuse a peerage." Not only is naval promotion secondary glory to these fictional characters, but there is also a long subtext centered on a young officer whose social rank—he is *Lord* Geoffrey—gives him privilege among his seniors afloat. And it is Lord Geoffrey who, at the very close of the novel, provides continuity at a time when an old Sir Gervaise is unable to remember the friendship, loyalty, or even name of his subordinate, Richard Bluewater: "The gentleman is now at the tomb of his dearest friend," Lord Geoffrey observes, "and yet, as you see, he appears to have lost all recollection that such a person ever existed."

The Two Admirals is not history. It is neither the historic relationship between Nelson and his associates nor, except as sheer fantasy, is it the relationship between Cooper and his best friend, William Branford Shubrick, prophetic as that name may be for American admirals. Cooper's book is more nearly a Shakespearean comedy, consciously clinging to the unities of time and place. It is dark comedy, concluded by a marriage that does nothing to resolve the themes of loyalty and legitimacy that have been tested afloat and ashore. The generosity of Sir Gervaise extends to recognize the justice of a young applicant's claim to a baronetcy, but not the Stuart Pretender's claim to the throne. Ashore, law is paramount. Afloat, issues of legitimate command and obedience, while unclouded, are resolved only through the mechanism of personal loyalty. Bluewater's crisis is not so much one of loyalty as recognizing the conflict of these principles—and opting for the immediate "right" of friendship.

Had this book been written a year later, no doubt we would speculate about the Gansevoort-Mackenzie relationship as a source for Bluewater's dilemma. But *The Two Admirals* was published in early spring, 1842, and Cooper went right to work on *The Wing-and-Wing*, perhaps his most mature romance of the sea.[9] In it Nelson appears as a major character in a major episode that plays out the historical drama of the Caracciolo hanging, the darkest blot on Nelson's career. Cooper, after all, saw Nelson as a highly questionable—if de facto—role model for the rising American Navy. *The Wing-and-Wing* came out in November of 1842, just as the next chapter in Cooper's life as a naval historian was beginning, not far to the east of the Lesser Antilles, in a brig named the *Somers*.[10]

Notes

1. See my introduction to the abridged *History of the Navy* (Delmar, N.Y.: Scholars' Facsimiles & Reprints, 1988) for a fuller analysis of the earlier naval writings.

2. For a complete discussion of Cooper's proposal for a novel with no human characters, only ships, see Don Ringe's introduction to the State University of New York edition of *The Two Admirals* (Albany: 1990). Cooper's intention may also have been sublimated in his unfinished "biography" of the USS *Constitution*, a long essay he had intended to publish alongside his human biographies in *Lives of Distinguished American Naval Officers* (1846).

3. Tom Clancy's *Hunt for Red October* (Annapolis, Md.: Naval Institute Press, 1984) is largely written in this form, with obvious tremendous success. Cooper's publisher, a hundred and forty years earlier, balked.

4. One might cynically say these admirals are the Effinghams redivivi. One is a tactician, the other a seaman; one is laissez-faire, the other a micromanager; one loyal to the house of Stuart, the other loyal to the house of Hanover. Cooper enjoyed working with doubles.

5. "Origins of James Fenimore Cooper's *The Two Admirals*," *American Literature* 20 (1948): 20–30.

6. Cooper's essay "The Edinburgh Review on James's Naval Occurrences and Cooper's Naval History" appeared in the *United States Magazine and Democratic Review* 10 (1842), 411–35, 515–41. James was essentially "doubled" by Cooper's piece and the unsigned *New York Review* article of early 1842, an essay that depended extensively on Cooper's own *History of the Navy* (1840):

> The recent appearance of a new edition of James's *Naval History of Great Britain*, repeating all the former misrepresentations in his narrative of events connected with our country, seems to us to offer a fit occasion for examining its claims to the authenticity of history; and in doing this, we shall find no difficulty, we think, in convincing the writer not only of a uniform violation

of truth in his record of everything that concerns ourselves, but also of such malignity of spirit as must disqualify him for his office, and destroy his credibility as a historian. ("James's Naval History of Great Britain," *New York Review* 10 [January 1842]: 184. The new edition was edited by Captain Chamier, R.N.)

Neither Cooper's piece nor the *New York Review* essay handles James particularly delicately.

7. *The Life of Nelson* (Annapolis, Md.: Naval Institute Press, 1990), 240–41.

8. Such contributions include the lessons of the Nile (388), "Kiss me, Oakes" (442), anticipations of Nelson's flagship, the *Victory* (357), the duty of an Englishman to hate a Frenchman (181), Nelson's idea of the proper place being alongside the enemy (254), and the names of Parker and Foley (and probably others, including the similarity of Vervillin and Villeneuve). Southey's *Lives of the British Admirals* probably also ought to be examined, not only for its contribution to Cooper's naval lore but also as a model for Cooper's own *Lives of Distinguished American Naval Officers* (published with this title in 1846). The idea of ducking a shot (336) comes directly from the Perry-Elliott controversy. The horrid and ironic anticipation of the *Somers* hangings (341, 354) may indicate, along with A. S. Mackenzie's description of the hanging in *A Year in Spain* and Cooper's own description of the hanging in *The Wing-and-Wing*, a morbid fascination for hanging prevalent among antebellum naval officers.

9. *The Two Admirals* turned out to be a surprisingly popular work: it was reprinted two-volumes-in-one by Lea and Blanchard in 1843, by Burgess and Stringer in 1845, and possibly by Stringer and Townsend in 1848 (in addition to the printings mentioned in Ringe's introduction). Near the turn of the century, *The Two Admirals* was published as part of a British six-volume set of sea tales, which included George Cupples's *The Green Hand,* Frederick Marryat's *Mr. Midshipman Easy,* Michael Scott's *Tom Cringle's Log,* William Clark Russell's *The Wreck of the Grosvenor,* and, remarkably, Herman Melville's *Moby-Dick.* The inclusion of this work out of all of Cooper's maritime romances indicates the higher esteem in which the work was held in the land of its setting and main characters.

10. Cooper's vitriolic response to the *Somers* affair found expression in *The Battle of Lake Erie* (1843), *Ned Myers; or, A Life before the Mast* (1843), and, exhaustively, in "Review of the Proceedings of the Naval Court Martial" (1844) (Delmar, N.Y.: Scholars' Facsimiles & Reprints, State University of New York Press). His general antipathy to Alexander Slidell Mackenzie, whom Cooper must have regarded as a literary rival second only to Sir Walter Scott, found utterance in virtually all of his naval writings after 1839. But that's another—and another's—story.

"One had actually sunk, and five or six were round the spot endeavoring to pick up the crew." The *Crisis* emerges victorious from a battle with twenty-eight proas. *(Afloat and Ashore)*

10

Fact and Fiction: The Uses of Maritime History in Cooper's *Afloat and Ashore*

Thomas Philbrick

ooper's 1844 double novel, *Afloat and Ashore*, marks a major change in the course of his sea fiction.[1] The nautical novels of the first decade of his literary career—*The Pilot* of 1824, *The Red Rover* of 1827, and *The Water-Witch* of 1830—were works that helped to propel him into the front rank of the artists of the romantic movement that was then sweeping the Western world. When Cooper moved his family across the Atlantic to take up a residence in Europe that extended over the next seven years, he was quickly received as the coequal of Sir Walter Scott, with whom he almost immediately exchanged visits in Paris; of Coleridge, with whom he dined in England; and even of the supreme shaper of the new sensibility, the aged Goethe, himself an avid reader of Cooper's early romances.[2]

Those first three sea novels grew out of and gave expression to the same artistic culture as that which fostered Byron and Berlioz. In them, the ocean is significant chiefly as an embodiment of wild nature, grandly dwarfing the powers and intentions of the human actors who strut and fret upon its colossal stage. Those few superb seamen whose defiant unconventionality, enormous skill, and tempestuous energy fit them for a life at sea become exemplars of romantic heroism, darkly intense, morally ambiguous, sublimely egocentric.

In such a fictional world, history functions chiefly as a means of deepening the background, enhancing the aura of significance, and removing the action from the diminishing familiarity of the here and now. The evocation of the era of the American Revolution in *The Pilot*, of mid-eighteenth century piracy in *The Red Rover*, or of smuggling in early eighteenth-century colonial New York in *The Water-Witch* is there chiefly to surround the fiction in the atmosphere of legend. Paradoxically, history, the appeal to the actuality of the past, serves to distance the work from the reader's experience, to make the story in a sense less real, more shadowy, more in touch with the absolutes that underlie the world of mere appearances.

A much different program informs the three maritime novels that, after a ten-year hiatus, followed the three early romances. *Mercedes of Castile* of 1840, and *The Two Admirals* and *The Wing-and-Wing*, both of 1842, all evoke the historical past for its own sake, attempting to render it with scrupulous accuracy and presenting it as a major center of interest. These are the novels that follow in the wake of Cooper's great *History of the Navy*, the first edition of which appeared in 1839, and in them the historian competes with the romancer for control of the work, disastrously in *Mercedes*, interestingly in the other two. Although written after Cooper's return to the United States, all three are as much European novels as *The Bravo* and the other two books that usually receive that label, for all three turn to the European past for their materials—to the age of discovery, to the great fleet actions of the Royal Navy in the eighteenth century, and to warfare in the Mediterranean in the Napoleonic era—as if only Europe furnished the grand events and the colossal figures in which formal historiography, and the fiction that tries to imitate its tone and effects, should deal.

In *Afloat and Ashore*, Cooper once more turned to the maritime past, indeed, to the very period in which he had set *The Wing-and-Wing* of two years earlier, here defined as 1796 to 1804. In the new book, everything changes, shifting toward the familiar and near. Two examples may illustrate the tendency of the change. In *The Wing-and-Wing*, the love plot is kept roiling by the clash between the hero's French revolutionary atheism and the heroine's Italian Catholic piety; in *Afloat and Ashore* the lovers are both middle-class American Episcopalians from the Hudson River valley, kept apart chiefly by the young man's feelings of social inferiority. In *The Wing-and-Wing*, Nelson unjustly hangs the Italian admiral Francesco Caracciolo in the Bay of Naples; in *Afloat and Ashore*, the hard-faced acting master of an American merchant vessel unjustly hangs a shriveled old Indian on the Northwest Coast.

It is impossible to reconstruct fully the circumstances that turned Cooper from the glamour and pageantry of the European past to the bustling activity of commercial America at the turn of the century for the materials of his new sea novel, but one experience would seem to have been crucial. Writing to his British publisher, Richard Bentley, in June 1843, Cooper announced his intention to "come forth with a new nautical story, immediately."[3] In that same month of June, however, he brought to his home in Cooperstown a broken down and boozy old seamen named Ned Myers, who as a boy had been the writer's shipmate aboard the merchantman *Stirling* in 1806 and 1807 and who had written a few months before to ask if the writer was indeed his old boyhood friend.

As Ned spun his yarns in the course of a visit that stretched into a period of five months, Cooper soon abandoned his plans, whatever they were, for a new sea novel, and in late July wrote to Bentley that the new book would be Ned's story. It would be, he said, "*real biography*, intended to represent the experience, wrecks, battles, escapes, and career of a seaman who has been in all sorts of vessels, from a man of war to a smuggler of opium in China." Acting as Ned's amanuensis and editor, Cooper would "put nothing down that I do not believe to be strictly fact."[4] In early November, the book, entitled *Ned Myers, or, A Life before the Mast* (*pace* Richard Henry Dana), was published, and Ned himself, with "a handsome fee" in his pocket, was on his way back to Sailors' Snug Harbor on Staten Island.[5]

It was only after all that, in December of 1843, when Cooper began writing the novel that was to become *Afloat and Ashore*. I do not mean to suggest that the novel was to be simply a fictionalized version of

Ned's life, for almost nothing of the incidents in Ned's story finds its way into *Afloat and Ashore*. Rather, the five months with Ned turned Cooper's mind to his own early experience as a merchant sailor, encouraging him to remember the world as it was then and to imagine how it would have been if, instead of entering the Navy as a midshipman after his first voyage, he had, as his character Miles Wallingford was to do, remained in the merchant service and risen to the eventual command and ownership of a vessel.

Out of some such mixture of remembrance and fantasy the new book took shape. Cooper drew upon the scenes time and again, the happenings, and the feelings of his own youth for the materials of his fiction, especially in the account of Miles Wallingford's first voyage. Like Miles, Cooper himself, as Alan Taylor has recently demonstrated, ran away from his inland home to go to sea.[6] Like Miles, he had crossed the Atlantic to England, running the gauntlet of French privateers and British boarding parties. Like Miles, he had toured the seamy side of London under the guidance of a corrupt English customs officer.[7] And so it goes. No novel of Cooper's, not even *The Pioneers,* is as autobiographical as *Afloat and Ashore*.

Relatively extensive though they are, however, those autobiographical materials in fact make up only a small proportion of the total fabric of *Afloat and Ashore*. Nevertheless, they set the pattern for the color and texture of the entire work, for the fictional extensions and elaborations from which the novel is woven are held to a standard of plausibility consistent with the actuality of remembered experience.

The primary means by which Cooper enforced his own adherence to that standard in *Afloat and Ashore* was his use of first-person narration, a technique he had not employed before in a full-scale novel. In the course of Miles Wallingford's narration, the succession of fictive incidents blends indistinguishably with the autobiographical basis of the character in a seamless fusion of memory and imagination. Everything is in keeping with the likely scope of experience available to a middle-class child of the new republic. There are no Byronic gestures or superhuman exploits, no participation in great historical events, no glamour and no heroics, nothing of the heightened color and excited pitch of the earlier sea novels. There is in *Afloat and Ashore,* in other

words, a sharp turn toward realism, toward materials that are consistent with the reader's own sense of the way things are.

The novel is set in the past, the action taking place some forty-five
years before the book's first publication. Indeed, Miles's first voyage
occurs just about ten years earlier than Cooper's own first voyage, at a
time when the author himself was a child of seven. Moreover, Miles's
eight-year career as a merchant sailor carries him to parts of the world
unknown to his creator, to the coast of Madagascar, the West and East
Indies, the Pacific coast of South and North America, Hawaii, Canton,
the Baltic, the Dardanelles, and the Irish Sea. It thrusts him into situations and actions that Cooper had never experienced—the ordeal of
shipwreck, the anxieties of command, and the risks and uncertainties
of international commerce.

If these materials were to meet the requirements of plausibility
that the tonality of *Afloat and Ashore* demanded, then they had to have
the same aura of authenticity as those that derived from Cooper's
memories—fitting out at the wharves of Manhattan, say, or eating
from the common kid in the dark forecastle of a merchantman, or tid-
ing up the crowded Thames in the time before steam tugs. To imbue
the purely fictive elements of the book with the necessary verisimilitude,
Cooper surely relied chiefly on his unMelville-like powers of invention,
his extraordinary capacity to daydream with something of the clarity
and specificity of experience. But that had always been his own best
trick, as every reader of his Indian novels soon discovers.

For the new realism of *Afloat and Ashore,* he evidently turned to
sources that would supplement memory and imagination, sources that
were different, moreover, from the formal histories upon which his three
European maritime novels of the early 1840s had drawn. Although it is
impossible to identify the particular routes by which information came
to him in most instances, it is apparent that many of the details of incident and scene out of which the story of Miles Wallingford's voyaging
is constructed derive from Cooper's broad acquaintance with those
whose maritime experience went far beyond his own. Among such
sources were naval officers, like his closest friend William Branford
Shubrick and like Charles Wilkes, who was seeing his *Narrative of the
United States Exploring Expedition* through the press in Philadelphia at

the very moment when Cooper was there to proofread *Afloat and Ashore;* acquaintanceships, too, with merchant seamen like his nephews Morris and William Cooper.

More important, perhaps, was his familiarity with documentary sources pertaining to maritime experience, not only with those that had contributed to *History of the Navy* and to his ongoing series of naval biographies appearing in *Graham's Magazine* during the very months in which *Afloat and Ashore* was written, but with the huge literature of eighteenth- and nineteenth-century voyage narratives, made all the more plentiful by the success of Richard Henry Dana's *Two Years before the Mast* in 1840. The one explicit reference to such literary sources in *Afloat and Ashore* is to Frederick Beechey's *Narrative of a Voyage to the Pacific and Bering's Straits* of 1831, but the source-hunting reader can detect traces of James Cook's *Voyages*, Richard Alsop's *Narrative of the Adventures and Sufferings of John R. Jewitt*, Richard Cleveland's *Narrative of Voyages and Commercial Enterprises*, and so on, evidence, finally, not of any scene-shaping prototype à la Herman Melville, but of Cooper's saturation in the literature of the sea.[8]

Thus the historical element in *Afloat and Ashore* is powerful and pervasive, but it is of a sort that offers a special appeal to those who adopt a view of history that attends less to the march of great public events than to the texture of private lives, less to the doings of the great than to the enterprises of the ordinary. We view the undeclared naval war with France not through the eyes of a commander like Thomas Truxtun but through those of a merchant sailor, desperately trying to preserve his hide and his cargo from the grasp of a French privateer. In this book, the naval engagements of the Napoleonic wars are not the battles of the Nile and Copenhagen but infuriating encounters with the well-born younger sons who command British frigates, ever eager to press fresh seamen and to enrich themselves by confiscating American vessels. All in all, the book offers an extraordinarily wide and detailed panorama of American maritime activity in the era before Jefferson's embargo, everything from beating off proas in the Straits of Sunda to driving before a gale through the Straits of Magellan under bare poles; from bartering for sea otter skins with the natives of the Northwest Coast to making up a cargo for Hamburg in the markets of New York.

Afloat and Ashore is something more than a fictionalized evocation of a crucial period of American maritime activity, something other than simply a sea novel. In the last analysis, it is a book about property, a book in which nearly every motive, every action, every concern, has some vital relation to economic value. Just beneath the narrative surface of Miles Wallingford's vicissitudes by land and sea lies a deep stratum of thematic concern, a virtually obsessive interest in buying and selling, borrowing and lending, profit and loss, owning and being owned, prosperity and bankruptcy. In no other novel of Cooper's do incidents, situations, and dialogue so incessantly turn on issues that are in some way or other financial in nature. Everything—from Neb, who is Miles's beloved companion and also his slave, to a young girl's parting gift of gold coins—has an economic value and can be regarded as property; action becomes transaction, whether it is bartering with the natives on the Northwest Coast or mortgaging the family home in Ulster County; conversations, whether between businessmen or lovers, again and again refer to incomes, bequests, exchange rates, prices, stocks, or interest. Insofar as *Afloat and Ashore* is a sea novel, it is the first one of Cooper's in which ships are put up for sale, used as collateral, salvaged, insured, condemned—treated, in short, as economic instruments rather than as expressions of their commander's will, vehicles of personal freedom, or objects of aesthetic admiration.

This is to argue that *Afloat and Ashore* is far more than a tale of adventure in which maritime history is introduced chiefly in order to lend the action an air of plausibility. Maritime history is introduced into the what-if world of this fiction because it provides the broadest and most vivid tapestry of financial activity that Cooper could conceive of, generating the actions and images that sustain his prolonged meditation upon man as an economic animal.

Notes

1. In keeping with Cooper's own practice, I apply the title *Afloat and Ashore* to both the first and second parts of the novel. After his death, his publishers in the United States generally retained that title only for the first part, calling the second part *Miles Wallingford*. In Great Britain, the second part has gone by the name of *Lucy Hardinge*.

2. James Fenimore Cooper, *Gleanings in Europe: France,* ed. Thomas Philbrick and Constance Ayers Denne (Albany: State University of New York Press, 1983), 148–57; James Fenimore Cooper, *Gleanings in Europe: England,* ed. James P. Elliott, et al. (Albany: State University of New York Press, 1982), 122–28 and 260–62; Johann Wolfgang Goethe, *Tagebücher,* ed. Gerhart Baumann, vol. 3 (Stuttgart, Germany: J. G. Cotta'sche, n.d.), 485–88.

3. James Franklin Beard, ed., *The Letters and Journals of James Fenimore Cooper,* vol. 4 (Cambridge: Harvard University Press, Belknap Press, 1964), 388.

4. Ibid., 391–92.

5. James Fenimore Cooper to Susan Augusta Cooper, 22 Sept. 1843; Cooper to Paul Fenimore Cooper, 9 Nov. 1843, Beard, *Letters and Journals of Cooper,* 412 and 425.

6. Alan Taylor, "James Fenimore Cooper Goes to Sea: Two Unpublished Letters by a Family Friend," *Studies in the American Renaissance* (1993): 43–54.

7. James Fenimore Cooper, *Ned Myers, or, A Life before the Mast,* ed. William S. Dudley (Annapolis, Md.: Naval Institute Press, 1989), 22–40; Cooper writing an anonymous review of Basil Hall, *Travels* in *New Monthly Magazine* 32 (Oct. 1831): 309–10; and Cooper, *Gleanings in Europe: England,* 30, 192–95.

8. Thomas Philbrick, *James Fenimore Cooper and the Development of American Sea Fiction* (Cambridge: Harvard University Press, 1961), 132–40.

James Fenimore Cooper

11

Cooper as Passenger

Wayne Franklin

Scholars interested in the seagoing experience of nineteenth-century American writers tend to focus on the time those writers spent as common sailors rather than passengers, perhaps because sailor-authors such as Richard Henry Dana or Herman Melville themselves were somewhat uncomfortable in the latter role. On his crossing to London on the liner *Southampton* in 1849, Melville invested considerable effort proving to his fellow passengers that he really was not just their fellow: hence his "gymnastics" at the masthead, his scoffing at the "nausea noise" that oozed from the staterooms, his eagerness to demonstrate to the sailors that he was one of them, his desire to ride out on the bowsprit after philosophizing with Adler and Taylor ("splendid spectacle," he noted), and so on.[1] Dana on the *Pilgrim* in the 1830s was always aware of his middle-class origins and labored to conceal them or vacate them by adopting a forecastle perspective. At last, oppressed by the fear that staying longer in California would convert his temporary role before the mast into a permanent fate, Dana used his "connections" in the world of commerce to arrange for a voyage home, thus arousing the suspicions of his fellow sailors that he wasn't really, for all his hard labor, one of them. Such a sailor was at least partly a passenger, his presence on the vessel being a matter of choice rather than necessity. His voyage was a vacation rather than a mark of vocation.

James Fenimore Cooper preceded Dana and Melville in the forecastle, and in this particular problem as well: as Alan Taylor writes, "In 1806 it was very unusual for a well-educated son of wealth and privilege to assume the hardships, drudgery, dangers, and low status of a common sailor."[2] In such cases, we may suspect, with good reason, that the "assumption" of the common sailor's lot was less than complete, for the articles of what Hugh Egan has called the "gentleman sailor" often contained handy escape clauses.[3]

Cooper began his voyage on the merchant vessel *Stirling* in 1806-7 in just such a protected manner. As the reminiscences of the cabin boy Ned Myers, edited by Cooper in 1843, remind us, the sixteen-year-old Cooper was accompanied to the vessel by two grown men, one of them a quarter owner of the vessel and the consignee of its cargo, unnamed in *Ned Myers* but revealed by a descendent of the captain of the *Stirling* to have been the famous Quaker merchant Jacob Barker, who, Captain John Johnston's descendent stated, was the business associate of William Cooper.[4] Although neither Alan Taylor's research nor my own has uncovered evidence of a direct tie between Judge Cooper and Jacob Barker in the voluminous William Cooper papers, apparently something in the Johnston family archives—presently unlocated—indicated the link. However that may be, the Johnstons's identification of Barker as one of the two merchants who led young Cooper to the *Stirling* in 1806 is certain. James Cooper did not approach the *Stirling* on his own, cap in hand, begging for a chance to sail before the mast in her, but rather was brought on board by men with commercial interests in the voyage.

How did Jacob Barker become involved in helping to arrange for young Cooper's berth? James had run away from Cooperstown sometime in the early summer of 1806, probably heading first for New York, where his older brother William Jr. then resided. In mid-July, William wrote a letter to family friend Richard R. Smith of Philadelphia, informing him of James's flight and alerting him that the young fugitive was on his way to Philadelphia. Smith was a sometime Cooperstown resident and business partner of Judge William Cooper, who owed his appointment as the first sheriff of Otsego County to the judge's influence—and his eventual fame as the model for the authoritarian sheriff Richard Jones in *The Pioneers* to the Judge's youngest son. In 1806 he was being called on to act on behalf of the family's interests in order to resolve the crisis that James's flight from Cooperstown had precipitated.

In reply to the letter from young William Cooper in New York, Smith on 18 July wrote Isaac Cooper, another of the brothers, in Cooperstown, saying that he had that day received William's news and asking what he should do if and when the wayward youth showed up on his doorstep. James must have arrived there almost immediately thereafter, certainly before any answer could arrive from Cooperstown, and spent the next three weeks in the city before heading overland back to New York. While James was in Philadelphia, a letter from Isaac dated 30 July, and containing "the Judge's memorandum" regarding his plight, arrived for Smith. From a letter Smith sent somewhat later, in which he noted that one from Cooperstown had arrived in five days ("a very short time for the Mail to come if you date correctly"),[5] we can assume that Isaac's 30 July missive arrived perhaps around 5 or 6 August (Smith says it came "in course"—that is, in the ordinary time), just a day or two before James was set to leave. We also may assume that James received his father's "memorandum," either as a document or through Smith's rehearsal of its arguments. From Smith's answer to Isaac, written on 8 August, the morning after James left for New York, it is clear that the Cooper family prior to that time knew of the boy's intention of running off to sea, with an eye to a career in the Navy, which was not mentioned in Smith's first letter and perhaps had not been divulged in William's unlocated letter of mid-July to Smith.

In writing to Isaac on this second occasion, Smith filled in some details about James's plans. The Judge's memorandum must have contained an armory of arguments to be aimed at the heart and head of the runaway, but Smith, who himself already had sought to dissuade his "young Friend" from going to sea by applying all the arguments he could invent, evidently did not find the new weapons any more convincing. He urged James to consider what hardships lay ahead and sought to delay him until "some Plan could be arranged with the Judge." Well connected in Philadelphia's business world, Smith also offered to find James a safer slot in "a Counting House" there, as he earlier had done for Isaac. When James persisted in his designs on a career at sea, Smith tendered further help: "I then offered to introduce him to some shipping Merchants of my acquaintance in whose Vessels he would have been less exposed to insult and ill treatment. But it would not do."

Why would it not do? During the three weeks James was in Philadelphia, Smith had gleaned enough to suspect that James, taken with the romance of a momentary excitement, had even more dangerous plans buzzing in his brain: he hoped to find some means of joining Francisco Miranda's effort to liberate his homeland, Venezuela, from the Spanish crown. Miranda had secured a ship in New York the previous February and sailed it, with an American crew, south for the purpose. As Alan Taylor has noted, American newspapers of the period, including the *Otsego Herald* in Cooperstown, contained glowing reports of the expedition, and the liberal revolutionary's intent to spread New World revolution to South America clearly excited the ardor of many young Americans.[6] Although Taylor does not mention this further point, when Ned Myers himself decided to run away to the sea in the winter of 1805–6, he first served port duty on board Miranda's ship, the *Leander*, in New York before its departure but "became heartily tired of it" and left.[7]

Regarding Ned's future shipmate and "editor," Smith wrote Isaac Cooper on 8 August that the stint with Miranda apparently was to be a prelude to a naval career: "I suspect he wishes to join Miranda for the present, with some future Views to the Navy." Indeed, Smith learned that James already "had written to Mr. Simmons of the War Office to procure him a warrant, and had desired him to direct [his answer] to my care." From Smith's wording here, it would seem that James had written William Simmons, the accountant of the War Department, from New York City as he was preparing to leave there for Philadelphia, a point which, if true, would suggest how well formed James's overall plan was shortly after he had run away, or perhaps even before leaving Cooperstown. Smith added that young Cooper subsequently learned that Simmons was away from Washington at the time, in New York State actually.

The youth's return to New York City from Philadelphia in August was motivated in part by his failure to secure a berth in a Philadelphia ship bound for the Caribbean and in part by the hope that he still could make contact with Simmons before, as was now his intent, finding a berth on a ship there. James would not tell Philadelphian Smith his intended New York City address, but did tell him that he would check for mail at the post office each day. Smith reported this last fact to Isaac Cooper in the hope that letters from Cooperstown would reach James before he made any rash commitments, but James's reason must have been to allow word from Simmons, not Isaac or his father, to reach him.

James Cooper did not receive his midshipman's warrant until 1808, as it happened, but I presume his original plan was to attempt to secure one before committing himself to a merchant vessel in 1806. I also presume that he wanted one then in order to make his future seem more organized, as this would have been a good way to convince his family that the impulsive behavior that had caused his expulsion from Yale (and, to be sure, his running away this very summer) was a thing of the past, and that he was aimed toward a respectable, perhaps glorious career. Finally, if as seems to have been the case, Cooper thought he could obtain a warrant and then sail on a merchant vessel as a means of learning the skills any naval officer would need to know, he may have been counting on a warrant in hand to help protect him from possible impressment by the British from whatever American merchant vessel he might eventually sail on.

Cooper did not have a warrant when he departed with the *Stirling* around 1 September, but I think Alan Taylor's analysis of what he did possess rather astute. The Cooper family undoubtedly reached out via the channels suggested by Smith in his 8 August letter, perhaps following part of the advice Smith somewhat hesitantly offered based on his sense of the young man's apparent firmness: "I am not fond of giving advice, but were James my son and he was so resolutely bent on the Navy as he now appears to be, I would immediately apply for a Warrant." Smith went on to narrate James's attempts to get a warrant on his own, and then concluded with a point that I think motivated the Cooper family—surprisingly passive in dealing with James's crisis up to this point—to intervene more actively in James's plans so as to shield him somewhat from the hazards that lay before him: "He is certainly too young to be launched into the World without protection." If the link between Judge Cooper and Jacob Barker indeed existed, then Smith's earlier offer of easing James into a life at sea via commercial connections of his own may have provided them with the design the Coopers themselves followed.

Barker, like Judge Cooper, was of Quaker background, though not from Pennsylvania—he had been born in Maine of Nantucket parents. His long mercantile career, many times awash in controversies about the sharpness and indeed honesty of his dealings, began when he was very young. He was only in his midtwenties when Cooper shipped on the *Stirling,* but in his (not wholly reliable) *Incidents in the Life of Jacob Barker,* published in 1855, the assertion is found that he was "probably the largest [shipowner] in the United States, with the exception of William Gray, of Salem, and was conducting a large commission business when Jefferson's embargo was adopted [late in 1807]." His vast mercantile endeavors easily could have brought him into contact with William Cooper, although Barker was a Jeffersonian and as such hardly could have been fully intimate with Cooper. Barker, in fact, vigorously supported the embargo, speaking in its behalf at workers' and seamen's gatherings in New York even as it destroyed his own business. He was, however, close enough to one of Cooper's own associates, lawyer Miers Fisher of Philadelphia, for the link with Federalist Cooper to have been at least indirectly forged, perhaps merely for the purpose of seeing young James safely at sea.

Fisher, a Philadelphia mayor who had become Cooper's partner in land development, seems to have been especially concerned with the welfare of Judge Cooper's children, writing the latter's sons in 1809 on the occasion of the Judge's death a letter of pained sympathy that eulogized their father's accomplishments.[8] Given the closeness of his relationship to Judge Cooper, Fisher may well have been the person through whom three years earlier the judge had sought to exert himself on behalf of James. Indeed, it also is possible that it was Fisher who accompanied Barker to the *Stirling* later in the summer of 1806, with James Cooper tagging along, as the boy's fate, in the form of the papers soon to be given him by Captain Johnston for signing, came closer and closer. Fisher's home, to be sure, was in Philadelphia, but he is known to have been in New York later in 1807 and to have visited Judge Cooper in Cooperstown in 1808.[9] Of course, at this point all of what I say on the topic ends in speculation, rendered less than pure speculation perhaps by a few bits of circumstantial and associational evidence.

The Johnston narrative baldly asserts that "This Mr. Barker was a personal friend of Cooper's father, and through his influence young Cooper was shipped as a 'foremast hand on board."[10] Ned Myers, who had simply come on board on his own, and in fact lied his way into his berth as apprentice to Johnston, serving as cabin boy, provides an interesting version (presumably with the approval of his editor, Cooper) of the event. Myers only briefly described Cooper's coming on board, but it is significant, I think, that he recalled no detailed negotiations regarding James's addition to the crew. The *Stirling* was laden with its cargo of flour, so close to sailing that it departed only two days after James appeared.

As an indentured cabin boy of perhaps eleven, Myers cannot be expected to have seen everything or understood all he did see or to have recalled it nearly forty years later when he dictated his book to Cooper. He probably only slowly grasped what was happening, and may even have taken Cooper at first as a would-be passenger on the voyage. I suggest this last point because Ned rather curiously introduced his account of the episode by saying, "Passengers were not common in that day, while commerce was pushed to the utmost. Our sails were bending when the consignee, followed by another merchant, came down to the ship, accompanied by a youth, who, it was understood, wished also to be received in the vessel."[11] Myers did not directly state that Barker and the other "merchant" wished to book passage (and in fact his later census of the ship's population makes it certain that they did not), though he may have taken them for potential passengers as they approached the ship that day. Did he at first think Cooper was to be an "uncommon" passenger, too? Perhaps, though the "also" in his statement ("[Cooper] wished also to be received in the vessel") may more likely refer to Myers's own recent signing on, not to any possible wish on the part of the merchants to be accommodated on board themselves. And it may even be that the force of "it was understood" is to signify that word of Cooper's coming had been received before his arrival, perhaps through Barker or the other merchant, with whom Myers's account more closely associates him. In that case, we may wonder whether the merchants had not already reached agreement with Johnston (who was half-owner of the vessel as well as its captain) to sign Cooper on.

That conclusion is perhaps supported by Ned's further comment that "[Cooper] was accepted by Capt. Johnston, signed the articles, and the next day he joined us, in sailor's rig. He never came to the cabin, but was immediately employed forward, in such service as he was able to perform. It was afterwards understood that he was destined for the navy." In short, the whole process by which Cooper was shipped on the *Stirling* smacks of an arrangement concluded on shore: Cooper came on board with Barker and the other merchant so that Johnston, who had been party to the arrangement, could see him and judge him for himself. On this, Ned Myers and the Johnston narrative seem to be in clear agreement.

Cooper thus shipped not as a true forecastle hand but rather as a well-connected young man with a landed identity that would give him special status on board, a not uncommon figure in Cooper's sea fiction. If in no other way, the mere fact it was "understood" how he had come aboard and that he was bound for the Navy would set him apart from the rest of the crew. And, as Alan Taylor suggests, the social apparatus that surrounded Cooper's presence on the vessel carried additional significance. Taylor notes that although Ned Myers describes several encounters with British press gangs, he "never describes young James Cooper as in any danger of the impressment that imperilled all of his other shipmates, including the captain who was briefly detained." If Cooper was seemingly immune from such serious threats, why? Taylor continues, "It seems likely that he had papers, provided by his father and his father's friends, attesting that James Cooper was the son of an American gentleman and former United States Congressman: the sort of young man whose impressment would be more diplomatic trouble tha[n] it was worth to a British naval captain." [12]

That Cooper sailed under some such protection is suggested by the fact that he often was closely involved in the actual impressments that afflicted the *Stirling*—but in a charmed sort of way, being, for instance, the person sent ashore with Captain Johnston's traveling desk and papers when Johnston himself had been taken and was being detained there. If he indeed traveled under the protection of such documents, Cooper's potentially dangerous outburst against a British naval officer who boarded the *Stirling* and sought to impress a Swede among its crew—an outburst Captain Johnston cut short, presumably for Cooper's own good—seems less rash and more exultant: Ned Myers tersely recalled, "Cooper had a little row with this boarding officer, but was silenced by the captain."[13] Would Cooper have given such freedom to his indignation if he had not held a trump card among his papers?[14] And, again, Captain Johnston's intervention in the argument suggests that he bore a special charge to care for the young son of Judge Cooper.

In conclusion, I would like to emphasize how Cooper's somewhat complicated masquerade as a common sailor on the *Stirling* has its counterpart in his various writings about the sea. It is clear that for the rest of his life Cooper enjoyed keeping up contact with individuals he had met during his brief career in the merchant marine and in the Navy. It also is clear that his sustained interest in things nautical, which fed his imagination in the dozen sea novels and the historical narratives he penned across the three decades of his active career, became a permanent part of his intellectual and emotional character. If we probe how he imagined the sea, though, we are likely to find that his own rather mixed condition during his only transoceanic voyages in his youth in fact was reflected in his art.

When he wrote of his crossing of the Atlantic in the packet ship *Hudson* in 1826, his first as a genuine passenger, he stressed how his nautical knowledge helped the crew (and the other passengers, including his wife, those "land-birds" who "were driven below, before evening" the first day on board) see what set him apart from the landsmen. The mate on the *Hudson* was able to detect Cooper's maritime background by virtue of a single expression he used in boarding the vessel from the steam launch that took his family out to it from Manhattan: later that day, Cooper recalled, "The first mate, a straight-forward Kennebunk-man, gave me a wink, (he had detected my sea education by a single expression, that of 'send it an-end,' while mounting the side of the ship,) and said, 'a clear quarterdeck! a good time to take a walk, sir.'"

Cooper kept up this masquerade through the 1826 crossing, and during his time in Europe and on the Mediterranean, nurtured what he called his "nautical instinct" whenever he could: even digressive comments in his accounts of the time in Europe frequently situate him as an accomplished hand at sea, as when Cooper asserts in his French travel book that he had no difficulty ascending a "dark well of a staircase" when paying a visit one evening in Paris because he had "passed so much of [his] youth, on top-gallant-yards, and in becketting royals."[15] Everywhere he turned, he was able to find echoes of the world he ran away to as a sixteen-year-old boy from the inland depths of Otsego.

Cooper tended to deploy his nautical knowledge in life as he deployed it in his art—as a means of suggesting that he belonged to a world marked by arcane skill and physical challenge. Yet it is worth noting that many of his imaginations of the sea also bear the traces of the special status under whose aegis he himself had entered the sailor's universe. Cooper found most fertile the fact that he was familiar with the sailor's world without being wholly of it—in some sense, he enjoyed an artist's ideal liminality. In the novel that drew most on his experience as a passenger, *Homeward Bound* (1838), Cooper thus created in the many-named Paul Blunt or Paul Powis a seeming landsman who yet betrays, as Cooper had in 1826, the sure marks of his nautical past by the care with which he acts and speaks while on board the *Montauk*.

At the same time, however, Cooper gave Blunt an unmistakable doubleness that matched his own. If Blunt is no mere passenger, as Cooper was not in 1826, he is no mere sailor either. Captain Truck comments, "You have traveled this road before, Mr. Blunt, I perceive. I have suspected you of being a brother chip, from the moment I saw you first put your foot on the side-cleets in getting out of the boat. You did not come aboard parrot-toed, like a country-girl waltzing; but set the ball of your foot firmly on the wood, and swung the length of your arms, like a man who knows how to humor the muscles." Later,

Captain Truck comments to another passenger, "I perceive something about that gentleman which denotes a nautical instinct"—the same phrase Cooper applied to himself in his book of French travels, published only a year earlier than the novel.[16] For his own part, Cooper showed by his proper handling of nautical language in this book as in so many others that he, too, knew how to step about the ship. For instance, without calling attention to the practice, he referred to the crew as "the people" throughout *Homeward Bound* (for example, pages 93, 161, 258, 274, and so forth), as he had with similar lack of overt emphasis in *France* (page 5) or *Italy*.[17]

Again, if this pattern shows Cooper's abiding interest in keeping his nautical past alive, others reveal how much he valued having his other foot on the solid ground of a landsman's respectability. His sailor-passenger Paul Blunt is, of course, genteel, revealed to be—as layer after layer of his more recent identity is peeled off—none other than the long-lost son of John Effingham, and hence an heir of Cooper's own inland home. Cooper created diehard sailors such as Long Tom in *The Pilot* (1824), who like Melville's Bulkington could not stand to have the solid earth under their fluid feet. When he set his autobiographical muse adrift, however, Cooper was likely to reveal in a character such as Blunt-Effingham the liminality that made his own nautical experience a source of inspiration rather than, as it had proved for Ned Myers, a fate, and a pretty grim one at that. American writers of the nineteenth century kept what Melville called "the open independence of [their] sea" by going there in the first place with their landsman's freedom largely intact. They were anxious to prove they were not passengers precisely because they knew they were not just sailors, either.

Notes

1. "Journal of a Voyage from New York to London 1849," *The Writings of Herman Melville: Journals*, Howard C. Horsford and Lynn Horth, eds. (Evanston, Ill.: Northwestern University Press and Newberry Library, 1989), 5, 6, 8.

2. Alan Taylor, "James Fenimore Cooper Goes to Sea: Two Unpublished Letters by a Family Friend," *Studies in the American Renaissance* (1993): 43.

3. Hugh Egan, "Gentlemen-Sailors: The First Person Narratives of Dana, Cooper, and Melville." (Ph.D. diss., University of Iowa, 1983).

4. J. Fenimore Cooper, ed., *Ned Myers, or, A Life before the Mast* (Philadelphia: Lea & Blanchard, 1843), 22–23; Edith A. Sawyer, "A Year of Cooper's Youth," *New England Magazine* 37 (1907): 498–504. It should be noted that, while Sawyer's name is listed under the title of this article, most of her text was from the pen of Alexander Johnston, Captain John Johnston's nephew. Alexander Johnston in turn based much of what he wrote on information derived from his uncle's papers, which included a March 1843 letter from Cooper. James Franklin Beard, ed., *The Letters and Journals of James Fenimore Cooper,* vol. 4 (Cambridge: Harvard University Press, 1964), 374–76, for the corrected text of Cooper's letter; also for Beard's comments on the original publication of the "Sawyer" piece, including the version of the letter Beard reprints, under Alexander Johnston's name in the *Mt. Desert Herald,* 20 September 1883. Alexander Johnston wrote the essay sometime between 1854 and 1883. Taylor's article "Cooper Goes to Sea," 49, mistakenly asserts that Sawyer wrote the essay herself on the basis on Captain Johnston's papers.

5. Richard R. Smith to Isaac Cooper, Philadelphia, 26 August 1806, William Cooper Papers, Paul Fenimore Cooper archives, Hartwick College, correspondence, Box 22. Smith's two letters to Isaac Cooper of 18 July and 8 August are also quoted from this source; they are printed in Taylor, "Cooper Goes to Sea," 51–52.

6. Taylor, "Cooper Goes to Sea," 47–48.

7. Cooper, *Ned Myers,* 19.

8. Jacob Barker, *Incidents in the Life of Jacob Barker, of New Orleans, Louisiana* (Washington, D.C.: n.p., 1855), 31. On Barker's tie with Miers Fisher, with whom he vacationed at Ballston Spa in the summer of 1807, see 22–23. For Fisher's letter to Judge Cooper's sons, Taylor, *William Cooper's Town: Power and Persuasion on the Frontier of the Early American Republic* (New York: Knopf, 1995), 3–4.

9. Taylor, *William Cooper's Town,* 3, 317.

10. Sawyer, 499.

11. Cooper, *Ned Myers,* 22.

12. Taylor, "Cooper Goes to Sea," 49.

13. Cooper, *Ned Myers,* 36.

14. In his *History of the Navy of the United States of America* (Philadelphia: Lea & Blanchard, 1839), Cooper bitterly condemned British impressment practices as an "intolerable outrage" on American national honor and individual Americans' liberty (2:128).

15. Thomas Philbrick and Constance Ayers, eds., *Gleanings in Europe: France* (Albany: State University of New York Press, 1983), 7, 27, 221.

16. James Fenimore Cooper, *Homeward Bound: or, The Chase, A Tale of the Sea* (New York: W. A. Townsend, 1860), 206, 225.

17. John Conron and Constance Ayers Denne, eds., *Gleanings in Europe: Italy* (Albany: State University of New York Press, 1981), 63, 88.

Index

About the Contributors

Hugh Egan is Associate Professor of English and Director of the Honors Program at Ithaca College. His research interests focus on nineteenth-century American literature, and he has published on Irving, Dana, and Cooper. He is currently working on a project involving Cooper's midcareer works.

Peter G. Fish is Professor of Political Science and Law at Duke University. He received his B.A. from Princeton University (1960) and his M.A. (1965) and Ph.D. (1968) from the Johns Hopkins University, after which he was a guest scholar at the Brookings Institution and taught at Oberlin College, Princeton University, and, since 1969, at Duke University. His fields of interest are American constitutional law and judicial politics and institutions. He is the author of books on federal judicial administration and the American chief justiceship. He is currently engaged in a study of the United States courts in the mid-Atlantic South sponsored by the U.S. Court of Appeals for the Fourth Circuit from which is drawn the contribution to these *Proceedings*.

Wayne Franklin, a native of Albany, New York, received his B.A. from Union College and holds his Ph.D. in English from the University of Pittsburgh. Formerly Professor of English and Professor and Chair of American Studies at the University of Iowa, in 1994 he became Davis Distinguished Professor of American Literature at Northeastern University, where he also serves as chair of the English Department. He is author of *Discoverers, Explorers, Settlers: The Diligent Writers of Early America* (1979), *The New World of James Fenimore Cooper* (1982), and *A Rural Carpenter's World: The Craft in a Nineteenth-Century New York Township* (1990). One of the editors of the Norton Anthology of American Literature, he founded and continues as editor of the American Land and Life series (published by the University of Iowa Press), coedited *Mapping American Culture* with Michael Steiner (1993), and most recently has edited *American Voices, American Lives: A Documentary Reader* (1997) and Cooper's *The Spy* (1997). At present he is writing the first biography of James Fenimore Cooper to be based on full access to the family's papers.

Mary A. Y. Gallagher is Coeditor of *The Papers of Robert Morris* and has served as Adjunct Professor of History at Brooklyn College and Queens College of The City University of New York. She holds degrees from Notre Dame College of Staten Island, New York, and the University of Notre Dame, and the doctorate in history from the City University of New York. She has a number of scholarly articles to her credit, in addition to several volumes of the Robert Morris Papers project.

Christine F. Hughes is Assistant Head of the Early History Branch at the Naval Historical Center and Associate Editor of the multivolume series *The Naval War of 1812: A Documentary History*. She earned an M.A. in history from the University of Virginia. She coauthored *The Reestablishment of the Navy, 1787-1801: Historical Overview and Select Bibliography* with Michael J. Crawford.

Robert D. Madison attended the University of Rhode Island, Clark University, and Northwestern University (Ph.D. 1981), and specializes in nineteenth-century American literature. He has edited works of Southey, Cooper, and Melville, as well as the Penguin edition of Thomas Wentworth Higginson's *Army Life in a Black Regiment* (1997). He is Professor of English at the U.S. Naval Academy in Annapolis, Maryland.

Richard C. Malley currently serves as the registrar of the Connecticut Historical Society. Previously he served as curator at the Mariners' Museum and as assistant registrar at Mystic Seaport Museum. In addition to curating exhibitions on maritime and naval topics, he has to his credit books on the art of scrimshaw and articles on a wide array of maritime subjects. He holds degrees from Providence College and Fordham University.

Jim Mockford is Software Quality Engineer at Wacom Technology Corporation in Vancouver, Washington. He was formerly Executive Director of the Japan-America Society of the State of Washington and an instructor of Japanese language. He serves on the Advisory Council of the Grays Harbor Historical Seaport Authority, operators of the replica tall ship *Lady Washington* at Aberdeen, Washington.

Elizabeth M. Nuxoll is project director and coeditor of the *Papers of Robert Morris* at Queens College of the City University of New York. She studied at Marymount Manhattan College in New York and at the University of Wyoming and earned her doctorate at the Graduate School and University Center of the City University of New York. In addition to the several volumes of the Morris Papers she has edited, she has published the monograph *Congress and the Munitions Merchants: The Secret Committee of Congress during the American Revolution* and numerous articles in scholarly journals and reference works.

Thomas Philbrick is an Emeritus Professor of English at the University of Pittsburgh. He received his undergraduate education at Brown University and has an M.A. and Ph.D. from Harvard University. Although he has taught and published in several areas of eighteenth- and nineteenth-century American literature, his most persistent interests have been in maritime literature and the writings of James Fenimore Cooper. In recent years, he and Marianne Philbrick have prepared critical editions of several of Cooper's novels and travel books. They are currently at work on *The Water-Witch*.

Joshua M. Smith, a Ph.D. candidate at the University of Maine in Orono, earned his undergraduate degree in history from the University of St. Andrews, Scotland. He also holds an M.A. in Maritime History from East Carolina University. His doctoral dissertation, now in progress, is "The Rogues of 'Quoddy': The Moral Economy of Smuggling in the Maine-New Brunswick Borderlands, 1783–1820."